# SOLD

# SOLD

## THE RISE AND FALL
## OF THE HOUSE OF SOTHEBY

# Nicholas Faith

Macmillan Publishing Company

Macmillan Publishing Company
866 Third Avenue, New York, N.Y. 10022

Library of Congress Cataloging-in-Publication Data

Faith, Nicholas, 1933–
    Sold: the rise and fall of the House of Sotheby.

    Bibliography: p.
    Includes index.
    1. Sotheby's (Firm)   2. Auctions.   3. Art auctions.
4. Wilson, Peter (Peter Cecil), 1913–  .  I. Title.
HF5477.G74S673  1985  381'.1  85-15542
ISBN 0-02-536970-9

Macmillan books are available at special discounts for bulk purchases for sales promotions, premiums, fund-raising, or educational use. For details, contact:
  Special Sales Director
  Macmillan Publishing Company
  866 Third Avenue
  New York, N.Y. 10022

10 9 8 7 6 5 4 3 2 1

Printed in the United Kingdom

# CONTENTS

# ILLUSTRATIONS

Peter Wilson in action at the von Hirsch sale (*Popperfoto*)

Peter Wilson as his friends remember him

Sir Alec Martin (*Christie's*)

Peter Chance (*BBC Hulton Picture Library*)

Patrick Lindsay (*The Photo Source*)

Sale of Francis Bacon's Study for Portrait VIII (*The Photo Source*)

The exterior of Sotheby's (*The Photo Source*)

Peter Wilson selling a Van Gogh owned by Sir Alexander Korda (*The Photo Source*)

The Dowager Countess of Rosebery (*The Photo Source*)

Mentmore Towers (*The Photo Source*)

Two of the Rosebery racing trophies (*The Photo Source*)

*New Yorker* cartoon by Saxon

Jim Kiddell (*photograph by Frank Herrmann*)

Peter Nahum (*Peter Nahum. Photograph by Hugh Kelly*)

John Marion (*The Associated Press Ltd*)

Marshall Cogan and Stephen Swid (*photograph by Barry Swaebe*)

Alfred Taubman (*Times Newspapers Ltd*)

*Part I*

# A TRADEABLE BEAUTY IS BORN

# A TRADEABLE BEAUTY IS BORN

A retired museum director in the United States was asked by somebody what an object that he'd bought cost – $3000 – it seemed a very low price and when he was told this he said, 'Ah, that was B.S. Before Sotheby's.' I felt very happy.

Peter Wilson in a BBC television interview with
Edwin Mullins 1972

Seven simple words: 'What, will no one offer any more?' marked the crucial moment in a revolution which catapulted Peter Cecil Wilson into international stardom, helped propel Sotheby's, the auction house he headed, into an unprecedented dominance of the inter-national art market, and launched the market itself into an orbit it had never previously attained. The verbs, 'catapult', 'propel', 'launch', are entirely appropriate: for they all convey the feeling of a rocket, a dynamic force, leaving the spectator wondering whether the load being launched will return to earth safe and sound or remain, a burnt-out shell, stranded in space.

The words which finally ignited the rocket were spoken on the evening of 15 October 1958, when Peter Wilson accepted a final bid of £220,000 for a Cézanne, *Garçon au Gilet Rouge*. Only a few years earlier, experts had agreed that £30,000 was the outside limit for a picture sold at auction – it was assumed that pictures worth any more would automatically be sold privately through dealers. The price paid for the Cézanne, more than double the previous sale-room record, removed their previous monopoly at a stroke.

Not surprisingly, Peter Wilson later claimed that the infinitely appealing Cézanne was the best picture he ever auctioned, but none of the seven sold that evening, by Van Gogh, Manet and Renoir as well as Cézanne, were run-of-the-mill. They fetched £681,000, a record average for any sale. This was not in itself surprising. They were the second, and finest selection from the collection accumu-lated by Jakob Goldschmidt, a German banker who had taken refuge from Hitler in New York. Nor were they 'difficult' paintings. The late Gerald Reitlinger* put it with characteristic bluntness. To him they were all 'pictures that made no exacting demands on the eye'.

The manner of the sale mattered almost as much as the content. It was the first held in the evening in the history of the auction house, one of the first to be treated as a 'media event' complete with television cameras. And this is where the seven little words mattered. The Cézanne was the sixth picture to be sold, and the first five had already all fetched far more than the reserve prices – themselves unprecedentedly high – placed on them. Yet the atmosphere remained tense until the auctioneer spoke the magic words: 'What, will no one offer any more?' According to one spectator, his tone of voice was: 'that of a man genuinely astonished that a group of experts of such distinction would let a painting of this quality go for so paltry a sum. A roar of laughter relieved the tension'. The tension had spread to the man on the rostrum. PCW† may have been outwardly calm, but inwardly he was naturally nervous. He later confessed that he had totally forgotten the special instructions given by an important American client anxious to conceal his bidding intentions. 'Fortunately', said PCW, 'he had chickened out long before.'

The record price itself was obviously important for Sotheby's, and indeed for other auction houses in their eternal battles with the dealers, but the personality of the auctioneer added another dimension. Here was clearly a man made for the television age, uniquely capable, not only of enticing the finest works of art into the auction room and then selling them at record prices, but also able to convey to a much wider public the fun and the profit he himself derived from buying and selling works of art. The nature and timing of the remarks were ample proof of that.

But PCW's achievements were not primarily those of a great communicator. They were summarised by Earl Jellicoe in his address at the memorial service held on 20 June 1984, four months after his death:

---

* His three volume work on *The Economics of Taste* contains a mass of information about prices, together with a series of personal, pungent, irresistibly quotable comments that inevitably make him a crucial source. He came from a family of dealers and was himself a brilliant collector (his house was brim-full of marvellous Chinese porcelain). Not surprisingly he hated the post-war art market so his judgments often exaggerated and distorted trends.

† The initials by which he was known by most people at Sotheby's, and thus the natural way to write about him.

It was he, more than any other single being, who created the international art market as it exists today. His genius – a word not to be lightly used – was as influential in its sphere as that of a Henry Ford to mass motoring, or of a Rothschild to banking or a Fleming to medicine. He did more than any other man or woman in his day to stimulate and channel the human instinct to adorn and to collect. In so doing, he made London, for two or three decades, the centre of the international art market.

The changes he exemplified were so profound that they necessarily change the sort of book that can be written about the art market. Previous books have naturally concentrated on the fluctuations of fashion, the changing prices and objects involved, the collectors, like Pierpont Morgan, the dealers, like Duveen, or the experts like Berenson who validated them (and thus the prices at which they were sold). It is a tribute to PCW that any book about the post-war art market inevitably centres on an auctioneer. This book is not a biography nor a systematic analysis of individual trends in the art market, nor a history of Sotheby's*. It is a fascinated outsider's attempt to explain to himself the revolution that exploded into the open at the Goldschmidt sale and PCW's role in it. It is about the way this one institution, dominated by one remarkable man, captured so great a share of the world's art market, and in doing so not only enlarged our ideas of what constituted marketable art, but also caused us to attach precise financial values to the most ordinary objects around us. For PCW was that rarest of phenomena: a man who not only transformed a business, but also helped to change the way we look at the world, the assumptions on which part of our lives are based.

For 'Second Goldschmidt' marked a crucial moment in the revolution in the way we look at our personal possessions, the furniture, china, pictures and even the knick-knacks that surround us at home. Until then they had been cherished almost exclusively for their beauty, or their usefulness, or their emotional associations – with our own lives, or the history of our families. But a new dimension has now been added to our perceptions: each piece, each work of art, however sentimentally important, now invariably has a price-tag attached to it, and, more often than not, the value is related to what the object would fetch at auction.

PCW did not make the revolution alone and it had started before 'Second Goldschmidt', but he symbolized it. Even in narrow business terms he was a catalyst in three very different ways, institutional, geographical, social. He gave Sotheby's its first-ever lead in

* Frank Herrmann has already written an admirably thorough history of the firm.

its historic batle with Christie's. He permanently tilted the balance between dealers and auctioneers (Christopher Weston, who built up Phillips, London's third largest auction house, put it simply: 'But for PCW my company would not exist'). Jet travel probably played a greater role in internationalizing the art market than he did, but he ensured that it would be centred in London. This was not a natural development. Although England provided the biggest single source of raw material for the sale-rooms, for the first time in history the international art market was centred not where the bulk of the objects being sold originated, or at their final destination, but at an entrepôt.

It was the first time, too, that an auction house had been at the centre of the market and this in itself helped to destroy the previously unchallenged idea that there were hierarchies in the world of art, a natural – if changing – pecking order set by more or less universally recognized authorities. In previous periods there had been a select group of tastemakers who had determined what the majority of those who could afford choice in their surroundings would prefer to buy. They were a heterogenous group: dealers like Duveen, critics, writers and editors at every level, reaching into quite humble homes (like Anna Jameson in Victorian England, or the editors of the *Ladies Home Journal* in early twentieth-century America), but they had one thing in common: it was they who made the market. In the past quarter of a century the market has become the major authority, leaving the tastemakers to follow, to explain its dictates.

As a natural corollary, every previous period in the history of art had been exclusivist: you liked either Gothic or classical, Regency or Victorian, but not both indiscriminately. The postwar world therefore weakened the historical links between connoisseurs, collectors, dealers and experts which had formed the foundation for the art market throughout history. The market thus became more objective, less subject to the whims of individuals, experts or families.

PCW was the ideal propagandist for a period without external authority, which also lacked the confidence to reject any broad categories of artistic creation. In Joseph Alsop's words: 'with the former canon abandoned, in fact, all art gradually becomes equal' – as a natural corollary, authorities like critics and art historians became important mainly because they were prepared to authenticate objects, not in their former, oracular role. The market discriminated, but not between ages or categories, rather between what was good, or important, within categories, and the market was situated, not in dealers' private viewing rooms but on the very public trading floor provided by the auction houses. The new limelight obviously did not suit the dealers, but the theatre directed by PCW did suit the new rich, particularly the Americans, used to the idea of an open market in every category in which they dealt, art as much as commodities or stocks and bonds. As a consequence, it was the only period in which nothing went out of fashion – for there were no authorities to set standards – merely a constant flow of periods and categories that emerged into the limelight. Some consisted of objects which may previously have been collected but had not been generally marketable, some were returning to public favour after generations in the wilderness.

In the absence of objective authority, there is a necessarily increased reliance on market value, itself increasingly defined by institutional buyers (I nearly wrote investors) like museums and corporations, or individual collectors. A market in which demand so relentlessly exceeds supply requires a continuous stream of new categories. Many American collectors who came to buy the American nineteenth-century painters would probably have preferred to buy Impressionists, but found that these were reserved (as works by such artists as Church now are) for truly rich millionaires.

Of course an amazing number of unlikely categories have been the subject of collection passions over the centuries. In a book published in 1944 Douglas and Elizabeth Rigby* gave a list of over a hundred. These include such well-recognized categories as autographs, birds' eggs and lead soldiers, but they also include exotic items like golf tees, early watering-cans – and lynching tokens. But in the thirty years after the Rigbys compiled their list many of these hitherto essentially private obsessions were connected with a general, international market. To the Rigbys collectibles had a market value through their scarcity and their desirability to other collectors in the same field. PCW, by providing a world-wide, universal department store for collectibles, brought them into the open – and he, and his disciples within Sotheby's, ensured that thousands of objects, previously considered unmarketable, made money for owners and middlemen alike. Past and present blurred into a single mass of 'collectibles'.

As a result, the talk is now more of traded art, and for art to be traded (and thus valued in financial terms) it has to be available. Maurice Rheims quoted an old Alsatian art dealer as saying 'For something to fetch a good price, it must be rare, very rare', and then, after a pause for reflection he would add, 'but not too rare.' So there would be little talk of Greek classical sculpture or medieval artefacts where only a few examples come on to the market. In reality, of course, only a few people ever did discuss classical sculpture, and

* *Lock Stock & Barrel, The Story of Collecting.*

doubtless they continue to do so. But they have been overwhelmed by the newcomers.

The lack of discrimination – a market is never shocked, it merely adjusts to new circumstances – also twisted and diluted the public's reaction to art. The sort of public outcry that greeted a London exhibition of Picassos as late as 1947 would have been unthinkable thirty years later, not only because British taste had become more sophisticated, but also because anything valuable had been by definition placed on a pedestal, and had become uncriticizable. The average man could be shocked by the new only when it involved public money: no one in Britain cared if an artist made his living piling up bricks and selling the resulting collection until the Tate Gallery proposed to spend taxpayers' money on an example of the genre.

PCW would have found these notions portentous and boring. For him art was above all fun: his friends still have ringing in their ears his cry of 'Oh I do adore that' as he entered a room and spotted, as he usually did, at least one object or painting that pleased him (above all, they add, if he thought he could sell it). For art, to him, was tradeable beauty. He was instinctively opposed to William Blake's famous dictum that 'where any view of money exists art cannot be carried on'. 'I think the idea of art for art's sake is really awful rot', was a typical PCW saying, assuming that 'no one who has ever bought a work of art has been exempt from the feeling that it is going to retain its value. There are sanctimonious individuals who say this has nothing to do with it. I think they are wrong.'

PCW genuinely loved the decorative arts, he was an omnivorous, not enormously discriminating collector. But he loved dealing more than his collection – he even sold the only school prize he ever obtained, a fine botanical book. The things he liked best were not necessarily valuable, they included all periods and countries, Japanese ceramics before they were fashionable, *nature morte* (his brother's house is full of Neapolitan paintings of fruit and fish which he insisted on buying) decorative items at a time when decoration played less of a part in determining prices than ever before. He acted as the focus for the combination of fear and greed that transformed even the humblest of objects into investments for the ordinary man. He turned art into a participative sport where for most people it had been purely a spectator sport. Lord Duveen had made a handful of American millionaires feel that their life was not complete without what he happened to have to sell at the time. It was PCW's genius that he enticed a large segment of the British people into a similar conspiracy. For he felt firmly that art meant ownership: 'Nobody is a patron unless they're covetous. Without covetousness you're not going to have appreciation of art. And I think that if covetousness were destroyed by some magic art would come to an end. It's very rare to be able to appreciate art without wanting to own it.' It was the ideal mentality for the pied piper who led thousands of ordinary people to associate *objets d'art* with security against inflation. Yet his influence was partly accidental. He was in many ways a traditional auctioneer, thinking, not of the mass market, but of great past sales and how to emulate them. (He naturally compared one of his greatest triumphs, the von Hirsch sale, with the famous disposal of the contents of Hamilton Palace nearly a century earlier.)

Despite PCW's aristocratic background and demeanour, he was, above all, a dealer and a showman, both essentially classless occupations. Other auctioneers saw only potential buyers, he saw an audience, and so was ideally suited to convey the excitement attached to high prices in the saleroom. He was tapping a rich vein: in 1887 a journalist described a fashionable sale at Christie's, how, when the hammer fell on a lot 'for a lumping sum there is a perfect uproar, just as the crowd roars its delight when the Derby is run, for the Christie audience revels in high prices simply for money's sake, though of course some of the applause is meant for the picture'.

Most sales, of course, are not like that, they are really rather dreary, monotonous occasions. PCW had the capacity to make you feel that they were all as exciting as Goldschmidt, even if they were just a handful of bored dealers in dirty mackintoshes going through the motions. He appealed to the combination of greed and confidence in our own judgment which appeals to the gambler in most of us. To the dealer and journalist Robert Wraight auction rooms are 'half museums with constantly changing shows and they are also gambling dens so far as I am concerned'. So they were for PCW. He was himself greedy for money, so he empathized with that famous notional character, 'the little old lady with the Ming vase which had always been used as an umbrella stand'. The greed had always been there. He institutionalized it. PCW built a bridge between the public and the world of art, never previously the job of the auctioneer. Picasso remarked that the critic 'built a bridge people can walk over to join the artist'. As the critics ascended into elitist incomprehensibility there was a gap which PCW filled to perfection – a talent he first demonstrated at 'Second Goldschmidt'.

His temperament was ideally suited to deal with the many relationships involved in the auction business: with his own experts, the sellers, the collecting public. He was forever playing a part, for he clearly could not stand many of the people he had to deal with: 'We must get this man out of here, he's giving me a nervous breakdown' was a frequent plea. One of his closest associates summed it up:

'PCW loved money . . . he had once been poor and he never wanted it to happen again . . . he had no family life . . . he was an instinctive person, the best smeller in the world . . . commercial sense knowing what would sell . . . the telephone was like an arm for anybody else.'

He used this 'additional arm', like everything else, as a business weapon. But what made him so irresistible was his almost compulsive sense of fun. He had an amazing charm and enthusiasm, which ensured that virtually nobody who ever worked with him, however shabbily they were treated – and most of them were – is disloyal to his memory: 'He had this enormous manipulative charm, he made everything seem such fun, he generated such a sense of excitement', says one former employee. 'He made us all part of a great big conspiracy, he would give you a big wink even at the most formal dinner parties. He made you want to do things for him. We would go to the theatre on an impulse, he made even buying a ice-cream in the interval into fun. His whole sense of fun, of humour, was like that of an English school-boy, you were in his gang and it was such fun.' John Marion, who worked with him for fifteen years in New York, tells of his 'boyish enthusiasm, he was open to every new idea'. And Hermann Robinow, a banker who helped him in the 1960s thinks of him as 'one of those people who stimulate you and make you feel witty and clever'.

But the charm was backed by a steely determination. 'He had these piercing, darting, blue eyes, and that mobile, rather cruel mouth' is one memory of him. Like many compulsively gregarious people, he was, essentially, a loner. Typically, Stanley Clark, the public relations man who played an enormous part in promoting PCW, says simply: 'I knew a lot about PCW and very little about him.' All these memories return to his competitiveness: Eugene Thaw, the leading New York dealer, perceived the 'cold glint' in PCW's eyes, 'he was the most competitive animal I've ever met'. 'He had a killer instinct', says another associate. Guests to Clavary, his retirement home in the South of France, remember games of croquet or snail races, children's games like Snakes and Ladders, all played with ruthless, competitive passion. Not surprisingly he was also compulsively devious: 'If there were two ways of going about something, PCW would take the most devious', says a former director.

But, although he was a superb, cold-blooded, manipulator, he was not a long-term thinker. He was an instinctual animal. David Nash, another close associate says 'PCW never planned, he reacted.' 'You must pay great attention to your first impression' he once said, 'just like meeting people, your first impression is valid in the first tenth of a second and then you have to look at it technically and try and argue it out logically.' 'He was easily hurt, he expected too much from people', says his son Philip. 'The first time he met people he saw them in black and white.' Those less close to him are rather less sympathetic. 'He would take you up and drop you and you wouldn't know what had happened, when he dropped the charm it was a dreadful revelation', is one bitter reaction.

His physical presence helped him greatly. At 6 feet 4 inches PCW was bound to be impressive. At the Memorial Service Earl Jellicoe remembered 'that tall, elegant, aristocratic figure with that very personal pitch of voice and with that mischievous, slight smile flickering around the corner of his mouth'. The physical presence, the manipulative charm, the reliance on instinct, make him sound like a superb actor, and perhaps he is best compared with a handful of old-style, elegant English actors. One interviewer compared him to the late Cecil Parker, an actor with the same clear, high voice who habitually played judges, colonial governors and the like, in British films. But a more accurate comparison is with Sir John Gielgud. In later life they both combined roundness and beakiness of appearance; 'he was portly but conveyed such a feeling of elegance' could apply either to Gielgud or PCW. Both talked the same way, they gabbled clearly in a mixture more fashionable before 1914 than since, the idiosyncracies of pronunciation and vocabulary which come naturally to an older generation but which seem affected to a modern ear.

The enthusiasm and the sensitivity, the ruthlessness, the feeling of loneliness, can be traced back to his family. For there is an old saying recalling how England's first Prime Minister, the coarse, ruthless, hard-drinking Sir Robert Walpole had as a son a great collector, the sensitive, worldly Horace Walpole. 'All over England fathers like Sir Robert Walpole are having sons like Horace Walpole.'

11

*Part II*

# CREATION

# I THE MAKING OF PCW

PCW's characteristics are hidden, rather than revealed, by a recital of the basic facts about him. He was born on 8 March 1913, the third son of Sir Mathew Wilson, the fourth Baronet, Companion of the Star of India, who had just given up a promising military career and was about to enter the House of Commons as Conservative member for a London constituency, South-West Bethnal Green. His father came from an old Yorkshire family, which owned Eshten Hall, an ugly, if impressive neo-Elizabethan house in a magnificent setting. In his monumental work on Britain's buildings, the late Nikolaus Pevsner describes it as 'the finest county seat in Craven', designed by a local architect in 1825, 'a remarkably early date for a house in a pure neo-Elizabethan style. Not very large but decidedly out to impress'. He is being polite; the house shows only too clearly that it is an imitation, not an original Elizabethan house. Even though the family's title dated back 150 years before it was built, they clearly retained a trace of the *nouveau*, a desire to impress.

PCW's mother, the Honourable Barbara Lister, came from an even more distinguished family. She was a daughter of the last Lord Ribblesdale, Master of the Buckhounds – and thus a senior official in Queen Victoria's Household – in Gladstone's last administration in the 1890s and a Trustee of the National Gallery (the biographers do not mention that his artistic connections also involved acting as a runner to help Messrs Agnews acquire pictures). PCW's maternal grandmother was the eldest of the fabled Tennant sisters, the most famous of whom, Margot, PCW's great-aunt, was wife of the Prime Minister, H. H. Asquith, when PCW was born.

These facts omit not only the nature of his parents' characters and relationship but, even more crucially, convey an impression of security, which must have been almost totally lacking in the young PCW. His mother was an emotionally detached lady whose strongest feelings had been lavished on her brothers, Tommy the elder and Charles the younger, both of whom were killed in action. In one of her books, the imagined memoirs of 'Zellie', her much-loved German governess, she provides a chilling description in the third person of how: 'Tommy had been the close companion of

15

Barbara, almost to the exclusion of others of her own age'.* (Her mother 'would have liked her to consort with a lot of people' – the daughters of her old friends – 'who were not especially congenial to her'.) When Tommy first went away to school: 'Barbara's desolation was so great at losing her playmate that it was decided she should winter abroad with her grandmother Ribblesdale'. Tommy joined the Army, served with distinction in the Boer War and was then killed in Somaliland in a minor, long-forgotten expedition against a mad Mullah. She felt his death had changed for her 'the aspect of the earth and the imagery of heaven. During the months which followed she wished to be alone with her grief'. She and Zellie 'treasured all his possessions, these trifles of his everyday life too precious to be handled. His hunting-whips, his spurs (how early he had won them), his books and clothes. His room next to Barbara's became a reliquary to contain them.'

Tommy had died at Christmas-time. Wilson – a Yorkshire neighbour, from one of the few county families easily reachable in pre-motor car days – had served with him in South Africa and in a sense was the closest substitute she could find for the irreplaceable brother. Wilson spent the summer after Tommy's death in England, and asked her to marry him; she put him off for a year, but, according to her, he was: 'dearly loved already. He was ultra-violet light personified and the champion purveyor of larks . . . such a good kind husband who was universally adored.' In the book – and throughout their relationship – she called him 'Harry', but to the rest of the world he was known as 'Scatters', from his supposed habit of leaving money scattered carelessly around.

He spent a year instructing at Sandhurst and was then promoted to be the Military Secretary to the Commander-in-Chief in India. Like a dutiful army wife she followed him to what was clearly a totally uncongenial environment. The only compensation was 'her first appearance at a regimental concert given by her brother Tommy's old squadron, his men gave her a splendid ovation (it was worth coming to India for such a welcome)'. But Scatters was restless and resigned his commission to nurse his constituency, living 'in a pleasant Georgian house on Stanmore Hill'.

Her first mention of the young PCW is of him 'still in a blue-linen tunic; playing in deep meadow-grass or pasture-land, he looked like a speedwell or periwinkle flower that had strayed there', a deeply embarrassing image for anyone to live with, but not inappropriate, for he loved flowers even more than art throughout his life. After the usual miserable few years at a preparatory school, he went to Eton where he made absolutely no impression. He claimed to have

* *Dear Youth* by Barbara Wilson, Macmillan, 1937.

16

avoided football as much as possible to loaf round the village's antiquarian bookshops. His only mark was a special prize for assembling the finest collection of wild flowers gathered from the neighbourhood – an achievement guaranteed merely to arouse derision among his contemporaries.

By the time he left Eton his parents were, effectively, separated. His father was not in the least interested in his children nor in Eshton Hall. It had been occupied during World War I by a school evacuated from Scarborough and was let for most of PCW's child-hood, although it was available in the summer – and, as such, came to symbolize holidays for Sir Martin.* But the family remained very 'Yorkshire' especially in their extreme canniness about money. (They did spend enough time at Eshton for Scatters to perpetrate an extremely elaborate practical joke by inviting all the many people in Yorkshire whose name included the phrase 'bottom' to a party. He especially enjoyed watching their embarrassment as they introduced themselves.)

For most of the year family life, such as it was, was concentrated in London. This was ironical, for PCW's mother once wrote of town houses as 'camps only, pitched in one street or another'. This was only a small burden compared with her husband's behaviour. After the war he gave up politics and became a half-commission man with a firm of stockbrokers, but lived mostly on his winnings at cards. His main occupation, however, was the pursuit, generally successful, of a generous swathe of London society women. Philip Ziegler paints a vivid portrait of the memorably handsome Scatters in his biography of Lady Diana Cooper. He was 'the prototype of the Edwardian rake, described by Lady Cynthia Asquith as: "a fussy ebullient bounder with his blue eyes and hoarse whisper" . . . his tastes were as traditionally rakish as his appearance; he prided himself on being responsible for more divorces than any other man in London and liked playing poker for high stakes with rich but innocent young men' – another memory is of him at the bridge table, avoiding playing more than one rubber with a weak partner.

Among his attempted conquests was Lady Diana herself. Ziegler has a hilarious description of her future husband, Duff Cooper, fuming outside the door of a bedroom within which Scatters was doing his best to add Lady Diana to his collection. But perhaps the most vivid description we have is from the pen of another of his potential victims, the writer Enid Bagnold, then married to Sir Roderick Jones, chairman of Reuter's. In her autobiography she left a sketch in pure – if delicate – acid of a trip to Goodwood, smartest

* It was occupied by a school during World War II, left nearly derelict, and sold after the war for its present use as a nursing home.

17

and most delightful of race meetings, with Scatters. To her, he was typical of her husband's friends, unsympathetic, smart and worldly. She was gardening, 'nails full of earth', when he called. She hurried off to Brighton to meet him, decked up in untypical finery (but with only 10s in her purse). Trouble began before they got there.

'Half-way to Goodwood, Scatters said: "Of course you belong."

' "Belong where?"

' "You're a Member, aren't you?"

' "Goodwood? No."

' "Good God, I shall have to pay for you!"

'I felt shame. But immediately rebellion. It was his look-out: he oughtn't to have asked me.'

Worse was to come. Scatters not only had to pay the entrance fee but also for lunch. Despite long consultations with the jockeys, his bets went astray. No wonder 'we drove back gloomy as we came', separated, as on the journey out, by a man 'who had no name and slept throughout'.

PCW's mother, disappointed that her husband no longer resembled the dream-brother of her childhood, then transferred her hopes to her three sons, Martin (the present baronet), Anthony, and Peter. They, she hoped, would resemble her younger brother Charles, a brilliant young diplomat, who had moved with properly effortless superiority from Eton through a first class degree in classics and philosophy at Balliol College, Oxford, to a promising career in the Foreign Office. But he was killed in 1915, leaving her with a further incentive to turn her sons into deutero-Charleses. She force-fed them culture, recording proudly how Martin and Anthony had learnt several of La Fontaine's fables by heart. But, perhaps inevitably, none of her sons showed any of their uncle's academic prowess.

She, like her husband, was a compelling character: 'you were swept up in her conversation, and Peter admired and adored her' says his elder brother. She and her children were heartlessly witty, a 'funny gang', a tacit alliance against her husband – who was not himself funny, although he had a fund of anecdotes, a very different matter. She left her sons feeling that they had disappointed her, but they inherited from her a certain chilliness in personal relations. PCW would have echoed his brother's statement that: 'I care more about things than people.' The charm and enthusiasm inherited from the irrepressible Scatters provided some compensation, but they did not involve any genuine warmth even towards his family.

PCW was no more successful at New College, Oxford, supposedly studying history, than he had been at Eton. He is remembered as shy, awkward, unformed. Unable to pass even the simple preliminary examinations, he left Oxford after a year and went first to Paris to learn French in a vague attempt to prepare him for a diplomatic career. Then, in the house of a professor at Hamburg where he had gone to learn German, he was swept away by a strong-minded, feminist fellow-student, Helen Ranken, the first person in his life who had ever believed in him. She was a teacher, five years older than him, and to her, alone in his life, he showed to the full the genuine sensitivity behind the armour. He showed her the perceptive short stories he had written, and even now she cannot recognise the descriptions of her former husband as a ruthless tycoon. She regrets how in latter life he shunned writing things down, to avoid exposing too much of himself. She transformed him, gave him confidence in himself. 'He was nothing until his marriage', says his brother Martin. The marriage was an act of great defiance. His mother hated the idea: 'I felt she would have preferred him to marry a dancer rather than a solid bourgeois like me', she says.

In the mid-1930s jobs were very difficult to find even for the best-connected young men, especially if they lacked money and academic qualifications. PCW worked at Spinks, a small auction house specializing in coins but found it 'cold, snobby and beastly in atmosphere'. He got a job at Reuters – possibly through Enid Bagnold's husband – but was sacked because he wouldn't learn shorthand. Fortunately for him, Alice Head, who was in charge of the Hearst interests in Britain, knew the family and got him a job on *The Connoisseur*, then a minor Hearst publication. Even a humdrum job selling advertising space and making sure the magazine was properly displayed on the newsstands was better than nothing. 'In those days it was a triumph to get a job', he said. 'People got degrees and were very happy to go around selling silk stockings. I remember my mother telling me that.' The couple of years before he joined Sotheby's left him with a feeling that he had been poor, the ultimate humiliation for someone from such a cold, proud, aristocratic background. Once he joined Sotheby's he was faithful until, thirty years later, the memory of that early poverty overcame that loyalty and he ditched even his greatest love.

He was exceedingly lucky to get a job at Sotheby's. At a weekend house party the Wilsons had met Vere Pilkington, a new young partner at Sotheby's, a future chairman now rather overshadowed by PCW. But he was a genuinely sensitive soul, a respected music critic; and he immediately saw PCW's potential. PCW started at the bottom, as a porter, handling and numbering a wide variety of lots. 'Here, for the first time in my life was work that I loved doing, I couldn't wait to get back to it on Monday morning', he once told an interviewer, 'I had nightmares of getting the sack from Sotheby's. I remember one nightmare was that I went into the office, someone brought in a large object and I hadn't the faintest idea whether it was valuable or not – a large Chinese vase or something. A most terrible feeling in the dream: was it going to be valuable – was I going to get the sack or wasn't I?'

He was obsessed with Sotheby's. Even when he was asked to choose eight records to take with him on a desert island ('boring food, sand in your bed and all the horrors of camping') his thoughts naturally turned to Sotheby's: two of his choices were of music whose original scores had been sold through his firm, and one was of a piece of music (the Schumann piano concerto) he had heard being practised by his neighbours at Steinway's.

PCW joined Sotheby's at a good moment. The art market was beginning to recover after the slump, London was taking an increasing share of the international art business, and, for the first time, Sotheby's itself was making a major impact on the art market as a whole. Both the market and the firm had long histories: but the market began to assume its modern form only in the 1880s, while the 'modern' Sotheby's is an even more recent creation, first conceived just before World War I, but coming into its own only in the fifteen years before PCW joined it.

# 2  THE MAKING OF A MARKET

All great civilizations, Eastern as well as European, have involved an appreciation of the finest works of art in their own (and usually in other people's) civilizations. Such appreciation invariably brings in its train an active market with its inevitable accompaniment of museums, dealers, hype, the use of collecting as a means of social advancement, prices that seemed ludicrous at the time and a proliferation of fakes and forgeries. At any one period a steady flow of pioneers would be reaching out beyond the then-accepted frontiers of artistic appreciation, and a fashion-conscious mass would be ready to follow at a discreet distance.

The art market that developed in the last quarter of the nineteenth century combined a number of features, some familiar, some original, in a mix that added up to a different kind of animal, the first we can recognize as familiar today. It was international, it was based in London, it depended on a seemingly inexhaustible supply of objects from the homes of an increasingly impoverished British aristocracy. The buyers were private as well as institutional, foreign rather than British; and, although dealers played the leading part in the dispersal of British artistic capital, an auction house was an integral part of the process.

British buyers – and the London market – had absorbed much of the mass of material thrown up (and usually out of France) by the French Revolution. At the end of the Napoleonic wars there was a fitful boom in pictures of varying descriptions and, although pictures continued to come to London through the century, London did not really want them. Prices of painters as universally admired as Rubens, Van Dyck, Rembrandt and Titian were miserably low, and even the works of Claude, which had fetched record prices during the revolutionary wars, were not in demand. For most of the nineteenth century the best hope of sellers lay with foreign monarchs, the Tsar of Russia, the King of Spain or Holland or Prussia. English buyers retreated into insularity for over sixty years. They concentrated on the works of living native artists who could charge prices far higher than those paid for foreign Old Masters – a relationship which started to change only in the 1880s, and then only because of demand from foreign buyers.

In the third quarter of the century Paris was the centre of the international art market, and even the defeat of 1870, civil war and occupation by the Prussians provided only a temporary break in its supremacy – a few foreign buyers even managed to take advantage of the panic times of 1870, including the Marquis of Hertford, creator of what is now the Wallace Collection. But once the Salle Drouot, the great auction rooms, had re-opened in the winter of 1871, Paris was again the bazaar of Europe. The French clung onto their artistic supremacy at a time of profound national humiliation. In the self-pitying mood of the day the *Chronique des Arts* declared, 'here at least was something the Prussians could not take away', heralding a decade when the country's apparent economic and political decline created a general hankering for the relics of the country's heroic past – a foretaste of the London market after 1945. But the French soon regained their confidence, and in the words of the great art dealer René Gimpel: 'People didn't want anything old after the war of 1870, it was all gold and red plush'.

It was only the break-up of the great English country houses that tilted the balance in favour of London; English capital had made London into the financial centre of the world, the apparently inexhaustible supply of art from aristocratic collections did the same for the London art market. Before the 1880s, the few major collections that were sold had usually belonged, not to aristocrats, but to speculators down on their luck or to scholars whose descendants were impoverished or simply uninterested. Not surprisingly, the most important auction house in London specialized in the sale of botanical specimens, dead and alive.

All this was dramatically transformed by the appalling agricultural crisis of the 1870s. Cheap imported wheat – two-thirds of it from American prairie farms – led to a drop of nearly 50 per cent in the price of native grain. As a result, a quarter of the country's arable land went out of production. The British aristocracy, which relied for the bulk of its income on the land, faced its worst financial crisis for a century. Most noble families had guarded against the depredations of improvident offspring by locking the family fortunes away in trusts. To meet the emergency the Settled Lands Act of 1882 allowed the trustees of such settlements to sell off lands and chattels, including works of art, providing that the trusts retained the proceeds.

The Act triggered off a series of sensational sales; most British aristocrats clearly prized their artistic treasures far less highly than their land (or their luxurious way of life). In the half century before 1880 only one sale a decade at Christie's had fetched more than

£50,000. In the thirty years before 1914 there were nearly fifty above that figure. The crucial year was 1884 when the 'traditional' Victorian market for modern art collapsed, but fortunately Agnew's clients were still rich enough to be able to support the market. That year, too, saw the first of many panics that the National Heritage was in danger when the Duke of Marlborough sold the fabled picture gallery at Blenheim Palace.* When he tried to sell his finest pictures to the National Gallery, he was able to ask £400,000 for twenty-three of his treasures (or £165,000 for six of the finest) even though only one picture in history had fetched more than £20,000. *The Times* was worried because of sales by people whom 'most persons would have supposed to have been as likely to part with the bones of his ancestors as to part with the family collection to a foreigner . . . the tide has set in a contrary direction, but not as yet in overwhelming force. The nation must make up its mind to buy the treasures or see them lost for ever.'

The theme has become familiar since then, as has the increasing importance of taxation to the art market, for a new type of death duties was introduced in 1894. The rates – 1 per cent on the first £10,000 rising to 8 per cent on estates of more than £1 million – were naturally felt to be intolerable. (Pierpont Morgan may have started to move his collection to New York in the last years of his life because Lloyd George was threatening to increase death duties.) But not only direct taxes were involved. American buyers were restrained because of the twenty per cent tariff on old works of art levied by their government in 1882. That year the French had exported ten million francs worth of works of art to the United States. In 1883 the figure was under seven million, the next year halved to a mere three-and-a-half million. The tariff was repealed in 1911 and after 1913 American imports of modern French paintings increased when the duty was reduced on the works of living artists.

The agricultural crisis removed for ever the British landowners, the biggest single force in the international market in the previous 150 years, so the market had to find new buyers. In Britain the socially-aspiring rich traditionally spend the bulk of their surplus cash on houses, land – and discreet political contributions to help them acquire titles. And if they did buy art, the 'new rich', the industrialists and manufacturers, continued to Buy British, albeit at a declining rate, until 1914.

Fortunately for the impoverished aristocrats – and for the London art market – the sheer quantity and quality of the goods on offer helped to attract a wide range of foreign buyers. Until the turn of the

* The only alternative solution to their financial problems, employed by the Churchills amongst others, was to marry an American heiress.

century American buyers – subsequently so dominant – were too busy buying modern French pictures, mostly 'safe' ones from the Barbizon school, to be a major factor. The biggest individual buyers were French dealers, bringing back home some of the 'national heritage', the mass of furniture and *objets d'art* imported in the previous hundred years.

But they faced stiff competition. For the first time institutional buyers were emerging as major forces in the market. The institutionalized megalomania of the well-funded museum curator, typified now by the Getty Museum had its first precursor in Dr Wilhelm von Bode, most distinguished of all directors of the Kaiser Friedrich Wilhelm Museum in Berlin. He came to London several times a year. He not only bought superb pictures at auction at what he considered ridiculous prices, but he also made the rounds of the major exhibitions at Burlington House each year quietly marking his catalogue, and subsequently used a German dealer living in Paris to offer the owners prices they found impossible to resist.

But not all the buying was institutional. Trends were still set largely by the way a select handful of the influential rich decided to live. Earlier in the century names like William Beckford and the Marquis of Hertford had been crucial. They were followed by Russians – Demidoff and Saltykoff – and by 1900 a number of individual Americans, especially James Pierpont Morgan, loomed even larger. Morgan, described by René Gimpel as 'the last American grandee', spent over £10 million between 1900 and his death in 1913.

The rich still set the tone of the market, but the nature of their purchases was altering, and the shift produced a fundamental change in the relative prices paid for different classes of objects. Our present scale of values, in which genius is prized above craftsmanship or the materials in an object, is a recent development. So recent that it is ridiculous to gasp at the low prices fetched by so many Old Master paintings – the very image of genius – before the 1890s. Before that date the work of even such a universally admired painter as Raphael rated lower than that of a great eighteenth-century *ébéniste* or Renaissance silversmith. To say that the price of a Raphael or a Leonardo multiplied a hundred-fold in a hundred years (even after eliminating the effects of inflation) is a meaningless statement. For only in the past hundred years has the market ennobled paintings to a rank above objects whose major virtue was the lavish materials, skill and ingenuity that went into them.

Before the 1880s the costliest work of art ever sold was a parcel-gilt and enamelled standing cup, made in Nuremburg in 1550 by Wenzel Jamnitzer, 'an inconceivably hideous object' in Reitlinger's words, for which Karl Meyer Rothschild paid £32,000.* In the following thirty years a few paintings fetched more than any objects. But in general, even after 1919, the highest prices were still being paid – with some regularity – for objects rather than pictures. The transition can be seen clearly through Christie's major sales between 1880 and 1914. Only three were purely of Old Masters, the majority were of 'Modern' pictures or *objets d'art*. These often fetched more than the pictures (the Huth collection of Oriental china, furniture and works of art fetched over £67,000, the pictures a mere £50,000).

The most obvious genre in which lengthy, painstaking and labour-intensive craftsmanship counts for everything, and genius does not enter into the equation, is tapestries – a category which also implies that the purchaser has acres of soaring walls to fill. The tapestry tradition is particularly associated with Pierpont Morgan, whose money, said Reitlinger, 'was spent avowedly for patience, hard labour and richness of material, as if these things were the highest essence of art'. But the fashion was not purely personal. After his death the great New York dealers, French and Co, paid $2.5 million (£515,000) for forty of his tapestry panels – four of which fetched the equivalent of a mere £30,000 in New York in 1957. And in real terms the record of $113,000 (£46,000) paid for a late Gothic Tournai tapestry at Sotheby's in Los Angeles in the mid-1970s was below the prices paid sixty years earlier.

The revolution which eventually substituted Impressionists for tapestries was triggered by one man, Joseph, later Lord, Duveen. His father and uncle had made their fortunes selling porcelain and other *objets d'art*.† He turned his talents to selling pictures as well. But even Duveen, with all his salesmanship, succeeded only partially, with a handful of collectors and relatively few pictures – only a select few Old Masters and eighteenth-century English portraits fetched more than major works of skill and craftsmanship like French eighteenth-century furniture. The prices paid at auction in the first decade of the century show the limits: Duveen bought a Turner, *Rockets and Blue Lights*, for $129,000 in New York just below the record auction (also in New York) set when his great rivals,

---

* The Rothschilds provided solid support for German Renaissance silver for a whole generation. There is only one good thing to be said about their taste: Philippe de Rothschild used two massive silver drinking cups he inherited from the family collection as the foundation for the superb Musée du Vin he created at Château Mouton Rothschild.

† In his lovely, entertaining book on Duveen, S. N. Behrman under-estimates Duveen's originality. He assumes that other dealers were making more out of the American plutocracy than his father and uncles, by selling them pictures rather than works of art and that Duveen was merely following them. I believe that Behrman was wrong: that Duveen was a genuine innovator.

Knoedler's, paid $137,000 for Hals' *Portrait of a Woman* at the 1913 Borden sale. (The same year a Rembrandt Lucretia went for $130,000 and three English pictures for over $100,000 each. The higher prices paid in private deals were exclusively for Leonardos or Raphaels.)

Duveen had to use new techniques of salesmanship: he persuaded a few American millionaires to pay fortunes for pictures which would ensure their immortality, first by associating them with an aristocratic past, and then, more permanently, by turning them into public benefactors celebrated for the collections they bequeathed to museums. It was the competition he engendered between his clients that set off the unprecedented upward spiral in picture prices.

Joseph Alsop spotted at least one precedent: 'just as Duveen was an Englishman peddling English and European old masters to American multimillionaires, so Damasippus was a Greek peddling Greek old masters to Roman multimillionaires of the first century B.C.' Damasippus ended up broke. But he was important enough to star in one of Horace's satires.

Despite Duveen's efforts most of the major collectors who set the pace were still not exclusively, or mainly, interested in pictures. Just as the Rothschilds had made the market in German silver, so Morgan single-handedly transformed the price structure of Chinese porcelain, on which he spent £2 million (then $10 million) in the first twelve years of the present century, far more than anyone spent on pictures at the time.

Some buyers were self-confident enough not to require advice, to set trends rather than follow them – hence the frisson that ran through the market a generation later when the great couturier Doucet completely changed his lifestyle. He sold his collection (and thus depressed the price of eighteenth-century French furniture), and moved out of an eighteenth-century town house into a modern villa in Neuilly, filled with art nouveau wrought ironwork and Lalique glass panels as a setting for Cézannes and Rousseaus and even a cubist Picasso.

'Creative money' like Doucet's had a confidence that did not require guidance from dealers or experts, and some rich men, of course, did not need art at all. (When a group of dealers presented a sumptuous volume to Henry Ford showing the finest works they had to offer, he thanked them, but saw no need to buy any of the originals. He was satisfied to browse through the magnificent illustrations. His grandson, Henry II, has been a notable collector.) But most of the funds coming into the market belonged to people who required the guidance, commercial and artistic, which could be provided only by dealers.

Even laymen can distinguish skill, craftsmanship and precious raw materials. Genius was more difficult to spot, so the buyers required some guarantee of authenticity. Until the Duveen era 'Old Masters' had so frequently been dubious that the best dealers, like Ernest Gambart or the Agnews, preferred to commission living artists. So Duveen helped promote a new breed of 'authenticating experts' like the young Bernard Berenson. The prototype had been Dr von Bode. Dealers would 'tip' him by donating one or two pictures to his beloved Museum. But most other 'authenticating experts' were more mercenary. Berenson demanded 25 per cent of the profits whether he was helping to buy, or sell, or merely giving his all-powerful opinion. Nevertheless he – and others of his ilk like Roger Fry – considered themselves a cut above the dealers, who were naturally infuriated by their moral and intellectual pretentions. René Gimpel (Duveen's brother-in-law, a passionately scholarly dealer who disliked and despised Berenson) recounts how Berenson once told an extremely knowledgeable antique dealer called Bauer: '"A man as scholarly as yourself shouldn't be a dealer, it's horrible to be a dealer." To which Bauer replied: "Between you and me there's no great difference; I'm an intellectual dealer and you're a dealing intellectual." Berenson never forgave him for that.' Another dealer once complained to Gimpel, 'We are the prey of German experts ... The incorruptible Friedlander (director at Berlin) now has a mistress and for her he acknowledges all the pictures he had previously condemned.' Gimpel's unbounded contempt was soundly based, for he had seen for himself the number of fakes bought on their say-so by sophisticated collectors like Jules Bache. 'The certified swindle', he had concluded, 'the hugest swindle the world has ever seen'.

The idea of authentification, that paintings were valuable only, or mainly, because they were the work of a given artist, is generally thought to be a mark of progress in the appreciation of art. We wonder at the naivety of the age of Sir Joshua Reynolds when we read that the executors of his estate believed his studio contained forty-four Michaelangelos, twenty-four Raphaels and twelve Leonardos. A tone of condescension underlies the comment that 'Corot painted five hundred pictures, of which ten thousand are in the United States'. But there is a very real loss of innocence mixed with the new purity. We sneer at fakes and those who admire them, but it is a little curious to belittle people who judged by the beauty of the object alone, not the signature attached to it. Once you look at the signature before the object you are abandoning the basic quest for beauty in favour of snobbery, price-consciousness, a whole slew of unworthy motives.

My attitude was shared by Geoffrey Hobson, probably the most scholarly and scrupulous director Sotheby's ever had: 'Knowledge does not make it easier, in my experience, to enjoy works of art', he once wrote. 'One of my earliest enthusiasms was for Japanese colour prints; I had not the slightest knowledge of what they represented, but they seemed beautiful to me; they did not seem more beautiful when I learnt whether the girls were goddesses or geishas, the men samurai or comedians.'

The changing scale of values was fully reflected in the catalogues and importance of Christie's, which dominated the auction scene in London. Its founder, James Christie, had secured the entrée into the mansions of the English gentry through his friendship with Thomas Gainsborough and this proved invaluable to his successor, 'Old Woods', a century later. Auction houses were not, in general, frightfully reputable, and rarely the medium for truly important transactions (Old Woods did many important private deals – like the sale for 25,000 guineas of 'Raffaelles' *Grace* from the Earl of Dudley to the Duc d'Aumale – because he was, personally, such a trusted intermediary). But Christie's was fashionable, a fixture in London's social round. Not surprisingly, when London Society started to go away for the weekend, it was forced to abandon Saturday afternoon sales.*

Christie's success showed up the inadequacies of the very different auction system in Paris – itself similar to an earlier one in Amsterdam. In both centres the authorities had established an elaborate licensing system, designed to control the market and protect buyers by providing some form of official guarantee that the goods on offer were genuine. This sort of strictly-supervized clearing house prevented any individual auction house from building up its business, the only entrepreneurs it permitted were necessarily small-scale, operating in what remains, in Paris anyway, a marvellously cosy covered bazaar. In the end a system designed to regulate the market (combined with a 10 per cent tax and the auctioneer's percentage, inevitably a high one because he was operating on such a small scale) served only to stifle it.

This became apparent in the 1880s. Unless a *commissaire priseur*, one of the auctioneers licensed by the state, could sell a specially important collection in the mansion where it was housed it had to go to the dirty dilapidated Hôtel Drouot. The French recognized the problem. As *Le Temps* said in 1886: 'in no country do the public sales cost so much as in France, and in no country are the arrangements so bad'. Since the French Revolution anyone had been allowed in, so there was always a great mob of unwashed Kibitzers at any interest-

---

* As late as 1907. PCW's mother, for instance, always considered the idea of the 'weekend' rather vulgar.

28

ing sale, although the situation improved somewhat in the 1890s when a special entrance was provided so that ticket holders could escape the mob.

The conditions at Christie's were not much better. When Gimpel went there in 1919 he declared that nothing had changed for a hundred years:

The main room, which is very dirty, not very big, with the walls a wine-red, in the middle of which rises up a sort of jack-in-the-box in poor condition but of good wood with a fine patina on it. It's the auctioneer's seat, and in front of it a long table stretches out at right angles to it, surrounded by hard wooden benches, with an odd one caned, but both sorts battered. It's wonderful! Here there is no need to pander to the clients paying twenty, forty, fifty thousand pounds for pictures! In Paris Georges Petit begins by attracting customers with comfort in his immense gallery, providing hundreds of velvet armchairs. He shows them the picture the way a goldsmith shows a jewel. He furbishes and gilds the frames, and of course cleans and varnishes the canvasses, which are then spaced out harmoniously on the walls. A sale is more consummately got up than a first night, with good carpets too on the floor. Even at the Hôtel Drouot, that squalid hole, sales are got up a bit better. Christie's in England, in the country of comfort and cleanliness, has the audacity to offer sheer discomfort and a parquet floor thick with dust. Pictures worth a few pounds alternate with hundred-thousand-pound works, and are sold along with them, everything 'just as it comes' on the walls. Three, four rows, the pictures one above the other, the finest sometimes perched just below the roof. With us, catalogues are superb. Before the war they cost an average of 50,000 francs to produce, here, not even fifty. No explanation or reference, no expert opinion or guarantee. What does it matter, since people still come!

The squalor helped the dealers compete by offering infinitely more elegant emporia, but Christie's could rely on London's unequalled combination of aristocratic supply and international demand – one catalogue even listed the times of the boat trains. London soon started to eat into even the specialist markets where Paris had remained supreme. The move to London may have signified the moment when a particular type of object changed from being of purely specialist interest and started to be collected more widely. In 1896 a big Viennese collection of medieval and Renaissance art was sent to London rather than to Paris. Similarly Paris had been the centre of Japanoiserie. Then in 1909 Sotheby's sold a major collection assembled by a New Yorker, John Stewart Happer, after which similar material, especially prints, flooded to London. The *Chronique des Arts* predicted that the international market would shift to London completely. This was rather premature, but the art business – including auctioneering – was so personal and entrepreneurial that any closed corporate system was bound to be defeated in the long run.

Arguably the most important long-term trend did not touch London at all. In the 1880s Durand-Ruel, the great patron of the Impressionists, found himself owing more than a million francs. With regular customers broke, other dealers ganged up on him, hoping he would have to dump his whole magnificent stock on the market. So he organised group shows in London, Rotterdam and Boston; crucially in 1886 he opened a gallery in New York, which, within a decade, became his most important market. His rivals learnt a lesson and Impressionists sold for previously unheard-of prices at the Victor Choquet sale in 1897.

Prices for an ever-widening range of objects continued to mount. In the four years before 1914 records were set for virtually every type of painting and work of art. In Reitlinger's words: 'There was next to nothing in the collector's repertoire of the period that did not have its share in the prosperity of the times'. Prices were so high that, allowing for inflation, virtually nothing was sold above the 1913 level for forty years: some categories (like Victorian paintings) had to wait sixty years to catch up, and a few others (like tapestries) probably never will. The long slump, combined with inflation, a factor which never entered into the price equation at all before 1914, left a curious legacy. In the 1950s and 1960s the art world was sure of a marvellous couple of decades when the world's wealthy classes finally regained their liquid funds and their confidence and returned to the art market. For two decades. journalists, dealers and auctioneers could all talk of the same transaction as involving both a 'record price' and being a 'bargain' without stretching the truth.

# 3  THE MAKING OF AN AUCTION HOUSE

Despite its long history, Sotheby's had played only a minor, specialist role in the great art boom before the First World War. The first auction conducted by Samuel Baker, Sotheby's founder, had been in 1744 when he had already been selling books for a dozen years. His firm passed through the hands of Samuel Leigh and the Sothebys, father and son, and by the 1840s was established as the premier London book auctioneer. In the 1850s they were also selling engravings, pictures and antiquities, as well as 'fictile manufactures' like porcelain, china and maiolica, but in the last forty years of the century concentrated almost exclusively on books and coins, together with some marginal items like arms and armour, etchings, prints and engravings. Christie's recognized its rival's supremacy in the books' field and, as a matter of course, handed over the library of any great house whose other contents it was selling. The tradition lingered on. As late as 1958 the catalogue for the Goldschmidt sale announced that Sotheby's were 'Auctioneers of Literary Property and Works illustrative of the Fine Arts'.

The books business was reliably cyclical: just as Agnew's used to trade with generations of the same families, so with books, as *The Times* put it in 1911: 'All great libraries are built on the debris of others'. One of the greatest of all collectors, Robert Hoe, recognized that, 'If the great collections of the past had not been sold, where would I have found my books?' Sotheby's was especially used to dealing with Americans, not only great collectors like Hoe, but with ordinary millionaires as well: for rare books and, more particularly, illustrated manuscripts, were considered very important adjuncts to the super-rich way of living. As a result, the book trade was a close-knit international clan, and Sotheby's was used to intricate and continuing financial relationships with dealers here and abroad – all useful, if intangible assets.

The firm took its modern form only in 1908, when a group headed by the remarkable Montague Barlow bought the business from Tom Hodge, who had nearly sold it to Hodgson's, a rival firm of book auctioneers. But there was no inherent reason why Sotheby's, rather than any of London's other auction rooms, should emerge as the major challenger to Christie's – which had itself seen off earlier challenges. These – notably from George Robins in the mid nineteenth century – had been personal, but, once the 'Barlow group' had taken over, Christie's was faced, for the first time, by a growing team of rivals. Barlow, the architect of the challenge, was a truly remarkable man, a versatile Victorian born out of time. He was the son of the Dean of Peterborough and, in deference to his father's wishes, started life as a barrister. But his real career started with the takeover of Sotheby's. He transformed the firm while using it as a stepping stone to political advancement and became an enlightened Conservative Minister of Labour. In the late 1920s he abandoned politics and helped develop what was then Malaya as vice-chairman of the Perak Hydro Electric Company.

As his widow (a former Sotheby's secretary whom he married late in life after a fifteen-year courtship) told Frank Herrmann:* 'he was determined to make the art auctioneering business a gentleman's business, you know. He had the vision of putting it on to an entirely different social status because I remember one of his friends in Society saying, "Oh, he's an auctioneer". He was resolved to remove the slur of the auctioneer business and to bring it on to a higher level.' The status was indeed low, both here and in the United States. When G. T. Kirby, son of the owner of New York's leading auction house, wanted to marry the adopted daughter of a merchant prince, the wedding contract allegedly contained a clause forbidding the bridegroom ever to become an auctioneer. As late as 1951, when Christopher Weston, the present chairman of Phillips, announced his choice of career, the headmaster of his public school, Lancing College, trumpeted: 'I am not having any of my boys becoming estate agents.'

Within a dozen years of taking over Sotheby's Barlow was not merely a Member of Parliament but a junior minister. In 1920, he could write confidently enough to Charles des Graz, then a civil servant, in persuading him to join the firm:

In the first place it is absolutely a gentleman's business ... Of course we are auctioneers, and it is necessary that the partners should be prepared actually to sell in the rostrum, as I do myself. But I find the auctioneering itself of great interest and the business which deals all the time with fine books, fine pictures, fine prints, furniture, coins etc, is absorbingly attractive ... work at Sotheby's brings one into pleasant social relation with most of the leading Statesmen of the day, such as Lord Curzon, Lord Harcourt, Lord

* All quotes in this chapter come from his invaluable book on Sotheby's unless otherwise indicated.

Lansdowne, the Speaker, Sir Alfred Mond, and others, all of whom are great collectors and drop in constantly: and in addition one gets into pleasant social touch with most of the big houses in England, such as Chatsworth, Wilton, Holkham and others in a way which I believe you would appreciate

Barlow was not himself wealthy, so he brought in two rich partners. The younger, Geoffrey Hobson, was a brilliant scholar and linguist and was destined for the Foreign Office. But he was deaf so could be neither a diplomat nor an auctioneer; nevertheless the respect he gained over the years as a bibliophile provided the firm with a scholarly respectability unprecedented in auctioneering history. Social respectability was provided by the third partner, Felix Warre, scion of a distinguished Somerset family and son of the headmaster of Eton, who fortunately turned out to be a brilliant auctioneer.

Barlow decided to widen Sotheby's activities in 1913 when he literally stumbled across some paintings in the firm's premises in Wellington Street. Previously all the pictures had been passed on to Christie's as part of the unequal swap arrangement by which the bigger house passed on the books in return. But pictures were only tacked on to sales of drawings and engravings until 1917, the year Barlow moved the firm to its existing premises in Bond Street (this was less foolhardy than it sounds, the auction business had held up surprisingly well during the war). The premises themselves had no great pretensions. They had been the Doré Gallery, dedicated to selling the works of the one artist, Gustave Doré. Below were capacious cellars belonging to a wine merchant. Yet, although they now seem picturesquely cramped, they were far more spacious than those at Wellington Street, and for the first time Sotheby's could physically handle heavy items – particularly furniture – on the spot.

Setting up in the centre of the art-dealing world was a clear challenge to Christie's, which was not going to take the challenge lying down. Its 'friends' almost certainly tried to sabotage Sotheby's first major general sale – of some of the riches of Wilton House, the ancestral home of the Earls of Pembroke, which included two magnificent suits of sixteenth-century armour. Only a couple of days before the sale Charles Ffoulkes, then Keeper of the Armoury of the Tower of London, declared in a joint article with his predecessor, Lord Dillon, that the suits were of later origin. In the event the Sotheby partners did not lose their nerves and went ahead. The suits were bought in after final bids of £14,000 and £10,000, far above the price paid for any armour before. (To give some kind of perspective to the sale a marvellous Rembrandt portrait of his elderly mother, still at Wilton today, was bought in for £11,500.)

This pretty piece of sabotage set the tone for the rivalry between the two. Barlow cut rates, charging vendors of more than £100 worth of pictures or works of art a mere 7½ per cent. The rivalry extended to the sale-room correspondents, who got a great deal of space in the serious papers. Barlow carefully cultivated the garrulous A. C. R. Carter of the *Daily Telegraph*, while William Roberts of *The Times* was firmly in the camp of Christie's (whose history he wrote).

The move to Bond Street was well-timed. In Reitlinger's words 'The London sales season opened four days after the armistice, and, for paintings at any rate, it proved the most successful season that had ever been known, with 100 works sold at upwards of 1,400 guineas each. Fifty-two lots of French furniture made from 1,000 to 9,000 guineas each.' Fortunately for Sotheby's, armour, in which they already dealt, had replaced tapestries as the fashionable decoration for millionaires' marble halls. The fashion had been set in 1917 largely through the enthusiasm of two Americans, William Randolph Hearst and Clarence Mackay, 'the cable and telegraph king'. Between 1920 and 1929 at least eight lots of armour were sold in London at above £2,500.

In the 1920s both firms prospered. When Barlow offered des Graz a partnership, he asked him to put up £15,000 for one ninth of the firm, capitalizing the whole at the highly respectable sum of £135,000. In 1908 Tom Hodge had valued the business at £30,000, and eventually took £25,000 for the goodwill and took out £60,000 worth of capital. Not surprisingly Christie's was even more profitable. In 1928–29, the year it disposed of most of the famous Holford collection, its profits amounted to 7½ oer cent of the turnover (itself more than £1 million), half the nominal revenue, for the overheads were minimal. When Barlow retired in 1928, Sotheby's employed a mere fifty-five people and when Arthur Grimwade, Christie's great expert on silver, joined the firm four years later it employed only six secretaries and two office boys; he also found that one man, Arthur Abbey, who had just retired, had catalogued all the applied arts except books and jewellery.

Nevertheless Sotheby's made very little impact on the central citadel of Christie's strength. In Reitlinger's lists of paintings and drawings sold between the wars, Christie's name occurs 721 times, Sotheby's a mere 189 – and even this comparison overemphasizes Sotheby's strength because drawings, a field in which they were relatively important, did not fetch as much as paintings. What does not emerge, either, is that the most important sales tended to take place out of the saleroom.

34

The Holford sales came just before the onset of the slump, which gradually froze the whole market. Sir Geoffrey Agnew, remembers how in his early days with the family firm he joined in 1931, not a single buyer would cross the threshold for months at a time, 'when the market goes down, it's not that you're selling at lower prices, you're not selling at all', although the general freeze did prevent too profound a slump in prices. Nevertheless, the number of pictures reaching the important figure of 1,400 guineas dropped from 130 in 1927 to 63 in 1930, to 13 in the season ending July 1931, and to a mere 8 the following season, even though foreign buyers should have been tempted to London when sterling was floated in the autumn of 1931. In the season ending July 1933 only four lots of French furniture made over £200. Inevitably both houses had to sack some of the staff, and cut the salaries of the survivors (in Christie's some of the wages were paid personally by Lance Hannen). In 1934 the two tried to merge, but the proposal came to nothing largely because Christie's was burdened with what then seemed like an overwhelming sum of rent and mortgage payments.

Christie's faced other problems. Power increasingly passed to Sir Alec Martin – the second figure of working-class origins to dominate this supposedly aristocratic firm in the past century. His qualities had been spotted by a Christie's director, Bill Anderson, while he was still a youthful choirboy at the fashionable church of St Columba's, Pont Street. In 1896 he had been engaged as an office boy. By hard work (he once took a holiday job washing dishes in a Montmartre café to learn French) and sheer force of character he became a major figure in the world of art. He was a friend of Ramsay Macdonald and his work for the National Art Collection Fund preserving the national artistic heritage – for which he was knighted – clearly seemed more important than selling it. In the words of *The Times*' obituary: 'he always considered the crown of his business career was the successful outcome of the lengthy negotiations for the acquisition by the nation of the chief works of art at Chatsworth'.

Christie's could still mount spectacular sales – the most famous in the 1930s was Sir Ernest Oppenheimer's collection of Old Master drawings, maiolica and bronzes. But Martin increasingly antagonized the dealers, especially crucial clients in bad times since they were prepared to buy for stock. He competed with them, advising clients to sell through auction, sending photographs of forthcoming lots to museum curators and other key clients before they went to the trade, trying to deprive the dealers of their role as middlemen. The Agnews, in particular, reacted badly. Their hereditary connection with Christie's had been diluted, for an outsider, R. W. Lloyd, a wealthy businessman and collector, had been invited to invest in the firm.* So Agnew's started to direct business to Sotheby's, often through Vere Pilkington, a young man whose father, a wealthy stockbroker, had bought him a partnership, and he naturally approached other dealers as well.

Some categories, notably those going out of fashion, were hard hit by the slump. The most spectacular examples came from Victorian painting, in decline since 1918 anyway, and the 'Duveen' market. A Lawrence head of Lord Castlereagh, bought in 1928 for 4,200 guineas, went for a mere £540 ten years later.

Nevertheless, the depression did create a feeling that works of art had a certain defensive worth, that they lost their value less than stocks and shares. The rich noticed cases like that of Arthur Hind, an industrialist from Utica in up-state New York. He was wiped out in the slump and after his death his widow found that only his stamp collection (which included the then most expensive postage stamp in the world) had held its value. Prices of art (although artificially supported because so little came onto the market) had held up surprisingly well. When the collection of an American banker, George Blumenthal, was sold at the depths of depression for 30 per cent less than he gave for it he was asked if he felt depressed :'Not at all', he replied, 'I'm losing 75 per cent of my securities.' The leading French dealer Maurice Rheims even claimed that he heard a Renoir described as a 'blue-chip investment' in the mid 1930s.

Despite the slump, Sotheby's was steadily moving towards a depth of professional expertise unprecedented in the auction business. Geoffrey Hobson's position was, of course, unique. In Tim Munby's words: 'no more striking example can be imagined of the ideal interaction and alliance between bibliography and business', for Sotheby's was literally the centre of the world's rare book business. But this was exceptional. In other areas Sotheby's started from a very low base. Their first 'expert' on Old Masters, William Mason of Mason & Philips, was really a valuer. 'The temptation was to use attributions suggested by the owner, or to lean heavily on provenance if it happened to be known, or if it could be deduced from old labels if they were clearly discernible on the back of frames'. Mason had only one virtue: 'Many of his catalogue entries were written – presumably unwittingly – in a delightfully rhythmic style that often resembles blank verse'. But he made major howlers and was eventually sacked when he simply overlooked the four most important paintings in a major collection. In the early 1920s he was replaced by Charles Bell of the Ashmolean Museum in Oxford, a much more substantial figure, who walked out in a huff and in 1924

* Originally because Christie's hoped to sell his famous collection of Turner watercolours. In the event they were bequeathed to the British Museum.

Sotheby's acquired the services of a man whose name, Tancred Borenius, was as improbable as his character. He was a sharp, quarrelsome fellow, a proudly nationalistic Finn (with an Italian grandmother and an appropriately flamboyant side to his character). Borenius served as part-time adviser for over twenty years. He did very well out of it – in the peak year of 1928–29 his commission income amounted to £3,000, more than the partners were getting.

It was far more difficult to cover Works of Art. Sotheby's defined these as everything you might find in a really good antique shop: furniture, tapestry, carpets, needlework, glass, pottery, porcelain, pewter, silver, bronzes, enamels, clocks and watches, stained-glass windows, old musical instruments, as well as jade, hardstones, lacquer and ivory, 'anything and everything that had been made by skilled craftsmen in the field of the decorative arts since the time of the Renaissance'. There were no specialist sales, most of these miscellaneous categories were lumped together in sales which started at 1.00 pm on Fridays (so that collectors could come in person).

Hobson looked for advice from the more erudite dealers and museum curators, as well as watching out for new cataloguers outside the book business, but the trend to general professionalism was hampered by Felix Warre. He believed that 'no expert is worth more than a fiver a week' and his reluctance in the later 1930s to compensate the staff for the salary cuts they had been forced to accept during the slump did not help morale. Even before the move to Bond Street his lack of understanding had created a new rival. He refused to pay the subscription of J. B. Caldecott, the firm's expert on many forms of antiques – including, especially, coins – to the Numismatic Society. Warre took over the business himself, but his lack of knowledge led the trade to depart, initially to Switzerland, where the sale-rooms illustrated every coin in the catalogue. Then Douglas Glendining set up his own coin auction house and competed successfully with the simple formula: he knew more and cut commissions.

Not surprisingly, Sotheby's lost its two best recruits, although this is inevitable in a business where the rewards for an expert who has any of the instincts of a dealer are so much greater outside the auction business than they can be within. One was Tom Lumley, who formerly worked for a rival house, Puttick & Simpson. He was the very model of the young men brought in a quarter of a century later. 'Lumley at nineteen was mercurial, ambitious, lively and had an unusually good eye for spotting pieces of quality in unlikely places ... the older partners soon found him something of a trial for he was

quite unabashed about questioning existing methods of procedure
... but, although they rarely said so, they were impressed by the fact
that he was often right ... he established a regular routine for the
circulation among directors of obituaries of people known to the firm
who had recently died' ('coffin power' is always vital in the auction
business). Among other gems he found a Franz Hals portrait, the
most expensive painting sold in London in the whole of the 1931–32
season, although it fetched a mere £3,600.

A visit by Lumley to an irascible colonel living in solitary splendour in a mansion in North Wales with fifty-seven bedrooms led to
the introduction of the biggest single novelty between the wars, the
'country house sale'. Until then London auctioneers had not normally sold the contents of relatively run-of-the mill houses on the
spot. Vere Pilkington was put in charge of a flying squad of three,
himself, Lumley and Temple Williams, a member of Spilman's, a
family firm of antique furniture dealers.

Temple Williams resigned in 1937 after eight years with Sotheby's
and joined Blairmans, where, almost single-handed, he created a
taste and a market for Regency furniture, which was then totally
unappreciated. Lumley had left the year before, soon set up on his
own and became one of London's most respected silver dealers (such
departures were not pure loss, since, as happened on a bigger scale in
the 1960s and 1970s, ex-Sotheby's people often became some of the
firm's best customers).

But one key man remained, Jim Kiddell, recruited by Barlow in
1921 as works and office manager. He had spent virtually the whole
of the First World War on the Western Front, including a spell
co-operating with the notorious Mutiny Breaking Staff. Indeed in
his first years at Sotheby's, he was something of a martinet, but
during his fifty-eight years with the firm (he died in harness in 1980)
he was transformed, leaving behind a feeling – throughout the
antiques trade as well as within the firm – of being, if not a saint, a
deeply lovable man, 'Cuddles' or 'Uncle Jim'. One useful friend
was Queen Mary, a regular client, buying under the *nom de guerre* of
Dawson. But he also 'had more friends among collectors and dealers
than any man in London. He was always about (even at eighty-four)
peering benignly over the half-moon lenses of his glasses. He had the
alert quizzical look of the scholar who has strayed into the non-
academic scene, though he was more the senior schoolmaster than
the absent-minded professor, for he exuded benevolent discipline,
efficiency and a sense of order.'

His first service – instilling some order in the chaos – was the least
he rendered. His major – and incalculable – contribution to
Sotheby's was to provide the firm with some of the scholarly

respectability in works of art with which Geoffrey Hobson had endowed it in the field of books and manuscripts. Barlow had set up the first auction house to be run like a properly-structured business, Hobson and Kiddell invented the equally revolutionary concept of the auction house as a repository of reliable, objective advice on every type of object. At a time when even dealers, let alone auctioneers, were rather looked at askance, Kiddell was asked to join the English Glass Circle and was the longest serving President of the English Ceramic Circle.

The standards which Hobson tried to impose made Sotheby's an increasing force in such disparate fields as Egyptian antiquities and antique firearms. The power of sheer expertise was shown in the 1930s when Geoffrey Hobson secured the sale of the library of Anton Mensing, a leading Dutch auctioneer. This was a major coup, for the Dutch had pioneered the sale by auction of books, as of other artefacts. Sotheby's also made a systematic attempt to get through to German dealers and collectors, while Christie's remained firmly insular. For the twenty years after the move to Bond Street had provided a firm foundation for Sotheby's future greatness.

PCW's timing was perfect. He joined Sotheby's, officially as a trainee in the furniture department replacing Temple Williams, at the end of 1936. That year only twenty-seven pictures and drawings had reached the magic £1,400 mark. In the seven remaining months of the 1936–37 season there were forty-nine at that level or above. Only a few months after PCW joined the firm it mounted the biggest non-book sale in its history, when Vere Pilkington's friend Lord Rothschild sold the contents of 148 Piccadilly, which he had just inherited.

At the time of the sale large numbers of wealthy foreigners were in London for the coronation of King George VI. The Rothschild name alone would have guaranteed the success of the sale, and the prices were high enough to ensure wide publicity. For the first time Sotheby's used a modern loudspeaker system and the most exciting moments of the sale were broadcast live on the BBC. The commentator was helped by Henry Rham, the firm's cashier, whose 'precise, rather dry manner' came over well; so the experiment was repeated a couple of months later. The Rothschild sale showed that Sotheby's could now compete on equal terms with Christie's for the few spectacular sales on which both firms still depended – there were none the following season and so the profits of both firms slumped. Indeed it took Christie's a quarter of a century for their sales – let alone their profits – to recover to the levels attained as a result of the first, record-breaking sessions of the Holford sale in 1928–29.

Later in 1937 PCW had the opportunity to catalogue the sale of a unique collection of rings originally accumulated by a Parisian, Edouard Guilhou, at the end of the nineteenth century. He threw himself into the job and produced a magnificently detailed catalogue – he also ensured that the sale was widely publicized. The collection fetched £15,000, more than was expected, and the young porter was beginning to make his name. It took him less than two years to become a partner, but not because of his (undoubted) talents. It was simply that his wife had inherited enough money for him to spend £5,000 on some of Felix Warre's shares and thus buy a partnership – it was still a feudal firm, Jim Kiddell was made a partner only after the Second World War.

But the three years before the war were also a crash course in works of art of all ages. He worked like a demon, for the first time in his life, taught, not only by Jim Kiddell, but even more by Jack and Putzel Hunt. They were remarkably knowledgeable antique dealers, one of the few specializing in medieval artefacts, advisers to the great Glasgow collector, Sir William Burrell. They became, and remained, very close to PCW. The sheer spread of his knowledge owed a lot to them, and to another couple of knowledgeable dealers, the Feilchenfelds.

The education was interrupted by the outbreak of war. PCW and his wife went off to join Sotheby's own branch of the war effort, the Postal Censorship at Liverpool headed, in the Second World War as in the First, by Charles des Graz. In early 1940 PCW moved to Gibraltar in charge of the 'Special Examiners' who opened diplomatic and other suspect mail, devising tricks like substituting anti-German propaganda for the anti-British material the Germans were sending *en masse* from neutral Spain and Portugal to Latin America. After the fall of France in June 1940 he moved to Bermuda, the centre of the postal interception traffic – his only connection with the world of art came when his boss, H. Montgomery Hyde, confiscated the Vollard collection of 500 paintings, mostly Impressionists, being sent by the Germans to New York through a Paris dealer, Martin Fabiani. Later he transferred to MI5 and finished the war in Washington doing much the same sort of work.

Sales went on in war-time – the marvellous Eumorphopoulos collection of porcelain was sold, inevitably for derisory sums, during the evacuation from Dunkirk. But the next year Christie's historic premises in King Street were burnt to the ground. Martin showed himself at his best. He firmly refused an offer of help from Sotheby's (let alone the proposal for a merger), borrowed a chair, a desk and a typewriter, and accepted the hospitality, first of Lord Derby at Derby House and then of Spencer House.

During the war PCW and his wife had drifted apart. After 1945 she wanted to live in the country, whereas he was firmly wedded to London and to Sotheby's. He was also discovering a previously latent homosexuality and for the rest of his life he had a series of relationships with men. But PCW was never remotely camp or overtly gay, unlike many homosexuals he was not overly interested in casual encounters, not even bothering to take advantage of obvious opportunities when travelling in the Middle East. Sotheby's was simply more important to him than relationships of any sort, sexual or platonic, with either sex.

41

After the war he moved around. Within a few years he rented Garden Lodge in Kensington from Thomas Harris, a dealer who was a friend of Burgess, Philby and Maclean. This connection produced the rumour, assiduously spread by his many enemies, that he was yet another of the Russian spies produced by the British upper classes before the war. Stories like this are inherently impossible to contradict with a hundred per cent certainty, but it is highly unlikely. He was never at Cambridge, where the notorious Russian recruiter was operating; he had never shown the sort of promise for which the recruiter was looking; and those closest to him say that he was never remotely interested in political or economic questions. (Of course he knew the curators of Russian museums, but that was a different matter. It was a source of great amusement to his colleagues, who bet each other that Moscow was one place where he did not know everyone who mattered in the art world. Needless to say he did.)

He allowed his wife to divorce him in 1951 to enable her to remarry a farmer, Philip Ballard, who lived in Herefordshire (after their retirement she developed a flourishing business in propagating and selling new varieties of hellebores, 'Christmas Roses'). PCW became a great friend of his successor and remained closer to his former wife than to anyone else for the rest of his life.

Although Christie's had twenty sales in the autumn of 1947, not having a home hurt them, but both houses suffered from the legacy of wartime strains. Geoffrey Hobson, who had succeeded Felix Warre as chairman, enjoyed one last triumph in persuading the Board of Trade to allow the import of a major collection, the Finaly library, for sale in 1948. He died, worn out, the same year and was succeeded by Charles des Graz, by this time embittered by the lack of recognition for his wartime services. Hobson's son, Anthony, himself a distinguished bibliophile, became a partner, as did PCW's friend Tim Clarke, and, belatedly, Jim Kiddell. The experts were beginning to take over from the gentlemen. When he returned from Washington, PCW had been put in charge of works of art, while Vere Pilkington took care of the pictures. Des Graz swapped them round with momentous consequences.

After the war Pilkington, looking for a new expert on pictures, was recommended to take on a brilliant German Jewish refugee, Hans Gronau. He fell ill and died, and his place was taken by his wife, the remarkable Carmen. Though not herself Jewish, she was – and remains – the very archetype of the indomitable Jewish mother, training a whole generation of young disciples in the disciplines she had herself absorbed from her husband and his world, the incomparably learned group of German art scholars and curators. She and

42

PCW worked very closely: he strongly backed her claims to a partnership when she was offered a better job elsewhere, and for a long time she was the biggest influence on him within the firm – more decisions were made when she gave him a lift in every morning from Garden Lodge than at official board meetings. At these she was not at her best, talkative and tactless. This was a permanent trait – one of her pupils fondly remembers how she told one vendor of a particularly awful picture: 'Oh yes, I'll take that picture and put it into a really bad sale.'

Recruiting the Gronaus was typical of the firm's unusually cosmopolitan outlook. Before and during the war Jim Kiddell extended a warm welcome (and often a helping hand with the authorities) to the numerous well-known Jewish dealers who had fled here from Germany with nothing save their knowledge; in later years, their businesses rebuilt, they naturally turned to Sotheby's. Kiddell was a genuinely good man; PCW, unusually for a British aristocrat, also liked Jews, as he liked all quick-witted, internationally-minded people.

But even Carmen Gronau will freely admit that Sotheby's could never match the strength of Christie's contacts and their muniment room. Safe in a steel-lined strong room, and thus protected from the bombs, all the firm's catalogues have survived, together with the famous collection of silhouettes of every picture the firm has ever sold, an invincible weapon when dealing with prospective vendors of Old Masters. Christie's never really lost the business – even when they didn't have a major picture sale for a whole summer.

For business in the early 1950s was very slow, so slow that Sotheby's eagerly accepted one of the most bizarre propositions ever placed before an auction house, the sale of the contents of the palace of King Farouk of Egypt, the very model of the fat playboy monarch, overthrown by a group of young army officers in 1952. The sale occupied most of the firm's brightest talent – including PCW and Tim Clarke – for nearly two years, as well as experts drafted in from other auction houses to fill the gaps in the Sotheby armoury of knowhow. Over the next couple of years the sales generated an immense amount of international publicity, but very little, if any, actual cash.

For the sales contained a high proportion of farce – and even danger. General Neguib, the original figure-head of the revolution, was overthrown by Colonel Nasser the day the sale started. Farouk had a number of important collections (the ever-bitchy Maurice Rheims alleges that Sotheby's sold a gold and agate scent-burner without anyone realizing that it had belonged to Marie Antoinette). But there was also a great deal of junk, including a famous collection of pornography (which proved rather disappointing under closer inspection). When Tim Clarke came to catalogue the contents of Farouk's bedroom he discovered objects whose nature he will not discuss even now, papers whose importance he understood because of his work as a senior intelligence officer during the war, massive numbers of old aspirin packets – and valuable paperweights on the loo.

The Farouk sale helped PCW learn the trick of attracting international publicity, but the crucial lessons he had absorbed were internal. For all the increasing storehouse of knowledge within the firm, it was an auction house, dependent on the skills of a few partners. And in his first years with the firm PCW developed into a great auctioneer, in many people's eyes the best, most sensitive in the world. He had a considerable tradition to go on – unlike his competitors at Christie's. The founder, James Christie, had been a master of the florid style: 'let me entreat – Ladies and gentlemen – permit me to put this inestimable piece of elegance under your protection – only observe – the inexhaustible munificence of your superlatively candid generosity must harmonize with the refulgent brilliance of this little jewel'. His most famous successor, Old Woods, stood at the opposite extreme. He started every sale by simply announcing, 'Lot One'. Sometimes, when in a particularly expansive mood, he would add, 'it's a nice picture'.

The 'gentlemen of Sotheby's' had developed their own style, largely thanks to Charles des Graz whose 'drier, more precise' manner had considerable influence. Tim Munby wrote in *The Book Collector*, 'the real test of this most exacting of roles is not in the selling of works of the very first importance. Long practice made des Graz perfect in the more difficult art of selling secondary material fast without missing a bid. Uncertainty or delay by the seller is soon reflected in lethargy and inertia on the part of the bidders. Des Graz kept the room on its toes. He knew the value of what he was selling and the personalities of the buyers; thus he was able to adapt the pace to the needs of each individual lot.' Tim Clarke analysed the auctioneer's role more poetically: 'He's the conductor of the orchestra. The objects are the score, the buyers at the sale are the musicians' – implying that the 'conductor' should know both.

The style was particularly suitable for book sales attended mostly by professionals, but was adaptable enough to encourage amateurs. The tradition was maintained by Lord John Kerr, head of the book department from the mid-1960s until 1982. According to Frank Herrmann: 'He is the quickest caller of bids in the business, very quiet in voice (which helps to rivet attention) yet infinitely authoritative. It is a style of auctioneering for professionals ... The amateur has to keep on his toes ... As soon as Lord John senses that a collector is genuinely involved in the bidding, the pace slows down, he cocks his head gently to one side, smiles expectantly and waits for the more hesitant reaction of the untrained cerebral processes of the amateur.'

PCW built his own, deceptively casual, informal style on the des Graz model. Unlike his predecessors, his generation of auctioneers could assume that they would be using a microphone. So it was entirely suitable for radio or the TV screen, just as television comedians, who know how close they are to their audience, can discard the outsize gestures natural to older performers reared in the theatrical tradition. At the same time, Bill Brooks of Debenham and Coe kept the old music-hall tradition going. According to Jeremy Cooper, Coe 'used to announce the lots with the adjectival relish of a master of ceremonies at Collins Music-Hall', threatening to describe music stands as 'mellifluous' and Chinese vases as 'full of occidental promise'. The style was not confined to minor London sale-rooms. PCW's style never went down in New York, where he took only one sale. The New Yorkers preferred auctioneers like John Marion telling them: 'Come on make it a hundred thousand, it'll sound better when you tell your friends'. But the 'huckster' tradition was equally professional. Marion once sold a major picture – a Turner formerly owned by Pierpont Morgan – amidst great applause, even though it had in fact been bought in since it had not reached the seller's reserve.

PCW himself always emphasized the informal nature of his style: 'You see a lot of familiar faces, it's rather like going to a friend's wedding', he said. But the informality was matched by the professionalism. Jeremy Maas, London's leading dealer in Victorian pictures, says firmly that he was 'the greatest auctioneer, he knew who should buy something, his effortless charm was such that you'd make another bid just to please him. He wouldn't allow you to bid against yourself – unlike Alec Martin who was a brutal auctioneer.' The ultra-critical Sir Geoffrey Agnew agrees: 'He was far and away the best auctioneer I've ever known because you always felt he was on your side. He was terribly good at changing foot when he sensed you were bidding up to a limit. Other people tried to work you up, refusing bids if they weren't far enough above the previous one. PCW coaxed you with small advances.' Peter Nahum talked of PCW conducting 'in large nonchalant leaps leaving people gasping before reducing the jumps to much smaller ones, others were far too monotonous' – at the sale of exciting pictures owned by Norton Simon in May 1971, 'the bidding moved up in lots of $500, the crowd rustled restlessly, ruffling the pages of the catalogue'.

To PCW: 'Onlookers help to create an atmosphere, which is necessary if you are to have a successful sale.' But the bidding itself was cruiously intimate, a conversation between three people: 'It's a curious thing that if you are sitting a long way from someone, if he is looking at you you are absolutely aware of that' – some would call this PCW's feminine sensitive side – 'and therefore if someone in the audience wants to bid on a lot he somehow conveys that by the way he holds his head or by his concentration that he wants you to look at him and you glance in his direction. The moment he sees you are looking at him he makes a nod or some other sign. You look away from him and see if there is a second bidder and once there is another bid you immediately look back to him. The courteous way to conduct an auction is to treat it as a ping-pong tournament, a series of duels, x takes on y and beats him and someone takes on x. You don't take bids from all over the room. Having only two people at a time makes it easier because you can recognize that some imperceptible sign is obviously a bid.'

PCW – in public anyway – was modest about his ability to increase the bids. He told one interviewer: 'The auctioneer can only boost the bidding by having faith and believing in the object he sells. I think that is communicable and infectious. I would not be able to sell things. I don't care about, like motorcars . . . He's got to believe in what you're selling even if he doesn't show it outwardly . . . he has to be courteous and bustling . . . he mustn't show in his voice that he considers the price a high one. This is very important, because it's counter-productive, showing that the price has gone beyond the point he expected.' Less convincingly, he also claimed that the auctioneer was a mere croupier: 'the figures are like telephone numbers, they go to a point and then stop'.

The professional coolth was well cultivated. In the introduction to Sotheby's *Annual Review* for 1961–62 Frank Davis describes how in an evening sale, amidst the paraphernalia of television and cine-cameras, 'a calm, slightly sleepy voice, apparently doubtful that all this amount of filthy lucre is actually going to be handed over in exchange for a few square inches of canvas, registers the bidding as it soars upward' – the croupier at work. But everyone knew better. Whenever PCW handed over the gavel prices tended to fall.

But there is an alternative theory, put forward by a number of former close associates: that he wasn't a great auctioneer at all, but rather a great dealer negotiating from the rostrum. The secret (and no one denies the partial truth of this) was exact preparation. When PCW went into an auction room he knew who would bid, how much, and for what, the deals merely had to be orchestrated. His sales were pre-sold, structured lot by lot. The weeks spent on the phone before a major sale were to match lot and bidders. At the sale all he was doing was reminding bidders with his eyes of what they had promised him previously, calling in his credit notes as it were. And even hardened dealers and collectors responded.

He was an arbiter of what people would buy, setting the priorities by what he had to sell. For PCW was a compulsive dealer. Julian Agnew remembers a deal struck after one sale in which Sotheby's turn was a mere £1,000 on an item worth £75,000. 'I want to do a deal' was the simple reason. Having a born dealer at Sotheby's was a permanent threat to dealers, they did not like having a born poacher acting as gamekeeper. For his character and inclinations perfectly fit Robert Wraight's description of a really successful dealer: 'A man who combines something of the psychologist, the stockbroker, the impresario, the public relations man and the detective, with a touch of aesthetic sensibility and some knowledge or artists' methods of working. He has insight into the buyers' mentality; the ability to aniticipate price trends and the power to create them; a sense of showmanship in presenting his wares and an understanding of the value of publicity.' It was these talents that helped Sotheby's triumph in the four years after the Farouk sale.

# 5  THE MAKING OF A TRIUMPH

In the glossy art magazines of the 1950s the 'Holy Trinity' was the Impressionist painting, the French commode and the Meissen figure (or T'ang ceramic horse). But the Impressionists were the central figures in the triptych. And it took only four magic years for Sotheby's to dominate the trade in them. The change was a sudden one. At the end of 1955 *Fortune* magazine could still dismiss auctions as outlets which settled 'the average price levels for low-priced works of similar size and quality over a period of years. . . . in New York the auction is more often a means of disposing of a collection after its prize pieces have been privately sold'. An anonymous American auctioneer admitted, 'an auction price must never be confused with a *market* price'.

But even *Fortune* acknowledged that special sales, properly orchestrated, could establish maximum prices for a category. And PCW was a master of orchestrating sales. As a result, and for the first time in art market history, the works of art most in demand from the international super-rich were being sold through the auction rooms. Bigger deals were still being done outside the sale-room. In 1957 a small Head of a Girl by Vermeer was sold by the Duc d'Aumale to an American collector, Charles Wrightsman, for £350,000 ($980,000), and the National Gallery of Stockholm paid £250,000 ($700,000) for a Lute Player by Watteau, both more than the top prices at the Goldschmidt sale. But Vermeers and Watteaus came on the market only rarely. Supplies of Impressionists, the favourite of the newly-rich, if not unlimited, were freer.

In this race Christie's enjoyed none of its usual advantages – and during these years there were none of the disposals of major British aristocrats in which it specialized. Christie's specialized in a field in which the supply was limited and the proportion frozen in museums high even then. Potential sellers were also discouraged because prices had still not regained their pre-1914 level. This was admitted even by Reitlinger, who saw the duality of the period. It was 'totally different from anything in this book, a market created by inflated currency, topsy-turvy financial controls and topsy-turvy systems of taxation, the market of the declining Roman Empire of Western man'. But at the same time he produced ample evidence that the period greatly resembled its predecessors in that demand was still highly selective.

Even after Christie's moved back into its rebuilt galleries in 1954 it was in no condition to compete. Sir Alec Martin was worn out, an ageing, irritable autocrat, unwilling to allow any initiatives, for he had been marked by the Depression, exhausted by the war. Profoundly pessimistic about the future (one veteran vividly remembers him insisting on the re-use of old envelopes), he was unwilling to expand Christie's areas of expertise – Arthur Grimwade, the fabled expert on silver, remained virtually unique, many other specialities were simply farmed out. There were occasional glimpses of the old style: in November 1954 Martin sold seventeen pictures, among them a Matisse, a Derain and a Bonnard for the British collector Rees Jeffries. They had been spurned by the trade but, nevertheless, fetched £44,320, twelve times the price Jeffries had paid. But this was an exception: Martin simply did not believe in modern pictures.

Traditional sources of business were still being tapped – one of Sotheby's best efforts in 1953 had been the sale of the magnificent contents of Ashburnham House after the death of its owner, Lady Catherine Ashburham, and the 1955–56 season had opened with the sale of the contents of the home of a Lieutenant-Colonel Sotheby (no relation), but there was little, if any, free cash within Britain; without American business, recovery was going to be slow.

But in November 1954, after a long campaign, in which Anthony Hobson played a prominent role, the market was freed. The British government finally allowed the free import, even from the United States – for dollars were still in short supply – of 'antiques and works of art'. Although rare books and sculpture were excluded for the time being (because the civil servants had problems defining them), London could now compete freely with Paris and New York. This applied to dealers as well as auctioneers: in 1956 Geoffrey Agnew bought two highly important Turners (including *A Scene on the French Coast*) and a Constable from the New York Public Library for a mere £47,000 ($131,600).

At first, Sotheby's relied on old contacts. In a series of sales starting in 1955 they secured £196,454 ($552,800) for the collection of documents and autograph letters assembled by a banker, André de Coppet, formerly a good customer of the firm. His widow remained loyal to Sotheby's, or rather to the legendary senior cataloguer in the book department, John Cameron Taylor. He had some scientific training and, between the wars, had pioneered the proper cataloguing of scientific and medical books. He also found time to write some of the first plays ever performed on BBC radio (and, in the late 1930s, on television as well). During the war, while working in the Postal Censorship, he had invented the system by which the information normally reproduced on a full-sized film could be photographed on a micro-dot.

Jim Kiddell was responsible for another early capture, the Arnold Schoenlicht collection of Chinese porcelain. This provided a good start for John Carter, the old school friend Vere Pilkington hired to represent the firm in the United States. Carter – universally known as 'Jake' – was an inspired choice. He had first found fame in 1934 when, as a young antiquarian bookseller, he had helped Graham Pollard expose the powerful and sinister Thomas James Wise, self-made bibliophile and mass forger. Carter was working as personal assistant to the British Ambassador when, a year before the restrictions were removed, Pilkington asked him to become Sotheby's representative in the United States.

In the event he started work only in October 1955, using his unequalled connections to the full. His first base was in the office of an old book-collecting friend, Donald Hyde, who also happened to be a distinguished Wall Street lawyer. Friends at the British Consulate ensured that the tiny office was listed in the Manhattan telephone directory under the grandiose name of Sotheby's of London. Most of the art business was then concentrated in mid-town Manhattan and Carter soon found a proper office in a 'cosy attic' in the Waldorf Towers next to the Waldorf Astoria, where he had frequently stayed in his previous job. The manager (who 'had been connected in some subtle capacity with the British Embassy during the war') was happy to offer Carter a diplomatic discount for accommodation.

The New York market had been self-contained, isolated from the world market, even though its participants were so often refugees from Europe. In his own specialized field he knew that Sotheby's could secure a higher price than Parke-Bernet, the only New York auctioneer of consequence. Lack of competition meant that 'at least two important libraries had perforce been sold in New York recently which would obviously have done better in the European market and I could only suppose that the same would be true in other departments'.

These included a curiosity, Baccarat paperweights, which at one time accounted for a quarter of Sotheby's total turnover. Tim Clarke had learnt a lot about them when cataloguing the Farouk collection (which temporarily depressed prices), but within a few years he attracted more than £250,000 worth from the United States alone. They were not universal favourites. *The Times* reported disgustedly on 27 February 1957 that 'The craze, now dignified into a cult on

50

both sides of the Atlantic for nineteenth-century French glass paper-weights shows no sign of diminishing. At Sotheby's yesterday eighty of these curious examples of the glass-maker's ingenuity realized a total of £13,466, and one of them, a St Louis piece, the only yellow example of its type yet recorded, changed hands at £2,700.'

Carter had his sights on bigger game: the many collections of Impressionists and Post-Impressionists either bought by Americans, or, more often, brought from Europe by refugees. The sellers knew the gross auction price would be the same in London, Paris and New York, but the net receipts would be very different. Sotheby's commission rates were half those of Parke-Bernet's, and even more favourable than those prevailing in Paris, where taxes had to be paid as well. The difference was considerable: 'when the dust died down, the seller would pocket $90,000 out of every $100,000 if he sold through Sotheby's, compared with a maximum of $80,000 at Parke-Bernet, and a mere $65,000 in Paris'. Moreover, and unlike Parke-Bernet, Carter's firm would provide reserve prices to ensure that the pictures were not given away below their real value. His biggest competition at the time came, not from rival sale-rooms, but from dealers – it was Knoedler's who negotiated the sale by the actor Edward G. Robinson of his marvellous collection to Stavros Niarchos.

Four months after his appointment, Carter spread the gospel in a three-week national tour – before the days of jet travel – which took him to Princeton, Philadelphia, Washington, Kansas City, Chicago, Cleveland, Boston, Cambridge, New Haven and Farmington. In these and subsequent whirlwind trips he combined the contacts he had made through the book trade with Sotheby's own, those available through his former colleagues in the consulate, and through his wife, the formidable Ernestine Carter, at the time curator of the Costumes Department of the Metropolitan Museum. In subsequent years his pitch was subtly blended with official propaganda. The English-Speaking Union, glad to find speakers not obsessed with Anglo-American relations, allowed him to make a number of tours, admirably designed as a series of puffs for Sotheby's, artlessly disguised as talks on 'Bull Market in Bond Street', 'Art in the market place' or 'A Renoir is a girl's best friend – or is it?'

The timing was perfect. For several years, especially in New York, the market in Impressionists had been building up – in 1942 the great Dr Barnes had paid $185,000 for *The Mussel Fishers of Berneval*, a record that stood until the Lurcy sale twelve years later. The wave caught the public consciousness on 14 May 1952 during the sale of the paintings accumulated by Gabriel Cognacq. The total for the sale was FF302 million ($860,000, just over £300,000). Inflation accounted for many of the prices: Degas had not recovered to the

£21,000 paid for *Danseuses à la Barre* in 1912. But the public brushed aside inflation accounting and concentrated on the cash sums being paid.

These culminated in the FF33 million, ($94,000, £33,700) paid for Cézanne's still-life *Pommes et Biscuits*. This should not have come as any great surprise. Cézanne had not been considered a bargain since the Choquet sale in 1899. In 1913 his *Garçon au Gilet Rouge* had fetched £3,600 (as much as the still-fashionable Alma-Tadema). At the end of the First World War, a good Cézanne was worth about £5,000. In 1922 $21,000 was paid for a *Still Life with Apples* formerly owned by Dirkan Kelekian. Prices had remained relatively static for the next, inflationary, thirty years. Moreover most of the painter's output, particularly his best works, was already embalmed in museums. The supply of Renoirs, on the other hand, was seemingly limitless, so the £19,500 ($54,600) paid for *Les Deux Soeurs* and £23,000 ($64,400) for a girl's portrait was even more significant than the bigger sum paid for the Cézanne.

The buyer was Madame Jean Walter, widow of a dealer, who subsequently married a wealthy mine-owner in Morocco. She was an unusually sophisticated example of the new rich who seized on Impressionists as status symbols in the 1950s. Thirty years on, they remain the rich man's introduction to art. In late 1984 the *Sunday Times* interviewed a typical newcomer to the art world, Cindy Spelling, the wife of Aaron Spelling, the producer of *Dynasty*. She was described as: 'thirty-seven years old, slender, sleek, manicured, exercised, massaged, well dressed and very glamorous. They say she wears $4 million worth of jewels for lunch: she was much taken with the Impressionist collection of a leading Hollywood grande dame: "I said to Aaron, let's cool it on the jewels for a while and get into art." A few days later they bought a Monet, their first painting.'

*Fortune* had mentioned Madame Walter as one of a relatively small group of major buyers at the time. They included Emil Buhrle, a Swiss armaments manufacturer, hailed as 'the only man in Europe currently able and willing to put down $500,000 for a painting'; Assis Chateaubriand, a flamboyant Brazilian publisher; Walter P. Chrysler Jnr (a mass buyer of Courbets and Millets); and a hangover from the Duveen era, the Foundation set up by the chain-store millionaire, Samuel Kress. The buyers did not all live in France, but according to *Fortune*, it was the supply of Modern Masters which 'put Paris in its absolutely pre-eminent position as center of the great international art market today'.

Within eighteen months the position had been transformed by Sotheby's – and a small group of Greek shipowners who had emerged as by far the most important influence on the Impressionist market; indeed the image of luxurious living in the 1950s was of Greek shipowners' yachts with a Renoir or some other simple, expensive splash of colour over the dining-table or the bedhead in the master bedroom. This was no exaggeration. At a 1968 sale in New York Aristotle Onassis bid up the price of a Renoir, *Le Pont des Arts*, to a record £645,000 ($1,541,550) because he wanted it as a wedding present for his new bride, Jacqueline Kennedy.

Initially the Greeks tended to buy in Paris: they often lived there, and had money in France that could not be exported any other way. Appropriately the greatest triumph of the Paris market came after the closure of the Suez Canal had provided a further boost to their fortunes. For the art market depends on the cash available, and this may well not be affected by a general depression. The mid-1950s showed that many operators who had either sold out or, like the Greeks at Suez time, who had benefited from other people's misfortunes, often had a lot of spare cash looking for an outlet. In May 1957 a Gauguin *Still Life with Apples*, formerly owned by Mrs. Margaret Thompson Biddle, was sold for FF104 million ($297,142, £106,000) to Basil Goulandris. This was three times the estimate, the result, according to Mollie Panter-Downes in *The New Yorker*, of 'a sudden desire to acquire the canvas which ignited simultaneously in the bosoms of Mr Goulandris and Mr Stavros Niarchos, another Greek shipowner, causing an explosion of human nature that blew the roof off the international art market'.

PCW was the ideal person to benefit from the new demand. His breezy, classy, aristocratic English attitude was entirely suitable for impressing the sellers – in those days it was profoundly chic to have an English accent in New York, and PCW's only real competition came from another Englishman, Leslie Hyam, the chief executive of Parke-Bernet, and a Cambridge graduate. Temperamentally, PCW was far more at home with the restless, rootless cosmopolitan tycoons of café society than with his fellow-aristocrats. For the Biddle sale was the swan-song of the Paris market. By that time the sellers, and the Greek buyers, had homed in on London, and not only to buy Impressionists.

In early 1956 Vere Pilkington had discovered a magnificent Poussin, formerly owned by Sir Joshua Reynolds, in the house of a retired naval officer near Norwich. A London dealer tried to abort the sale by offering £10,000 cash, a figure later raised to £15,000. So Sotheby's was forced to provide a guaranteed price, an unprecedented gamble. In July 1956 the painting (described by PCW from the rostrum as '*The Poussin*') fetched £29,000 ($81,200), the highest London auction figure since the war.

The price, and others in the same sale, were a watershed in the

53

market for Old Masters. The significance was explained by Denys Sutton in the *Financial Times*. He insisted that the price paid for the Poussin was no accident, it had been bought by a shrewd dealer for stock; nor was it an isolated case, for an Avercamp had also gone for a record price. It was a turning point showing the owners of Old Masters that a new scale of values had been established. The implications included a new threat to the National Heritage: 'If owners are as wide-awake as they ought to be . . . then the state will no longer be allowed to buy on the cheap as it has done so often in the past. . . . the Velasquez *Saint John on the Island of Patmos* will prove one of the last paintings to enter the National Gallery at below par.'

But the Poussin was a rarity. Between 1952 and 1956 only twelve Old Masters fetched £10,000 or more in the London sale-rooms, far fewer than the number of more recent pictures in the same price range. A simple shortage of supply meant that there was no immediate follow-up to the Poussin sale. But by that time the Modernist bandwagon was rolling, albeit at a pace that now seems sedate. Reitlinger noted advances by 'distinctly minor men', £7,350 ($20,580) for one Bonnard, and £5,000 ($14,000) each for another by the same painter and for a Vuillard, a sign that 'as a millionaire's market, the modern French school had now taken the place of the English eighteenth-century portraits in the 1920s'. The first pictures came from a German refugee, Alfred Schwabacher. Carter, helped by PCW's cheerily optimistic estimates, persuaded him to sell his collection through Sotheby's, appropriately enough on 4 July 1956. Sutton sniffed at the pictures, 'rather mediocre. . . . an insignificant Matisse Still Life had gone for £4,200. . . . the owner must congratulate himself on receiving £1,300 for Chagall's gouache and water-colour of *Clown riding a goat*'. Sutton gloated at how a Renoir Landscape failed to reach its reserve of £6,000 ($16,800). He did not mention that the sale also included a lovely Berthe Morisot and two other Renoirs, and that the proceeds, a mere £29,400 ($82,320), seemed satisfactory enough at the time.

The real breakthrough came in November with the sale of a number of pictures 'from the estate of the late Jakob Goldschmidt'. Geoffrey Hobson had met Goldschmidt, then one of the leading bankers in Berlin, while on a trip to Germany in the early 1930s. Unfortunately they had had a blazing row over the commission payable in a possible sale of Goldschmidt's collection of Oriental porcelain (Hobson admitted that Kiddell would have handled the matter more tactfully). Goldschmidt was one of the first Jews to leave Berlin, motoring through the night to the safety of Switzerland after repeated urgent warnings by an old friend, Baron von Thyssen, who knew that the banker was 'Public Enemy Number One' to the

Nazi hierarchy. In the late 1950s his estate was up for sale through two executors, his son Erwin and a New York lawyer, Jesse Wolff, who had befriended the father. Erwin Goldschmidt preferred to sell in Europe, and first negotiated with Maurice Rheims, king of the Paris art market, but was naturally deterred by the heavy costs. So he installed himself in a suite at the Savoy and started simultaneous negotiations with Sir Alec Martin in one room, and PCW and Carmen Gronau in another (they only knew of the competition when they overheard him say to a friend: 'Die hier gefallen mir viel besser' – 'I like this lot much better'). PCW and Gronau responded to the challenge by devising a flexible commission structure for the pictures (Gronau also helped by getting them cleared through customs). Fourteen of them – including a Delacroix, a Corot nude and a Murillo which had fetched £5,880 at the Holford sale in 1928 – were placed at the end of the Old Masters sale that November. The sale was a great success. A Greek shipowner, John Carras, paid £25,000 ($70,000) for the Murillo and, surprisingly, £7,800 ($21,840) for a Van Dyck, while the Maharanee of Baroda paid £27,000 [$75,600) for Goldschmidt's Corot (which, allegedly, she hung in her bathroom. The Greeks did not have a monopoly of conspicuous consumption).

Sotheby's triumph was confirmed a month after the Biddle sensation, by the sale of the collection of William Weinberg, another émigré financier, whose wife and three children had been caught up in the Holocaust. Inconsolable, he concentrated on collecting. His adviser, J. B. de la Faille, had compiled a major *catalogue raisonné* on Van Gogh, so Weinberg's collection was naturally rich in the painter's works. This was lucky: the British public's interest in modern painting had first been stimulated by an exhibition of Van Gogh's works which had livened the drab winter of 1946–47; by the mid-1950s a print of his *Sunflowers* hung on the wall of every student bedsitter; and some of the Weinberg pictures had featured in a recent film about the painter, *Lust for Life*. Erwin Goldschmidt had recommended Sotheby's to the executors of the Weinberg estate, and tipped PCW off about the collection. Early in 1957 Jake Carter, Carmen Gronau and PCW managed to inspect the paintings, although they were under dust sheets at the financier's house and lit only by hand torches. It was the chance PCW had been waiting for.

Once terms had been agreed he persuaded his partners to hire a public relations firm, J. Walter Thompson, part of the advertising agency. The executive in charge sent an invitation to the Queen (when shown the list, the partners thought he meant the magazine of the same name). Her Majesty graciously accepted, and the Weinberg executors were duly presented to her at the private view, thus launching the slogan – 'Sell at Sotheby's and see the Royal Family'. (True to form, the Queen's favourite picture had a horsy theme. It was a Degas: *At the Races: the wounded jockey*.) But three days before the sale the executors, inspired by the results of the Biddle sale, demanded far higher reserves. PCW play-acted at losing his temper and, although his antics were spotted by one of the executors, Richard Netter, the charade was effective and the auction itself was a triumph, lavishly described in the press.

Mollie Panter-Downes best understood how different the Weinberg sale was from the normal atmosphere at Sotheby's: 'as English as a London club in which most of the habituès know one another'. Normally:

> It is a soothing spot to drop in to for a browsing half hour or so . . . In the two smaller rooms . . . prowling gentlemen with umbrellas hooked over their arms earnestly examine cases of Meissen china and Georgian silver, or, snatching a small canvas from the wall, hold it a few inches from their eyes as if testing it with invisible antennae . . . in the book-auction room, on sale days studious men sit among the folios with the air of having been there for several months, and perhaps by now needing a dust.

The atmosphere, and indeed the characters, had not changed greatly since René Gimpel had visited Christie's forty years earlier:

> I can see an old Englishman with side whiskers and the eternal topper. A character out of Thackeray or Dickens, full of dignity and full of passion. All the men wear their clothes with an air. I notice two ladies looking at a male nude as if it were a stallion. An old woman wants to take their place: she is long and thin with a very small behind. The dealers have carnations in their button-holes. Their shops may often be revolting, but they remain gentlemen. Mysterious colloquies, one very secret-looking between two individuals, one of whom is wearing a form-fitting frock coat, while the other, red-faced and rustic, with his stomach protruding, looks like one of those figures who sit in taverns in sporting prints. The latter is a lord, the former an antique dealer.

But on the morning of the Weinberg sale the normally private world had gone public. The pavements were crowded. Inside, at Netter's suggestion, closed circuit television had been installed so that PCW could take bids from two other rooms as well as the main gallery – needless to say both the BBC and NBC were there with their cameras. All three rooms were crowded with the rich and the beautiful. But Panter-Downes knew these were merely spectators. The real action would come from 'the big London, Paris and New

York dealers who had been allotted ringside seats right under the auctioneer's mahogany rostrum'. They 'sat without consulting their catalogues, for they were men who had already decided on, and buttoned in their minds, the exact amounts they were prepared to give for what they were there to buy'. She noted, too, the particularly caressing style of PCW: 'alert in his mahogany watchtower ... a man with a gentle but remarkably carrying voice and a way of pausing almost affectionately to wait for the gentleman on his right – or left – to advance another thousand pounds'.

The total take, £326,000 ($912,800) was far above the Press estimates (although, even in sterling terms, it was still below the level of the 1928 Holford sale). To Panter-Downes, as to everyone else, the Weinberg sale had succeeded in putting 'London back in the position it held before the war as the center of the international art market'. Four months later, in Reitlinger's words, 'this now extremely popular drama transferred itself to New York' with the sale of the works of another refugee, George Lurcy, a Parisian banker born simple George Levy in Alsace. It was another trend-setter, with closed-circuit television to cover two side galleries. Although this produced a great deal of confusion as many bids were not properly received, the sale totalled a record $1.7 million (£610,000). Henry Ford paid the highest price, $200,000 (£71,400) for a Renoir, second place went to Goulandris, who bought Gauguin's *Mau Tapora* for $180,000 (£64,300).

Nevertheless, Sotheby's had shown its superiority in sheer sale-room hype by getting excellent prices for largely second-rate works, inferior to many at the Biddle and Lurcy sales. Not surprisingly, Reitlinger seized on the Weinberg sale to prove his general thesis about the decline of taste. Four years later he wrote about the 'homage paid to mere autographs ... seven early drawings and watercolours by Van Gogh aggregated more than £20,000. Drawn in Holland between 1882 and 1884, they offer not the least hint of Van Gogh's mature style. Provincial ... dull, barely works of art at all, they contain about as much promise of genius as the drawings of Adolf Hitler that came under the same hammer three years later.' To him this was a sign of a general decay of taste: 'another of these drawings, the *Paysan Béchant* of 1881, which looks like an unusually stodgy prize-winning drawing from a public school competition, made £6,500 in 1959 as if it were a Rembrandt or a Dürer. On the other hand, a beautiful and typical Van Gogh landscape drawing, in his developed style, made only £2,200 at Sotheby's in November 1960. There is no accounting for the philatelists of connoisseurship.'

He should not have been so surprised. Names have always been the stock-in trade of the art market. The small-time crook dealer in an eighteenth-century French pamphlet, *The Public Confession of a Dealer*, told how: 'I didn't sell painters, only their works; but most of us dealers only know their names and can't distinguish between their works. We're only interested in buying these strings of names, and selling them at high prices.'

(Things have got worse since Reitlinger's day. In early 1985 the owners of the artist's former summer home discovered an 'old fashioned three hole lavatory seat decorated by Willem de Kooning in a few minutes in a spirit of merriment' before a party to make it look like marble. Kooning's widow thought it was ridiculous to describe it as a work of art, but according to the new owners: 'the globs are reminiscent of Pollock'. The association was enough to lead to hopes of a million-dollar sale.)

The Weinberg sale marked the end of a record season. As part of his sales drive, Jake Carter had suggested the idea of an annual review with which to impress clients – an idea pioneered by Christie's in the 1920s. The first edition of what soon became the glossiest of annuals was a modest affair, with thirty-two pages of illustrations, only one in colour (Van Gogh's *Usines à Clichy*, sold for £31,000 ($86,800) at the Weinberg sale). But the tone was celebratory, with good reason. Sotheby's had sold a record £3.2 million worth of goods, a fifth from the United States, £900,000 more than the previous year and 80 per cent more than Christie's: 'the highest turnover of any fine art auctioneers in the world and a record not only for the firm but for any London art sale-rooms'.

Although there were no outstanding sales the following season, and Britain was still suffering from the economic hangover of the Suez affair, sales slipped by a mere £100,000. For by now Carter was in full cry. He failed to get the 'De Bellis incunabula' despite 'three blisteringly hot days in an unventilated room with every book thrice-wrapped in brown paper', but he bounced back, securing a magnificent group of seven books illuminated by William Blake which fetched £40,800 ($114,000). He had clearly seen off the competition provided by his transient rival, Bob Leylan, a well-known connoisseur and Christie's American representative for a short time.

The real action that winter was behind the scenes. For some time Pilkington had been getting on his partners' nerves, and when in December he resigned over a minor issue connected with salaries, the resignation was immediately and unanimously accepted – much to his surprise; like so many others in a similar position he had assumed that he would be invited back. *The Times* reported that Pilkington 'plans to retire next October. He is expected to be succeeded by Peter Wilson, the next senior partner'. According to

Carmen Gronau, PCW did not want the job and had to be persuaded by her into it – evidence to support the theory that he retained the modesty of the young man who had joined the firm twenty years earlier. In the event he allowed himself to be persuaded.

Pilkington's departure was hastened by his disastrous handling of the Cook collection, 'one of the greatest Victorian collection of Old Masters', according to *The Times*. The most important pictures had been sold through dealers, but, even so, Pilkington should have got more than £64,608 for the 136 pictures he sold on June 25th. Although some of the attributions were dubious, only lackadaisical auctioneering could explain the sale of a Van Dyck portrait for £2,800 ($7,840). Agnew's secured a Portrait of a Woman by Hogarth for a mere £1,900 ($5,320) – while a Rubens sketch for part of the ceiling of the Banqueting House in Whitehall went for only £1,100 ($3,080). Not surprisingly, when some of the more important pictures from the collection came up for sale a few years later, they were auctioned by Christie's. Pilkington's sheer professional incompetence, on top of his previous pettiness, ensured that PCW started his chairmanship at the head of a united partnership, although the partners must have felt rather guilty at their behaviour – several of them still remember the Cook sale as having been before the agreement to let Pilkington resign, as if to justify retrospectively a decision by which they were rather shocked at the time.

At Christie's there was a much more fundamental upheaval. Early in 1958 a group of the younger partners pushed through a forced liquidation of the old company to form a new one with rather different shareholders. They bought back control from the nonagenarian Lloyd and Sir Alec Martin. The latter was effectively kicked upstairs, 'to be available in a consultative capacity' (his son Bill remained as head of the paintings department). Lloyd naturally left and Sir Henry Floyd retired 'to devote his time to his other interests', although his young cousin, Jo Floyd, was one of the new group. The new chairman was Peter Chance, an upright, traditional, soldierly figure, very much in the mould of his ancestors, the Agnews. Chance's task was formidable: 'he had to resurrect the firm, and he still had Bill Martin, who was pretty useless, round his neck', in the words of one sympathetic observer. Chance was not naturally a man to hurry and, moreover, all the new partners had learnt two basic lessons. The firm had been laid low by the domination of one man; from now on it was going to be a team effort; and they had seen the problems created in the 1930s by the cost of servicing loans and mortgages, so were not going to go into debt. This conservatism proved enormously helpful in the long term, but at the cost of giving their rivals a clear run for several years.

With the opposition laid low, PCW's first season as chairman was triumphant. Sales nearly doubled to over £5 million and, for the first time, exceeded in real terms the record set by Christie's at the end of the 1920s. PCW scored a double triumph: in the second Goldschmidt sale in October 1958 he showed what he could do with really good Impressionists; and with the sale of the Westminster Rubens eight months later he firmly invaded Christie's territory.

Despite Erwin Goldschmidt's enthusiasm for Sotheby's, it was by no means a foregone conclusion that he would entrust his father's seven most precious pictures to the firm. They were all famous: Renoir's *La Pensée*; a marvellous Van Gogh, *Jardin Public à Arles*; three Manets: a self-portrait, a famous street scene on a public holiday, *La Rue Mosnier aux Drapeaux*, and a portrait, *Aux Jardins de Bellevue*; and two Cézannes, a still life *Nature Morte: Les Grosses Pommes* and the delightful *Garçon au Gilet Rouge*. Goldschmidt had allowed them to be lent for exhibition, and he was fully aware of their quality. So he drove a hard bargain with PCW. There was no question of a fixed commission payable whatever the eventual outcome. Sotheby's had to set high reserves, below which only a tiny commission would be paid, but would get a far higher rate after a certain level had been reached (at one mid-point Sotheby's would receive the whole of the proceeds).

There were two major hiccups after the agreement. An anonymous 'Greek shipowner' offered £600,000 for the collection – an offer which, to PCW, proved merely how much more it would fetch at auction; and a premature leakage of the news led to a last-minute attack of nerves. PCW was fully equal to the occasion. As a spectator at the Lurcy sale he had seen how the New York technique of an evening sale mounted as a social occasion for the beautiful people had boosted prices: so the second Goldschmidt sale was to be held at 9.30 pm, with evening dress compulsory. Even the catalogue was something out of the ordinary: the previous year, Richard Day, one of Carmen Gronau's protégés, had persuaded her to produce a catalogue for a magnificent note-book of drawings by Fra Bartolommeo in which each item was illustrated. The sale had been a great success. So for Goldschmidt they went one further: each of the seven pictures was illustrated in colour.

Nothing was left to chance. Another public relations agency was hired, but this was scarcely necessary, for public interest all over the world was intense – a month before the sale it had been written up extensively in twenty-three countries. Erwin Goldschmidt and his beautiful Canadian wife, Madge, had been endlessly interviewed, his passion for vintage cars noted, his father's career wondered at. PCW himself badgered Lord Beaverbrook, an old crony of his father's, to ensure that the Beaverbrook press gave the affair the maximum attention. He even took a dress rehearsal, during which he sold 'Poor Mrs Gronau' to an imaginary bidder for £42,000. But the sale itself was delayed by a nerve-wracking incident. A notoriously unbalanced anti-Semite managed to get in and started to insult Goldschmidt, who would have called off the sale if one of the senior partners, Tim Clarke, had not firmly ejected the intruder.

PCW was five minutes late starting the sale, but it took only five more for success to be assured. In those minutes he had sold three paintings; the best result was for the Manet self-portrait which went for £65,000 ($190,624) – £20,000 more than the reserve. At that point, reported the *Daily Express*: 'the grey head of Somerset Maugham shook slowly in amazement, Dame Margot Fonteyn, in an off-the-shoulder, eau-de-nil dress, stood on her famous toes craning with excitement. An iron-grey man dropped his monocle under foot.' It was that sort of occasion.

The Van Gogh was something of an anti-climax, with long pauses before it went – albeit for £132,000 ($369,600), a tenth above the reserve – while the Cézanne still-life went quickly for £90,000 ($252,000), a third over the reserve. The *Garçon au Gilet Rouge* had been widely tipped as the top picture, although the reserve, at £125,000 ($350,000) was only a little more than for the Van Gogh. True to form, PCW started the bidding low, at a mere £20,000, to give time for the rhythm to build up. The bidding quickly became a contest between two dealers, Roland Balay of Knoedler's and George Keller of Carstair's Gallery in New York, acting for the absent Paul Mellon. It was Keller's final bid of £220,000 ($616,000), twice the price of the Biddle Gauguin, which triggered PCW's famous remark: '£220,000, £220,000, what will no one offer any more?' The rest was anti-climax, with the last picture, the Renoir, going to the only successful English bidder, Jack Cotton the property developer, for a mere £72,000 ($200,000), only £1,000 above the reserve.

Mellon was naturally nervous about the price paid on his behalf. He need not have worried. Prices remained buoyant. When the travelling circus moved to New York a few weeks later, a Picasso at the Kirkeby sale went for $152,000 (£54,285), the highest price ever paid for a work by a living artist. For prices were still moving: Rheims reckoned that by the end of the decade the prices for the Cognacq pictures would have doubled. Since then, of course, they have moved much further. Only one of the seven Goldschmidt pictures has come back onto the market. the Van Gogh that had been so difficult to sell; it fetched $5,200,000 (£1,857,142), fourteen times its earlier price in dollar terms, when Henry Ford sold it – at Christie's in New York – twenty-two years later.

Sotheby's had done its sums well: its commission on the record £781,000 fetched by the seven pictures was only a fraction below its normal 10 per cent. In publicity terms the second Goldschmidt sale was unique – it even persuaded the National Gallery to increase the insurance value of some of its pictures. But far more important, historically, was the sale on the 24 June 1959 of the 'Westminster Rubens', a magnificent altar-piece painted in a mere eleven days for a Flemish convent. According to an employee of the Duke of Westminster, 'the Rubens was never very highly thought of by the late Duke or his advisers'. Otherwise he would not have insured it for a mere £7,000 or left it on the staircase at Eaton Hall – an enormous nineteenth-century country house near Chester – although the damp cold atmosphere characteristic of English country houses had kept the painting in perfect condition.

The death of the second Duke, Bendor Westminster, grandest of Dukes, former protector of Coco Chanel, created the need to sell. Fortunately for Sotheby's, Jim Kiddell was a long-standing friend of the estate's legal adviser, Sir William Charles Crocker. He insisted on an enormous reserve – £200,000, far more than any Old Master had ever fetched at auction, and double the figure allegedly offered by the National Gallery. For the sale created a major storm of protest, with allegations and counter-allegations about the number and quality of Rubens' pictures already in national collections. The final problem, which nearly gave Carmen Gronau a nervous break-down, was physical, how to get the enormous picture, measuring 12ft 9¼in by 8ft 1¼in, into the sale-room. In the event she copied a technique used to get Rembrandt's *Night Watch* into the Rijksmuseum, to cut a slit in the wall of the auction room. The slit was impeded by a number of pipes, but eventually twelve men managed to man-handle the Rubens inside – to the dismay of a group of press photographers who had been waiting for the painting, or the wall, to collapse. She then spotted a new crack in the picture and had to 'spend all her time boiling kettles to keep up the humidity level'. The Rubens was included in a superb sale of Old Masters and PCW was lucky in having a number of potential serious bidders. He tried his usual technique of starting the bidding low, at a mere £20,000, but a London dealer, Martin Asscher, rather spoiled the build-up by yelling an offer of £100,000. The eventual winner, Leonard Koetser, entered the bidding at £130,000. There was a pregnant fifteen second silence, which must have seemed an eternity, at £200,000, but PCW recovered by taking the next bid as £215,000. There were still four bidders – three dealers and Paul Getty, bidding in person. Geoffrey Agnew dropped out at £270,000 and PCW got Koetser to bid £5,000 more. His client was soon revealed as Major Allnatt, a virtually unknown property developer (the only class of person with spare capital on that scale in England at the time). Although the trustees of the National Gallery twice failed to keep appointments with him, the picture eventually found an appropriate home, adorning the interior of England's finest single ecclesiastical building, the chapel of King's College, Cambridge. On this occasion PCW had avoided any awkward questions about selling off the national heritage.

Other Old Masters – notably a Frans Hals and a Gainsborough – fetched high prices at the same time. For PCW had demonstrated that, for a select number of Old Masters as well as the ever-popular Impressionists, a new era had dawned; even allowing for inflation, prices had risen above those reached in the Golden Years before the First World War. But these prices were by no means general. In particular, furniture was still a depressed market: in 1960 two Louis XIV Boulle pedestals which had fetched £1,575 at the Hamilton Palace sale of 1882 were sold for a mere £1,155 ($3,234) at Christie's; and Rheims noted how the price of Louis XV screens and clocks had dropped by a half since 1913. The shadow of the long depression (and previously inflated prices) also hung over whole schools of Old Masters. Reitlinger noted how: 'the sale-room price of Guido Reni, the Carracci family, Guercino, Domenichino, Albano, Pietro da Cortona and Carlo Dolci are as yet scarcely up to late nineteenth-century levels'. The bull market was still very specialized. Whether it would become more general depended on the attitude of the growing army of collectors on both sides of the Atlantic.

*Part III*


# WHY BUY ART?
# USE OR SHOW OR STATUS OR
# PROFIT OR SECURITY?

## WHY BUY ART? USE OR SHOW OR STATUS OR PROFIT OR SECURITY?

The scope of the art market, and its scale of values, have both shifted over the centuries. Originally the price of objects was decided primarily by the value of the precious metals they contained. The expense of the workmanship that had gone into them gradually became even more important. It is only relatively recently – during the 1950s – that the supposed 'genius' of the creator of the object being sold – most obviously a painting – has assumed overwhelming importance. For the post–war period is the first in which the art market has been thinking in terms of pure 'artistic' value, however defined (increasingly by the market value). It was this revolution that provided the new chairman of Sotheby's with his opportunity.

The shift in relative market values was the outward sign of an even more fundamental change: in the motives for buying the objects in the first place. Until recently buyers had specific purposes for their purchases: for use, or show, or decoration, to match their way of life as well as their wealth. Motives are now less specific, and, as a natural consequence, the categories of goods being generally traded are more numerous and varied: once the reason for purchase has become mere 'collectibility' or, more recently, mere profit, there are, theoretically, no limits to the range of 'tradeable beauty'. As a result the market has been making enormous inroads on the hundreds of categories of objects that were already being collected but not generally traded. Indeed the story of the past twenty-five years is of a steady flow of general interest into previously narrow and specialized markets.

The urge to collect can be seen as one of the most basic of human activities; 'To collect nothing at all is to descend below the level of magpies and marmots', wrote Gerald Reitlinger. But there is no necessary connection between the urges represented by collecting and the 'art market'. Our present scale of values, in which the idea of 'collectibility' is intimately linked with market values is as new and revolutionary as the notion that genius should be prized above craftsmanship or content.

When Aline Saarinen studied some of the United States' most

remarkable collectors* she found that for all of them 'the collecting of art was a primary means of expression'. The love could be almost physical. Many of them 'responded particularly to craftsmanship and form'. Henry Havemeyer 'kept two handsome Greek fourth-century helmets and several Chinese bronze jars in the library. He caressed them frequently, like a blind man experiencing their shape.' They were echoing the feeling reported by the Chinese art historian Zhang Yanyuan. In a chapter entitled 'On Grading by Name and Price' he wrote, 'it is an inner necessity for collectors to feel scrolls in their hands and determine their value by discussion' ('and not to be stingy' he added).

The possessiveness can also be negative, protective: 'Art', said Leo Stein, member of a notably discerning family of collectors, among them his sister Gertrude, 'is what a man does with his loneliness.' For until recently the insecurity relieved by buying works of art was usually psychological rather than financial. That surprisingly neurotic Prime Minister, Stanley Baldwin, allegedly collected owls and insisted on taking some of his stuffed specimens away with him at weekends. The need, and thus the relief, was greatest in the United States. The nineteenth-century French novelist Paul Bourget wrote of 'the sincerity, almost the pathos, of this love of Americans for surrounding themselves with things around which there is an idea of time and stability' – in a raw new country old objects were indeed reassuring, although Bourget's remark contained a fair dollop of the condescension which still pervades European comment about American collecting habits.

In similar vein, the worldly-wise mother of William Randolph Hearst explained her son's super-magpie behaviour simply: 'Every time Willie feels badly, he goes out and buys something.' The idea that buying a painting cheers you up – in the same way that, in a pre-feminist days, women supposedly bought another hat – was not ridiculous. Theodore Pitcairn, a Swedenborgian minister – and son of the founder of the gigantic Pittsburg Glass Company – bought a marvellous Monet in 1927 when he saw it in a dealer's window in 57th Street in New York: 'We bought it in ten minutes for about $11,000 [then about £3,800]. I wasn't thinking of investment. We were both struck by its cheerful quality and thought this was the type of picture that would always give us a lift' – forty years later it was sold for £588,000 at auction.

The urge to collect is so basic that psychoanalysts have always found collecting a legitimate and fruitful source of enquiry. In the words of Frederick Baekeland, psychologist and art historian: 'psychoanalysts, who stress the sublimatory and expressive

* For her splendid book: *The Proud Possessors.*

68

functions of art, believe that all hobbies are sublimations of libidinal and aggressive impulses and that they are a refined form of play. They can discern other factors in collecting, such as exhibitionism, voyeurism and identification.'

The ownership of a particularly desirable object obviously provides the thrill of monopoly power, yet this did not historically lead collectors to think of their possessions in terms of possible profit or even, in most cases, of their monetary value. Desirable possessions (not just objects, Morgan was a great collector of beautiful girls) could be useful, or status-symbols, or both, but they were not investments.

In their admirable book *Lock Stock & Barrel* Douglas and Elizabeth Rigby regarded profit as only one minor motive among the many they give for collecting. The Rigby's provided a list of 113 categories, ranging from ice skates to old insurance policies, all of which 'claim a very real clan of devotees', and even today there is no profit to be found in collecting the majority of items in the list, there is no real market in many of them, they remain private obsessions. The motives for collection still remain in many cases, if not pure, at least largely untainted by pecuniary motives. The market may have made gigantic inroads but is not all-conquering.

Historically a lot of 'collections' would never have passed the Rigbys' criteria: 'the true collector creates an ordered entity ... an accumulation may not properly be called a collection when the assembled objects bear no intelligible relationship to each other'. For our definitions have become stricter. To Geraldine Norman 'there are at least two types of private collector, the one who collects on aesthetic grounds what pleases his eye and he who seeks to form the best possible collection representative of his chosen field'. Neither she nor the Rigbys would have counted 'poor Willie' with his infantile magpie purchases among the collectors. Yet he was not alone. The motives involved in collecting were as wide as the objects collected.

Sheer curiosity was an important motive. It even had a market value: the single most valuable object in the inventory of the legacy of Lorenzo the Magnificent of Florence was a whale tusk fondly supposed to be the horn of a unicorn. Throughout the nineteenth century the *cabinet des curieux*, a random assortment of oddments, remained an essential element in any gentleman's way of life. The nucleus of the British Museum was just such a collection built up by Sir Hans Sloane. As Horace Walpole put it: 'He valued it at four-score thousand: and so would anybody who loves hippopotamuses, sharks with one ear, and spiders as big as geese! It is a rent-charge to keep the foetuses in spirits.'

Curiosity value was naturally associated with the value placed on

69

objects associated with the famous. These could be valueless – like autographs – or objects that were themselves valuable but whose value was boosted because of the person – or the story – attached to them. The queens and mistresses of French eighteenth-century monarchs – Madame du Barry, Madame de Pompadour, Marie Antoinette – still exert their historic magic on market values. Reitlinger dismissed the worship of Marie Antoinette as 'a sentimental cult of an exceptionally silly woman'. One of the worshippers was the Empress Eugénie, wife of the Emperor Napoleon III: 'As the foreign-born consort of a tottering crown, the Empress must have felt some affinity with the unhappy Autrichienne' But Reitlinger was over simplifying: the market still reflects a mixture of motives, elegance by association is still powerful. In 1928 Duveen paid $71,000 for a marquetry table formerly belonging to Madame de Pompadour. The magic remains: in 1971 it fetched $410,000. Of course the association also reflected inherent values, the fact that the ladies had commissioned such luxurious and splendidly-crafted objects. More recently the name of Morgan has provided a similar boost, again partly because of the undoubted quality of everything bought by the old tycoon.

Value-by-association reached its zenith – or its nadir – with the recent sale of Sotheby's of 'Rock' n Roll memorabilia 1964–83'. The idea goes back to a question posed to PCW by a reporter from the *News of the World* as early as 1967: 'If you'll sell anything that has a unique interest then the Beatles' original song manuscripts ought to be worth selling one day'. At that point, according to the journalist: 'I heard a sound like an Old Master cash register ringing. He said to his colleague: "You know, they'd be worth quite a bit now."' He was quite right. When a collection of Beatles' memorabilia was auctioned at Sotheby's Belgravia, the manager of Liverpool's commercial radio station spent £36,000 on material destined for a proposed Beatles' Museum: Paul McCartney's upright piano fetched £9,900, while a self-portrait of the naked John Lennon went for £8,800.

But sheer quaintness, or even value-by-association, is a world away from general market values. Of course the objects were also status symbols. But, until recently, most of them were designed to be used: the Orientals were particularly good at turning into desirable artefacts even such mundane objects as kimono stands and spittoons (known as 'leys jars' in today's sale-rooms) – calligraphy was turned into an art form by the Chinese to elevate the basic skill of the governing mandarin class. Once an object ceased to be of use, it was abandoned, or broken up. Treasure, defined by Joseph Alsop as 'a device for storing liquid assets impressively and attractively', was precisely that. It was the content, the precious metals and stones, which mattered most to contemporaries, more than the – often exquisite – workmanship. In Renaissance Italy life was still so hazardous that it was useful to have gold or silver plate as capital. Lorenzo the Magnificent's Giottos, his Masaccios and his Donatellos were valued at a fraction of the jewels or (another sign of an insecure age, which traditionally values the past more than present artefacts) the relics of the past – Byzantine as well as Greek and Roman. The concentration on the content remained: until well after the war the auction rooms gave the weight of every lot of silver sold, however fine. Not surprisingly, in Millard Meiss's words, 'the life of goldsmiths was thus somewhat like that of cooks ... But the goldsmiths, of course, sometimes cooked an object for years.'

Because of the emphasis on use and inherent value, artists and craftsmen did not enjoy any real artistic freedom. There were a few scattered periods when artists had some liberty, but only when there was an art market big enough to allow them independence from their patrons. Of course they were also aware of the market, and altered their requirements accordingly. In Gerald Reitlinger's words: 'At a time when painters still charged a fixed rate for the job, as if they were making a pair of shoes, certain paintings began to acquire a prestige value. They were painted, not into the plaster of walls but on portable panels or canvases in order that their owners might trade them, if need be.'

But the products of this artistic freedom were not greatly valued. Use allied to precious raw materials and luxuriantly obvious craftsmanship was the outward and visible sign of greatness. The Oriental tradition was to elevate the humblest object; similarly in the West everything in a royal palace was a work of art in the sense that it was specially made by the finest craftsmen in the land out of the most precious suitable materials. The eighteenth century Kings of France, said Reitlinger, 'were not expected to display worn or second-hand articles in their palaces ... smart Parisians imitated their King ... In some cases the original basic cost of a work of skill, which has now become an "antique", will be found to have been astonishingly high ... Between 1775 and 1784 Reisener alone supplied the French court with £36,000 worth [of furniture] while between 1779 and 1785 Roentgen's bill came to more than £40,000' – sums that would have bought the world's two finest collection of pictures at the time.

Not surprisingly decoration went with craftsmanship: 'the dearest pictures of all were those whose neatness and glossiness came nearest to the surfaces of Sèvres porcelain and furniture mountings, for paintings were a relatively minor part of the total decorative scheme. In the Paris of the 1860s the grandsons and even the sons of the old craftsmen were still alive: the cost of production could be verified by simply having a copy made. Thus the first four-figure prices for *objets d'art* of the past were paid in some cases for things made in the memory of living men, because comparable workmanship cost that to procure.'

The value attached to craftsmanship and to sheer decorative effect was not confined to France. In Vienna pictures were often hacked around to fit the walls they were to decorate; in the eighteenth century English collectors even chose their classical statues to fit the niches available, rather than the other way round – and the paintings of the families and their horses were often matters of record, of family sentiment, rather than artistic worth. Was a Reynolds portrait worth much more than its modern equivalent – a 'passport photo by Cecil Beaton'?

Till the end of the nineteenth century, English taste favoured very large pictures, and payment by size was all to the advantage of the seventeenth-century Italians, among whom life-sized figures had been an occupational disease. Moreover the huge well-smoked altarpieces went particularly well with even smokier ancestors. The pictures most in demand, the works of contemporary British painters, were valued for their size, for their decorative nature, and above all for the painstaking craftsmanship they involved. Families would go repeatedly to Royal Academy exhibitions to examine in detail the faithful craftsmanship of the exhibits, many of which had taken years to complete.

(One of the few people who still looks at paintings with a Victorian eye is the nonagenarian Sir David Scott, who recently startled an art dealer fifty years his junior by noticing how one side of the arm of a serving-wench in a picture of Dr Johnson in a tavern was slightly scorched – because of its repeated exposure to the oven.)

The price of past skills tends to be limited, because it is always possible to relate their worth to the materials and skills originally employed. Multiplied into modern terms the value may be extremely high, but, unlike that attachable to works of genius, it is not limitless: 'the value placed on pure genius is limited only by the fluid capital available' said Reitlinger. 'Generally when a picture is stolen from a collection or a gallery it at once becomes, in the language of the popular Press, "priceless", though as often as not it is something that can be priced only too easily. Fundamentally, however, this word is perfectly sound, for the stolen picture has no commodity value.' But the change in valuations is comparatively recent. 'The distinction between skill and genius has not existed very long in the minds of men.' The concentration on Impressionists signified a revolution: these paintings were not artefacts made by

72

craftsmen, their value related purely to the supposed 'genius' of their creators.

The association of value and use was prolonged by the slump in the 1930s and the shortages which persisted in Britain until well after 1945. In the first London auction season after the war prices of pictures remained ridiculously low (the National Gallery snapped up the Dürer *Madonna of the Lilies* for a mere £12,000) but the *objets d'art* collected by R. M. Walker fetched £156,000. Reitlinger remembered how: 'during the war years when fine *objets d'art* were sold at what now appear to have been bargain prices, very ordinary carpets, glass, china and cutlery became excessively dear, because one had to seek at an antique shop the articles of the modern showroom, which under war conditions were either not worth buying or not to be had.' The same applied to motor cars until the mid-50s. Many late pre-war models had been laid up during the war and in the immediate post-war years and therefore had very little mileage. It took only a decade to transform the scale of values: a car valued in the early 1950s because it was a 'good runner' had often become a cherished collectable item ten years later.

In the late 1950s it was still natural for Denys Sutton, in his review of the art market since the war, to assume that changes in value – like the fall in value of tapestries or heavy oak furniture – was related to the size and style of the homes of the rich. Their decorative tastes were still dominant, and if these included Renoirs over the dining-table in the yacht, well, this was no more than a new type of decoration, 'light in colour, gay in subject-matter – works which impose no strain on the beholder'.

'The dwelling units of the Collector Class had changed', noted Saarinen in the late 1950s. 'The exodus from mansions to town houses and to apartments meant smaller rooms and lower ceilings, a shift from ponderous English furniture to lighter French furniture, from Persian rugs to gray wall-to-wall carpeting, from dark wood-paneled walls to pale painted ones. In these new living quarters, English eighteenth-century portraits, such as those with which Huntington filled his California palace, were too large; tapestries ridiculous; and most Old Masters too dark.' The change affected every market: the walls of apartments were too low for tapestries, so between the wars flower pictures were in great demand from interior decorators – Fantin-Latour was in a class of his own, the 1930s equivalent of hand-blocked wall-paper. Maurice Rheims noted that: 'the finest black-inlaid Boulle writing-desk is worth at most four million francs, whereas a desk of the same design but of light veneered wood by an inferior cabinet-maker might fetch ten million francs'.

Yet the rich who possessed precious objects were not necessarily collectors, or if they were, did not associate the precious objects with which they surrounded themselves with their collections. A whole generation of Rothschilds went in for collecting orchids, rhododendrons or fleas, and even the less scientifically-minded David Rockefeller accumulated a fabulous collection of beetles, 40,000 of them. But their Louis XV chairs, their T'ang figures, their Cézannes and their Manets were simply part of the décor. It was really rather vulgar to think of their value – a sentiment reinforced because so many of the splashiest buyers were using their money to gain social status. The insecurity relieved by buying art could also be social.

The existence of a flourishing art market did not, historically, assume that collectors were primarily (if at all) interested in financial gain. This was something of a paradox: these markets have always depended on a class of people whose wealth was available in liquid form. These were often nouveaux riches, their wealth acquired through socially dubious activities, and therefore anxious to improve their social standing. Art has always been a marvellous way of laundering money: Verres, greediest of Roman collectors, was a notorious war profiteer, and the first modern collector was a fifteenth-century moneylender from Treviso. Typically he started by trying to buy respectability through collecting – and then developed a genuine passion for his collection.

In eighteenth-century France the major collectors were not the aristocracy so much as the *fermiers généraux* whose fortunes were derived from manipulating the tax collection system. In Britain, as Denys Sutton pointed out, 'three of the main collectors, William Beckford, George Watson Taylor and Ralph Bernal . . . derived their fortunes from the West Indies and the fluctuation of property there and such factors as the emancipation of the slaves exerted a considerable effect on their position and thus influenced their buying and selling, as the case may be, of works of art.'

But the mainstay of the market has always, naturally, been bankers. The line runs clearly from the Medicis in Florence, the Fuggers in Augsburg, to the Rothschilds throughout Europe and Morgan in New York. Only when there was a large-scale stockmarket – and that usually meant New York or London – could ordinary industrialists sell shares in their own concerns on a sufficient scale to afford large-scale art purchases. Though the purest of capitalists, the bankers' art purchases usually reflected a love of beautiful objects or a love of show as well as a desire for increased respectability.

The temptation to speculation was, of course, always present. In the seventeenth century, Philippe de Voulanges promised the daughter of the redoubtable Madame de Sévigné that pictures were like golden bars and could be counted on to double in value. Paris has had an active art market for well over 200 years, but, in the eighteenth century anyway, it was very narrow – a quarter of the turnover of the leading dealer, Lazare-Duvaux, came from Madame de Pompadour alone. It was the Dutch who pioneered the modern, broadly-based art market.

The rise of the Amsterdam market dates from 1557: the previously dominant Antwerp market collapsed when the Northern Netherlands revolted and wrenched their independence from their former masters, the Spanish. The subsequent Dutch dominance in the world's trade was reflected in the art market. They did not go in for show in the objects they used (all those plain, scrubbed dressers). But they did have the crucial requirements: a lot of spare cash not tied up in land, a well-developed taste for pictures ('there was nothing unusual about finding from 100–200 pictures in a modest home', said Bredius) and solid capitalist instincts.

For over 200 years the Dutch showed how an art market can be socially broadly-based, and achieve an acceptable balance between collecting for pleasure and for profit. The market was of course rife with all the petty (and grand) trickeries characteristic of art markets throughout the ages, fakes and tall tales. More positively, later dealers like Durand-Ruel and Ambroise Vollard who financed their artistic clients had a predecessor in Hermann Becker. He had brought together a stupendous collection by advancing money to artists who paid him back in pictures – although some of the painters, eternally ungrateful, broke the code of conduct that bound them to the dealers and sold directly to the public.

When the young John Evelyn, the diarist, visited Holland in 1641, he noted that 'the peasants were so rich that they were looking for investments and often spent 2000–3000 florins for pictures'. There were also a few more professional collections formed by bankers and other serious capitalists looking for safe investments at a time when there was a glut of gold lying idle during the Thirty Years' War. 'In the middle of the seventeenth century', wrote F. H. Taylor*, 'this city became the liquidating market for Europe's princely collections, just as London was to be after the French Revolution and Napoleonic Wars, and New York following the World War of 1914–1918. The bankers invested heavily and their children and grandchildren reaped their reward in the eighteenth century by selling their works of art to the *curieux* of France and England.' Amsterdam was the centre not only for pictures; because of the Dutch dominance of trade

* *The Taste of Angels.*

with the Far East an amazing quantity of porcelain passed through Amsterdam (in the next century the Swedes also imported an enormous amount). Amsterdam's supremacy lasted right through the eighteenth century – even, significantly, after it had been surpassed as a commercial centre by London – and was terminated only by her unhappy involvement in the Napoleonic Wars. But, although people marvelled when collections were sold for large sums, there was no general feeling that investment or profit was a primary motive in the collection of art.

Taylor's book is one of a handful devoted to the study of collecting throughout the ages, most of which originate in the United States, a country that took up the Dutch tradition of popular interest in art. Unfortunately the condescension shown by so many writers on the subject has rather biassed our view of American taste. The authors often reflected the acute ambivalence of the experts who advised the richer American buyers in the late nineteenth and early twentieth centuries. Aesthetes like Roger Fry were simultaneously taking handsome commissions for finding pictures for the likes of Pierpont Morgan and sneering at their paymasters. In their position only a saint could have accepted that these millionaires cared as deeply about art, and were often as sensitive to it as their artistic mentors.

These massed sneers have obscured the fact that a select group of Americans showed a greater sensitivity to avant-garde French painters than did the painters' fellow countrymen. They not only bought the pictures earlier than Europeans, they also shared their knowledge – and their purchases – by endowing a group of American museums with collections often superior to those bequeathed to their European equivalents.

The transformation of American taste was amazingly swift. 'American private collections travelled with incredible celerity from the tenth rate to the best', noted the art critic Royal Cortissoz. For many Americans their first exposure to foreign art came with the Centennial Exposition held in Philadelphia in 1876. But the taste for modernism started in the mid-West, especially in Chicago, although the largely German city of Cincinnati had raised over a million dollars as early as 1886 to endow a museum and an art school, which soon attracted over 400 pupils. 'In the eighties and nineties', wrote Saarinen, 'the Middle West by-passed New York and looked to Paris. Middle Western manufacturers entered their reapers, plows and wagons in the great international expositions in Paris and went abroad to see them.'

They returned with the best of French art: 'In Chicago', a toffee-nosed visitor was told in the 1950s, 'we don't buy Renoirs. We inherit them from our grandmothers.' The same generation of millionaires financed the construction of the first, and most architecturally splendid, generation of skyscrapers – it was the architect Stanford White who encouraged the great dealer, Dirkan Kelekian, to promote his Persian rugs, early textiles and potteries in the Mid-West (he later used the entrée he gained to promote modern art – whereas Duveen had used the similar entrée provided by his father and uncle to sell safe, second-rate, British portraits).

The majority of collectors were naturally inspired by a desire for social correctness ('People in our position would naturally be expected to have a Corot', explained one lady), but Saarinen provides ample evidence of a widespread strain of cultural independence and adventurousness. None of her collectors was inspired by a desire for profit, or even a lust for improved social standing. Rich Americans – some of them anyway – had a natural, unselfconscious confidence denied to their European brethren, which enabled them to experiment, to chance their arms.

The problem is that we – Americans as much as Europeans – have been culturally conditioned not to take seriously characters like Mrs Potter Palmer, the social and cultural queen of Chicago at the turn of the century. We automatically associate her with one of the absurd dowagers immortalized by Helen Hokinson in *The New Yorker* (or even with Margaret Dumont in the Marx brothers' films). But she had 'an easy uncondescending manner' and got on well with the artists. Her friendship with Monet led her to buy enough of his work to make a frieze round her ballroom. Guided by the American artist Mary Cassatt she also bought Degas and four marvellous Renoirs (at a total cost of $5,000) which are now the pride of Chicago's Art Institute – itself a product of the 1890s.

Another of Mary Cassatt's friends, Louisine Elder, borrowed $100 to buy a Degas (a purchase which rescued the poverty-stricken artist from a decision to abandon art entirely). Later she and her husband, Henry Havemeyer, built up a fantastic collection, the best of which she conscientiously reserved for the Metropolitan Museum in New York. Their daughter Electra rebelled: at the age of eighteen she brought home one of the wooden statues of Red Indians which stood outside cigar stores, a first declaration of a taste that led her to build up by far the finest collection of Americana in the country, a generation before the majority of museum curators had become aware of their artistic and cultural importance. She bought on a breathtaking scale: her collection of 125,000 items included a lighthouse, a stone jail, and an early paddle-steamer which cost a fortune to transport to her inland home.

The young Electra's obsession with the American past was matched by the passion of an Oklahoman oilman, Thomas Gilcrease, for anything connected with real, rather than wooden Indians – 85,000 books and manuscripts as well as pipes, beadwork and jewellery. For Saarinen's list is diverse: Charles Freer, a tycoon of 'exquisite sensibility' and great friend of Whistler's, who had made his fortune employing starving Polish immigrants at a pittance to build railroad wagons; the splendidly independent corporate lawyer, John Johnson, who employed leading experts to find offbeat, difficult pictures, which are now the glory of the Philadelphia Museum of Art; the Stein family, who introduced Matisse to an apathetic American public; and John Quinn, the combative lawyer behind the famous Armory Show of outrageously modern art held in New York in 1913. The show aroused a predictable outpouring. *The New York Times* called it 'pathological' and particular scorn was reserved for Marcel Duchamp's *Nude Descending a Staircase*. One cartoon portrayed a rush hour on the subway called *The Rude descending a Staircase*.

Nevertheless, the show – which attracted a record number of 129,000 visitors – had an immense effect. A week after it opened Wanamaker's store ran an advertisement announcing: 'Color Combinations of the Futurist Cubist Influence in Fashions in the new Paris Models for Spring'. More serious was the visitor who noted: 'whatever you think of this show our art can never be the same again'. But the most fundamental comment came from a banker, John Spellman: 'Something is wrong with the world', he said grimly, 'these men know.'

René Gimpel had much the same feeling when he saw the work of post-war German painters: 'If France were to study it carefully', he said 'she would realise the dangers facing her.' This super-critical dealer fully appreciated the revolution in American taste. He recalled how his father had opened his gallery in New York only in 1902 and persuaded millionaires such as Jules Bache to buy pictures for the first time. By the 1920s he was marvelling at the intense 'movement in favour of modern art' and admiring many of the museums outside New York – one of which he advised. In Toledo, the curator, 'George Stevens and his wife, only moderately well off, gave up a good job ... This devotion to the cause of art is found throughout the United States ... Ralph Booth, President of the Detroit Museum, gave up the chance to run for the US Senate for its sake.'

By the end of the decade it was safe for a group of socially secure, if relatively unadventurous millionaires, the Whitneys, the Rockefellers and their like, to found New York's Museum of Modern Art. From the start it was one of the city's most chic institutions and, once the country emerged from the depression, the public returned in even greater numbers to art. Popular museum shows like that devoted to Van Gogh in 1935 attracted phenomenal interest. By the 1940s Taylor could explain the growing attendances by saying that 'a generation of philanthropy in the fine arts is beginning to pay off. A hell of a lot of money, you know, has been poured into institutions like this one, and we're beginning to collect the dividends', for innocent, non-profit oriented popular involvement in art purchases culminated with his fourteen-year reign as Director of the Metropolitan Museum between 1940 and 1954. 'The museum is the midwife of democracy', he said proudly.

The popular mood had changed. As the Rigbys put it: 'Modern art, instead of creeping along, began to hurl its influence into household furnishings, into architecture and popular literature ... the man in the street and his wife were becoming reconciled to the idea that art was not as bad as it had been painted.' This theory was subjected to a stern test with the disposal of the mass of material accumulated by the by-now financially desperate William Randolph Hearst (and also, to a lesser extent, with the collection of Clarence Mackay). Conventional auction sales obviously could not cope. So, in the Rigbys' words, 'first at Marshall Field's in Chicago in December 1939, then a few months later in a St Louis and in a Seattle department store, portions of the collection were offered publicly. These ventures attracted large crowds and resulted in a surprising number of sales. They were followed, early in 1941, by a genuine "blockbuster" dropped on the collecting front, when a larger portion of the Hearst collection was installed in two New York department stores at bargain prices ranging from thirty-five cents to hundreds of thousands of dollars.'

The choice was amazing, including not just a mass of bric-à-brac but hundreds of Turner watercolours, sold within a few hours at prices ranging from $6.76 to $298.50. Significantly, only a few buyers ventured into Saks Fifth Avenue where a select group of paintings had been hung in conventional gallery style. The crowds were attracted by Gimbels' sales pitch, which emphasized the accessibility of great art, how ordinary people could make their dreams come true. The pitch also appealed to snobbery ('Have you always wanted an ancestral portrait? We have some – and who's to care (or to know) whether it isn't your grandfather's aunt?'), and to historical curiosity ('Would it thrill you to cherish a bit of brocade that had paid glittering homage to the brilliant beauty of its wearer at Louis XV's court? We have it'). But the underlying, and exceedingly effective, call was to simple love of beauty. 'Do you want to touch, every day of your life, a silky satinwood table that Hepplewhite made ... beautiful precious old things aren't only for museums and art galleries and great hushed private collections. Artists never made them for museums and art galleries. They made them to be worn, to be used, to be looked at, to be appreciated, to be loved.'

The sale represented a high point: a unique combination of the love of art for its own sake, allied to a brand of high-pressure salesmanship which did not derogate from the value of the items being sold, but merely made great art accessible to an unprecedentedly wide public. It is difficult not to feel that the story since then has been a sad decline in the quality, the innocent mass love for art.

Although the tradition did not die out – Otto Bernet of Parke-Bernet had 'barnyard rallies' between 1943 and 1945 with middle-class buyers bringing in their sandwiches to sales in their lunch hour – he died in 1945 and the 'rallies' with him. After the war Sears Roebuck tried to attack the mass market again with the 'Vincent Price' collection of art, but by the end of the decade the President of Parke-Bernet, Leslie Hyam could lament: 'At the beginning the money aspect was a kind of pestilence one endured. Later it became ossifying.'

For Americans came relatively late to the idea that you could make money out of art. Even outside Holland it was nothing new. In his history of Christie's, published in 1926, H. C. Marillier writes of 'people who buy pictures as an investment or at least with the idea of an investment at the back of their minds'. At much the same time Gimpel was describing how 'inborn taste plus a taste for speculation have made him [Joseph Bardac] a collector'. During the Second World War many once-rich families from Continental Europe had learnt through bitter experience the importance of portable wealth – even the Rothschilds had been forced to carry portmanteaux full of gold coins when they fled from France in 1940. Not surprisingly, a survey conducted by the French magazine *Amateur d'art* in 1953 found that investment and speculation were overwhelmingly the most important motives behind art collecting. Only 7 per cent of those questioned mentioned a desire to embellish their homes, the same percentage as referred to their love of art. Profit was clearly taking over from use or love of beauty before the money motive had taken root in the United States.

The first American millionaire to take investment in art seriously was probably Charles B. Wrightsman. His purchase of the Duc d'Aumale's Vermeer in the 1950s was merely the most public demonstration of a total investment policy. Wrightsman's father had lost his all in the Depression, but had recovered to leave his son a major interest in Standard Oil of Kansas. In the late 1940s the son sold the bulk of his stock and sat back to decide where to invest the resulting millions.

Like a lot of other rich men he had noted Sutton's point: 'that major works of art could command hard cash at a time of universal economic distress – before the shortage of works of art had become so acute as is now the case – was proof of their financial strength under trying conditions'. But Wrightsman was thinking of the future. By 1953 he had concluded that inflation was here to stay, which precluded fixed-interest investments; and that there was a good chance of a glut of oil, so a return to his father's business did not make sense. He rejected professional advice to go for real estate or industrial shares. For, as he said in a deposition made in a tax court some years later: 'Charles had formed the belief that works of art were an excellent hedge against inflation and devaluation of currencies, that they represented portable international currency, since there were no restrictions on export from the United States and that works of art were appropriate assets for investment of a substantial portion of his surplus cash being generated'.

He and his wife Jayne concentrated on eighteenth-century French works of art. They knew nothing about the subject but immersed themselves in it, talking to anyone remotely qualified and reading omnivorously. Jayne even learnt French (or, in the language of the tax court, 'educated herself in the use of the French language') so that she could 'engage in discussions and reading of materials in that language concerning eighteenth-century French furniture and works of art'. Their learning curve led them to spend $5.2 million by the end of 1960 on works of art, and another $3.7 million by the end of 1967 – by that time their 'investments' were valued at nearly 90 per cent above their cost price. Although much of the Wrightsman collection is now in the Metropolitan Museum they were the models for the new investors (PCW knew them well, although he could be sharp, about Jayne in particular, in their absence), and a month before PCW died, Sotheby's sold the furniture from her home in Palm Beach for $4.8 million.

It is difficult now, as we look back on the Eisenhower years as a period of unrepeatable economic stability, to understand how deep was the fear of inflation. It wasn't the numbers but the idea, unprecedented in living memory, that prices were going to rise, inexorably, every year, which the rich found so frightening – Sutton talked about the preservation of capital 'in an era marked by a perpetual fall in the value of money', and that firm decadentist, Reitlinger, declared boldly, 'by the middle of the 1950s, after two world wars, a world financial depression, and a world wave of currency inflation, "art as an investment" had lost any stigma it had once possessed'.

But it took a change in the US tax laws to create a whole class of

Wrightspersons. Since 1954, as Sutton put it, 'the sale-room has been examined with a solicitude usually reserved for the stock exchange'. It allowed collectors relief from capital gains tax – and their heirs equal relief from inheritance taxes – on the full market value of works of art donated to a museum, even if the collector had kept them for his own enjoyment during his lifetime (although this particular loophole was closed in 1965).

The full consequences of this relief were spelt out by *Fortune* magazine at the end of 1955. 'Art stands out as one of the most attractive remaining targets for excess cash', said the authors. 'From the broadest point of view art is an investment: the prime investment that men of great wealth can make.' They talked of the 'world's hardest coin ... areas of canvas or wood overlaid, by some master hand, with the oxides of metals, all of them base' – a classic statement of the way 'genius' had taken over the market from craftsmanship or content. The magazine recommended 'gilt-edged securities', like Flemish primitives, 'Blue-chips', like the Impressionists, and 'speculative growth' stocks, like a great many modern artists. The investment was versatile, inflation proof and offered unique tax advantages:

> If a wealthy man whose taxable income is $500,000 a year owns a painting realistically appraised at $100,000 market value, a dealer might purchase it from him at one-third below that price – the discount being the dealer's commission. The relinquishing owner would then have to pay a capital-gains tax on the difference between $66,666 and the price, probably much less, at which he long ago bought the painting. But if, instead of selling, the owner gives his painting to a museum, he gets a tax deduction for the full amount of its honest $100,000 appraisal as a gift to a tax-exempt charitable or educational institution. The difference, to a wealthy man, may be considerable. Not only would he legitimately avoid a capital-gains tax: his taxable income that year could be only four-fifths of what it might have been without the deduction.

Chief Justice Stone, then chairman of the trustees of the National Gallery in Washington – a major beneficiary from the ruling – approved the practice and thus accelerated the trend. Of course, motives remained mixed. Richard Rush, an enthusiastic collector whose book on *Art as Investment* was published in 1961, had been through the whole gamut, starting as a genuine enthusiast, ending as an apologist for art as an investment medium. Many collectors felt like him that '"the investment value of art" provides not only a real reason for investing in art, but at the same time a splendid excuse for a person to buy what he loves'. For 'the purchase of art', he warned, 'is unfortunately, not the road to quick profits, at least for the inexpert collector'. He felt that his book 'may provide some excuse for the art lover to indulge himself with a little more freedom'.

The tax ruling, and press coverage like the articles in *Fortune*, had an immediate effect. 'In the recession of 1957 we were literally deluged with Wall Street brokers up here to buy paintings from us', one dealer told Richard Rush. It also upset the practice of hundreds of years. Historically the art market had been dominated by people who had a vested interest in keeping prices down – collectors and dealers alike were engaged in a tacit 'ring' because they both wanted to buy more of the same. Of course the new rich had a vested interest in keeping prices high, thus showing that they had consumed lavishly, but yet shrewdly and profitably. Nevertheless, their influence would not have been dominant without the tax change, which produced a new conspiracy, of rich 'benefactors' and museum curators, vitally interested in keeping market values up.

By the end of the 1950s, too, corporations had started to get into the act, partly in an effort to improve the working environment of their employees. The trend was set by David Rockefeller, himself a major collector, through the Chase Manhattan bank, which spent $500,000 on nearly a hundred paintings and pieces of sculpture.

But it was the increasing importance of museum purchasing power, boosted by the tax concession, which concerned observers at the time. *Fortune* talked of 'cold socialization' to describe the steady drift in ownership from – transitory – private hands into – permanent – public ownership. The market was affected not only by the increased purchasing power, but also because the new 'mushroom museums' as Reitlinger scornfully dubbed them suddenly widened the very concept of 'museum art'. Previously, in Geraldine Norman's definition, a 'museum picture' had been 'an important and successful example of the artist's work'. The new institutions could not afford to be so choosy, they had to compete with private buyers for less outstanding works. They also revolutionized whole markets. Reitlinger could remember that 'liturgical manuscripts of the twelfth century with simple rubrics, but no illuminations, could be bought in the early 1920s for £10 in fine condition. Today they are worth something in the region of £1,000, only for the simple fact of their being as old as the twelfth century.'

The increasing importance of museums and other institutional buyers further weakened the links between works of art and their practical usefulness. In the words of Professor Gombrich: 'Nearly all the objects in our collections were once intended to serve a social purpose from which they were alienated by collectors'. Art had become depersonalized, detached from human life. Joseph Alsop complained, 'too many of today's collectors think of art-as-an-end-in-itself, rather than art-for-use-plus-beauty ... The contemporary works they acquire are never designed with any specific use in mind. They have no purpose except to be art.' This applies also to many older 'collectibles' not just old furniture, but also artefacts from other civilizations, pre-Columbian statues or carvings from many West African kingdoms, originally designed as votive objects, symbols of other-worldly power, the pagan equivalent of crucifixes wrenched from their setting and reduced to – tradeable art.

For the swing away from craftsmanship and use led to alienation right through the system: the artist was responsible only to his own artistic conscience (with a peep or two at the market); the collector, the very opposite of a patron, was in no way responsible for the production of the works he was collecting – he was helping to depersonalize the process. So were PCW and the group of talented youngsters he had gathered around him.

*Part IV*

# TOMORROW THE WORLD

# I  MR WILSON'S ACADEMY FOR YOUNG AUCTIONEERS

The momentum generated by the Impressionist sales which culminated in 'Second Goldschmidt' was kept up for the next few years.
The year after Goldschmidt could have been an anti-climax. It
wasn't. Despite the absence of any major single item (apart from a
Louis XV silver dinner service which went for £207,000, showing
that craftsmanship was still highly valued) the sales total rose by
over £1 million and continued to rise steadily even though there were
few enormous sales.

Before PCW became chairman, the firm had no full-time public
relations advisers. In 1958 Christie's had appointed a full-time
public relations director, John Herbert, a former journalist and son
of A. P. Herbert, the famous playwright and humorous writer ('The
Board was reassured because I was a Wykehamist and so they
thought I was a gent', says Herbert). The next year, not to be
outdone, PCW made a less routine choice, hiring an adviser who was
to have an influence on Sotheby's second only to PCW himself. The
description most routinely (and rightly) applied to Stanley Clark
was that he was 'rumpled', a round, friendly, crumpled sort of man,
looking very much the journalist he once was. Clark already had a
distinguished career before being hired by PCW (who did not even
bother to interview any other candidates after he'd seen him). A
journalist before the war, he had shown extraordinary powers of
organization as an officer in the Royal Army Ordnance Corps, a
normally unglamorous service responsible for the Army's supplies,
which he managed to enliven with his particular brand of initiative
(he was several times promoted on the spot by an unusually far-
sighted quartermaster-general). His most notable service was performed during the long siege of Tobruk in 1942. He ended the war as
a Brigadier, but the phrase 'Brigadier Stanley Clark' conveyed an
entirely alien impression of military (and when combined with the
name of Sotheby's) social correctness. After the war he had risen to a
senior job at Reuter's, had left after a flaming row and had started his
own PR company just in time for PCW to hire him.

After the Goldschmidt sale it had become relatively easy to

guarantee publicity for major sales of the possessions of famous figures like Somerset Maugham or Sir Alexander Korda. Stanley Clark's particular contribution was to use the relatively new medium of television to persuade the general public that the auction business was not only glamorous, but accessible as well. He provided a receptive press with a steady stream of stories concentrating on a few key themes: that the vast majority of the items auctioned at Sotheby's went for prices well within the reach of the average man; that there was some chance that even the most neglected household object could be worth infinitely more than the owner had ever suspected; and that Sotheby's, far from being the toffee-nosed institution it seemed, welcomed all comers.

The Clark formula was first expressed in the 1958–59 edition of the firm's year-book: 'The prosperity of the Art market depends not on spectacular figures but on the thousands of lots which change hands at prices between £20 and £200.' The average was still low. Turnover in the year was around £5.75 million (virtually double anyone else). Excluding the Goldschmidt sale, the Westminster Rubens, and a diamond tiara which went for £110,000, the average for the 45,000 lots was only just over £100. Even five years later 70 per cent of all the lots went for below the magic £100 figure. So in the early 1960s PCW (and occasionally other Sothebyites) appeared on TV with some regularity, not only on the occasion of major sales, but also in general current affairs programmes – most noticeably on the BBC's *Tonight* show, a pioneering and highly influential news programme.

Clark was an ideal propagandist, the very model for the £100 buyer (although he himself bought quite a lot, at least one friend said simply: 'He didn't know any more about art than I did'), but then it was part of PCW's genius to enroll in his crusade outsiders like Clark and Jesse Wolff, who were not remotely part of the art establishment. Initially PCW was hesitant about Clark's ideas for democratization, he thought that everyone with money was already aware of Sotheby's. But he was soaringly ambitious: 'We want to talk about £100 million turnover', he told Clark, who persuaded him that the only way to reach an apparently ridiculous dream target was to aim at the mass market. Clark had seen the then-President of the Royal Academy, Sir Gerald Kelly, talking to the Queen about a typical Dutch genre picture, and Kelly's enthusiastic remark, 'Isn't that interior a bloody marvel?' seemed to him the key to the popular approach required.

Clark immediately became very close to PCW – in later years he was the only person with automatic, immediate access to his office. More importantly, he changed the direction of the whole firm, he was the only person who actually influenced PCW's policy. For PCW would never have thought of democratization himself; indeed there are those who believe that Clark was a sort of Svengali, manipulating PCW, using his passion for Sotheby's to turn him into a sort of missionary, eternally preaching the gospel of profit through art. It would be truer to say simply that Clark enabled PCW to preach his own gospel to a wider audience.

He shared PCW's sense of fun: he was responsible, for instance, for the Ian Fleming story, *The Property of a Lady*, which appeared in the year-book in 1962–63. It's a splendidly tongue-in-cheek affair involving James Bond and the bidding for a 'very important Fabergé terrestrial globe' – for convoluted reasons the resident KGB director in London ended up as underbidder.

But in the end Clark paid for his loyalty. He found himself dependent but without the security of full-time employment. He was one of those who came too close to PCW, as to the sun, and was duly burnt. The same applied to some of the small group of recruits who joined Sotheby's between 1955 and the mid 1960s. Together they had an even greater impact on the firm. They were recruited by Jim Kiddell and Carmen Gronau as well as PCW himself in a successful effort to increase the pool of experts available within the company – which continued to rely on outside help in some subjects throughout the 1960s. For Sotheby's was still a tiny firm with only eight partners at the time of the Goldschmidt sale and only 220 employees even eight years later. Second to PCW was Cyril Butterwick, formerly a housemaster at Eton, with a passionate love of silver – and the entrée into the houses of his former charges (he combined the two assets by attracting the fabulous Berkeley silver to Sotheby's). Third was Anthony Hobson, very much his father's son, a severe, remote, brilliant, intolerant bibliophile. Tim Clarke, the expert on ceramics, was, and remains the classic British eccentric, a man who has spent thirty years studying the rhinoceros in relation to the imagination of European writers and artists. He, like PCW, had spent the war in Intelligence. He was head of M15 in Aleppo, an influential figure and expert interrogator and had joined Sotheby's at the suggestion of PCW – then a close friend – just after the war. Apart from Jim Kiddell and Carmen Gronau the only other partners were Fred Rose, the expert on silver, and another close friend of PCW, and Richard Timewell, in charge of furniture, a man who felt himself increasingly by-passed as time went on.

But they needed help, and showed enormous flair in their choice of new recruits: they were invariably young, untrained, brilliant. Many of them were promoted to the board at what seemed an absurdly young age, often while still in their twenties, but they tended to drift away for one reason or another, unlike the rather less glittering group of young men enlisted by Christie's during the same years.

The first recruit was the sensitive, tragic, figure of John Rickett. He was a Wykehamist who joined Sotheby's in 1953 straight from New College, Oxford – where he had founded the Oxford Society of Bibliophiles. His obituary spoke of his 'many and varied interests such as horticulture, geology, ornithology, literature and music', he collected cacti, had 'an extraordinary understanding of music', and had managed to pursue his interest in archaeology and astronomy while he was doing his National Service in North Africa. He was one of the select few who measured up to Carmen Gronau's exacting standards and within six years he was a partner, the first appointed after PCW became chairman.

Even more important in the long-term was Peregrine Pollen. Unlike most of the others, he was neither an expert nor an auctioneer, but they tended to look to him for leadership. He was older than the other 'new men', twenty-nine when he was recruited as PCW's personal assistant in 1957. His family were bankers with a splendid house in the Cotswolds, a background less distinguished, although infinitely more secure, than PCW's. Pollen looks every inch the English aristocrat with long hair outlining a severely sculpted – albeit unaristocratically mobile – face. But his most noticeable physical features are his long, bony, expressive fingers.

Pollen had been conventionally educated at Eton and Christ Church, Oxford. There he beat a century-old record by running a mile, riding a mile and rowing a mile, all within the space of fourteen minutes. After Oxford he spent a restless few years, as a schoolmaster, then bumming round the world filling in with a variety of jobs (ranging from filling station attendant to playing the organ in a Chicago night club). He was well-connected and became aide-de-camp to the governor of Kenya, Sir Evelyn Baring, who tried to get him a job at Christie's through Lord Crawford (whose younger son, Pollen's cousin, the Hon Patrick Lindsay, succeeded Bill Martin as head of Christie's pictures department in 1962).

Another 'grown-up' was Richard Day, a particular protégé of Carmen Gronau's, who took charge of drawings when these were separated from paintings. The dozens of new departments created by the many amoeboid splittings of the 1960s provided the young entrants – like Michael Webb in furniture, and Michel Strauss in modern paintings – with unprecedented opportunities which they took with both hands. The process was remarkably quick. The 1958–59 edition of the firm's year-book was divided into a mere four categories: Paintings and Drawings; Jewellery, Silver and Gold; Books, Manuscripts and Engravings; and Works of Art, still covering an immense range of objects. Within three years the year-book itself had been transformed from a rather drab, utilitarian production to a thick glossy volume with over 200 pages of pictures illustrating some of the major lots of the year. It was now divided into fifteen sections: pictures and drawings (prints, modern and Old Master pictures), silver, which had been separated from jewellery, and works of art divided into twelve categories, from scientific instruments to Oriental art. Even then, although Sotheby's claimed as one of its major assets 'sound scholarship in the compilation of a catalogue', yet the term Antiquities was simply 'a convenient term which may denote anything from a Sumerian clay tablet to a carved head from darkest Africa'. There were still plenty of opportunites for ambitious new boys.

The first was Marcus Linell – one of the few still with Sotheby's. He had been recruited in 1956 by Jim Kiddell who needed someone with the keen eyesight of extreme youth to help examine the intricacies of ceramics. The sixteen-year-old Linell hated school and Kiddell simply asked him: 'When are you free to start?' He spent two years dusting and numbering, and a further spell cataloguing a whole range of wares, bronzes, maiolica, Persian pots, and African artefacts and by the mid-1960s was running the Chinese department.

If Linell was the youngest, Howard Ricketts was considered by his contemporaries as the most original and important talent among them. He had been fascinated by arms and armour since the age of seven and in his teens developed a number of other interests, including one in sixteenth-century bronzes. He had won a place at the Courtauld Institute of Fine Art and while waiting to go there took a temporary summer job as a porter in the furniture department (not a natural role for someone as slightly built as he). He realized that 'I would only have been given the Blunt party line about the seventeenth century if I'd gone to the Courtauld' and remained at Sotheby's. Within a few months he was given musical instruments to catalogue largely because he played the violin. He was moved to the works of art department to take care of gold boxes as well as his first love, arms and armour, while Tim Clarke was away. Clarke was naturally annoyed because he had not been told of the arrangements (a foretaste of later, more serious manoeuvrings in which PCW acted behind his partners' backs). When John Malet left in 1963, Ricketts, still in his early twenties, was given additional responsibilities – although he relied heavily on outsiders, like PCW's old mentors, the Hunts – and the next year was made a director. His first initiative (originally intended to teach himself) was to institute a proper 'blue card' filing system for the gold boxes the firm sold, to provide a comprehensive card index, still not a usual practice.

Ricketts had had 'an old headmaster who used everybody. I saw this aspect of PCW and kept my distance from him'. One recruit who didn't was Bruce Chatwyn, who lasted only a couple of years, but made a deep impression on everyone, especially PCW, who grew very fond of him. He married PCW's secretary, the daughter of a leading US steel magnate, and was thus able to leave before he had made his name as an expert: for although his colleagues usually came from public schools, they were not wealthy. PCW was deeply upset when he left to start a degree in archaeology before wandering about the globe and (under the slightly changed name of Chatwin) writing a number of brilliant books – the only one of the original group to escape entirely from the art world.

The youngest director, appointed at the age of twenty-four, was the remarkable Derek Johns. Without any social advantages his father had risen to become managing director of Knoedler's and the son had strayed accidentally into Sotheby's in a temporary summer job as a porter (he had intended to study horticulture). He too grew fascinated and took advantage of the enormous wealth of material, good bad and indifferent, pouring through. For if the pupils in the Sotheby's school were remarkable, the teaching was equally brilliant. Almost every morning Jim Kiddell would give the youngsters one of his famous 'one-minute seminars' discoursing briefly but learnedly on some newly-arrived object, and a select few were sent on study trips round Europe, to museums and galleries. For they were encouraged to get out and about: 'We could go on swanning tours', says Richard Day, 'we were encouraged to stay with people, that's how I got some marvellous Rembrandt etchings.' In Bond Street 'it was more like a college than an auction house' remembers one of them, 'every morning we would assemble in the little cupboard at the top of the stairs where Mrs Janner, the cleaning lady, kept her brooms and boast over the coffee of our latest discovery.' 'We were all frightfully over-enthusiastic', says Richard Day recalling his early days at 'Mr Wilson's Academy for Young Auctioneers'.

Outsiders felt the same electricity: 'In talking to Mr Wilson or any of his colleagues or his staff, one has the feeling frequently of being at a university or in a college common room rather than in a way of business', noted Goronwy Rees in the early 1960s. The tone was set by Kiddell: 'When I came to Sotheby's', says Marcus Linell, 'it was made clear to me by Jim Kiddell that if I wanted to get rich I shouldn't come to Sotheby's.' This is the eternal theme of both houses. Peter Chance used to remind recruits that he himself had started at £150 a year and that they shoudn't come into the business if they wanted to make money. A former Christie's director, Anthony du Boulay, adds that the auction houses are often going to attract people without commercial instincts, or they would become dealers.

The fact that their 'headmaster' was himself temperamentally a dealer rather confused the situation, for they looked to him for a code of conduct and his differed from that of his predecessors – or indeed his contemporaries at Christie's. 'If PCW saw something good, he bought it', says a friend, 'he was sometimes short of cash and then he sold it, he bought and sold a lot, but remained an amateur, a passionate collector.' 'I don't want anyone on my staff who doesn't collect', he used to say, 'I wouldn't believe in them if they didn't.' Even Old Woods, who believed that auctioneers should not collect, could never resist a bargain, buying a Hoppner for 23 guineas at one sale, a Romney for 28 at another.

But despite PCW's own greed, Jim Kiddell ensured that the moral code they were taught was remarkably strict. Only a handful of people had to be sacked for succumbing to the most obvious temptation, diverting material brought in for sale to dealers and acting as middlemen (although even Christie's would not sack a really valuable expert if he was caught siphoning off a promising item: they would simply compensate the vendor, on condition that he did not mention the subject, and reprimand the culprit).

They were even forbidden to sell objects they owned themselves – although Derek Johns remembers auctioning his own pictures (even though they were entered in the name of his mother-in-law) as one of the greatest thrills of his life. But the basic code remained. It was, for instance, strictly forbidden to look in the 'bid book', which recorded the bids made in advance of a sale. A glance would tempt anyone looking for a bargain, but it was sternly guarded (in New York the bid book was guarded by a formidable lady, Sandy Carroll, who was quite rightly trusted by many collectors). They also learnt early on that it was silly to force prices up to the bids left 'on the book'. Most of them, like Richard Day, 'had this little group of dealers' on whom they depended for a substantial part of their turnover: 'I worked with Hans Kalman and Jim Byam Shaw, PCW used John Hewitt, they were another eye for us'. For if any dealer found he had secured every lot he wanted, but at precisely the prices he had left with the sales clerk, he would simply not return – although PCW himself was not above using the proverbial chandelier to nudge upwards a lot left by a friend.

The 'headmaster', PCW, was genuinely interested in almost every artefact coming into the building. Carmen Gronau remembers how 'when something came up he would look for the expert, he was always willing to learn' – of course his knowledge was encyclopaedic and Tim Clarke or Jim Kiddell could cover his few blind spots, like Chinese works of art or porcelain. But even where he did not know the field his commercial imagination remained impeccable. David Nash remembers dealing with George Ortiz, owner of a marvellous collection of African art: 'PCW discussed prices way above the market, I thought he'd lost his judgment, he was putting crazy reserves onto the lots. But he said simply, "I thought I knew the market", and of course he was right.' He taught this same arrogant confidence to his pupils: the youngsters noticed how in traditional departments like silver and furniture, dominated by a small group of dealers, the imagination of the old-timers was bounded by historical values. The newcomers refused to accept that past experience was valid. The sheer – if impersonal – greed imparted by PCW was a major force in upsetting historical values in every category of traded art.

PCW's ideas about education were naturally simple and direct: 'You've got to look at museums, you've got to look at fakes, you've got to look at copies. It's fatal only to look at the finest things, it's most misleading ... an auction room is a very good place to learn because you have things of all kinds coming in and every object that comes in may prove, in fact, to be a winner or the reverse.'

The youngsters who started as 'numbering porters' had an even better opportunity. Numbering involved handling each object twice, and examining it to ensure that it corresponded to the description in the catalogue. This intensive and severely practical training, supplemented by short periods of study in foreign museums paid for by Sotheby's, gave them enormous confidence. Derek Johns remembers going round an exhibition with some students who had been through an orthodox art education and seeing them laboriously going through the motions of narrowing down the definition of a picture, where he, accustomed to instant judgments (which he knew would be costly if they were proved wrong) could at once home in on the painter, the period, the condition – and the value – of the painting. (He once valued a picture through a drawing-room window when unable to gain access to a house. He had some difficulty in persuading the owner that the somewhat dismissive valuation resulting from his quick peep was in fact reliable. It was.)

But it was the 'headmaster' who set the tone: in Sotheby's *Annual Review* for 1961–62 Frank Davis gave a rather glamorized description of the informal, almost country-house atmosphere prevailing at the time:

> The more innocent visitors tell me that they find the place at first glance startlingly casual. It is not just the unemphatic voice from the rostrum, but the apparently higgledy-piggledy display, the sprawling dead-pan audience creeping in and out, the paintings

hung from door to ceiling, the dust of ages, almost the odour of sanctity; everything played down, they say, as if each actor in the drama were determined to throw away his lines. All this, no doubt, is true enough, though unrehearsed; just an old Spanish custom as it were, which, combined with an underlying efficiency of which the record is sufficient witness, has grown up with the years.

Davis omitted the role played by the front counter, still one of the most extraordinary entrepôts in the world, where greed meets reliability, respectability and – Stanley Clark's special contribution – accessibility. For the art world in general does its best to make the outsider feel like an intruder. The classier establishments specialize in deep pile carpets, hushed tones and a general air of reverence, but the atmosphere in even the humblest antique shop exudes an air of mystery, intensified by the absence of clear pricing and the habitual tone of insufferable superiority born of a know-how that is usually only skin-deep, if that.

The front counter at Sotheby's, as seen so often on television, is more welcoming. The range of visitors is astonishing: sad old men in mackintoshes with bulging brown paper parcels containing every sort of object from unsaleable photographic prints to valuable old artefacts, lovingly woven silk pictures, carefully cherished china; casually arrogant Continental persons in belted leather coats, vaguely reminiscent of Herbert Lom playing a senior officer in the Gestapo; dealers, instantly recognisable from their theatrically shabby appearance and their sharply darting eyes; ladies from the shires trying to pretend they don't actually need the money they hope to get for some of the family silver. A spell at the front counter was once part of the general education of young recruits. It is now acknowledged to be a rather specialized job in itself. The youngsters behind the counter – Fiona lots one two and three they were once called – summon equally adolescent 'experts', who are surprisingly gentle with their more vulnerable visitors. In most cases they can tell the value of an object at a glance, but they have been taught not to say anything until they have counted to ten. They know that they have to: 'tread softly for they are treading on people's dreams'. They are also trying to follow PCW, to see some monetary value in any work of human hands, and to follow him too in being optimistic, without providing too precise or exaggerated a valuation.

Davis, the sales room correspondent of *The Times*, was an insider. So he did not comment on the importance of the layout, or rather the lack of it, the casual confusion of the place, the nooks, crannies, winding stairways and confusing corridors, which made the casual visitor feel that there were discoveries to be made and scholarly experts hidden within the old college walls. PCW's own office contributed to the general feeling of shabby antiquity. 'The walls are a dirty hessian yellow', reported one visitor, noting the desk top in very old scratched leather' – for he was the untidiest of men. A former secretary remembers the 'mummified sandwich' in the desk drawer. For the immaculate appearance hid a great deal of muddle: friends remember the chaos when his suitcase burst open at an airport and they spent half an hour scrabbling for the contents and sitting on it to try and squeeze it shut.

The atmosphere was intensified by the dark green walls. In the 1950s John Fowler, one of London's leading interior decorators, had been asked to advise on a suitable colour. Crimson, he suggested. PCW preferred a dark green. He was obviously right. In English minds this is associated with Wimbledon, or the green baize doors that separate the servants from their betters in country houses (or the boys from the masters in public schools). Mollie Panter-Downes found the walls depressing: she did not appreciate the classiness conveyed by the colour.

By then the lessons taught at Mr Wilson's Academy were growing increasingly complex. The mass of material enabled him to increase the number of sales separated either by category or by quality. By the early 1960s, for instance, there were three levels of print and picture sales, junk, middling and star. But even more important was the orchestration of the seasons, and weeks within them. Sales had traditionally followed a pattern, with Mondays reserved for books, Tuesdays for *objets de vertu*, Wednesdays for pictures, silver and jewellery on Thursdays and furniture on Fridays. There were times to avoid: Budget Day, the period of the Grosvenor House Antique Fair, and religious holidays – silver and jewellery were obviously almost impossible to sell on Jewish Holy Days. Equally weeks like Ascot when a large social crowd was going to be in London anyway, were obviously desirable. Whereas Vere Pilkington had no sense of the dramatic, PCW tried to inject an element of climax by bringing together a group of related sales, to attract as many buyers and as much interest as possible – again a process that became easier as more material poured in from a greater variety of sources. Orchestration within the individual sale was equally important, starting with an easily sold lot and then building up to the most attractive at about lot 15. For Mr Wilson's academy also taught the elements of drama, that each sale must have a beginning, a middle and an end.

But PCW's ambitions were not confined to the local academy. Although American sellers accounted for about 30 per cent of the firm's record sales of £8.8 million in 1961–62 he was not content. He wanted to dominate the business there as well.

96

## 2 A VERY DIFFERENT KIND OF AUCTION HOUSE

PCW, that born hustler, naturally felt thoroughly at home in New York, he was always convinced that the city was the natural centre of the world art market. Jake Carter clearly needed reinforcement. So early in 1960 he sent Peregrine Pollen to take charge of the office. PCW was naturally nervous about how Jake Carter would react, but he need not have worried. Carter behaved with enormous generosity towards Pollen, expressing a wish not to 'breathe down his neck or jog his elbow', a vow to which he scrupulously adhered

Pollen and Carter set up a small, if ever-expanding office on the corner of Fifth Avenue and 55th Street and played the 'cool English charm' game all over New York, bagging a number of mouth-watering sales from the local competitor, Parke-Bernet, not only Impressionists but also drawings, Renaissance jewellery and a group of twenty-nine Picassos and other modern works from Jacques Sarlie. Their biggest coup was the collection of another refugee, René Fribourg, the Belgian-born owner of one of the world's largest firms of grain merchants. The contract, which ran to fifteen pages, showed how sophisticated the market had become. Sotheby's was to pay the first $120,000 of the enormous expenses involved – for the sale was to be in London and more of Fribourg's wealth had been invested in fragile furniture and eminently breakable porcelain than in pictures. No commission was payable if the proceeds were below $1.5 million, 15 per cent between $1.5 and $3 million, and 11 per cent above that. Sotheby's had to adhere to a strict, tight timetable and the executors could (and did) call on an independent valuer to check on Sotheby's estimates. In the event that sales realized well over $3 million – although it then took four years to tidy up the accounts.

But Carter and Pollen lost the big one, the disposal of the paintings owned by Alfred W. Erickson, head of a major advertising agency. The executors' patriotism ensured that they went to Parke-Bernet instead. In November 1961 the pictures fetched a record of nearly $4.7 million – PCW, who attended the sale, estimated the staggering total within a few thousands. By far the highest price – $2.3 million – was paid for a Rembrandt, *Aristotle Contemplating the*

*Bust of Homer* (it had cost Erickson $1 million before the war so, allowing for inflation, the price was low. But at the time no one did the sums). The successful bidder was the Metropolitan Museum, which already owned – reports varied – was it twenty-three or thirty examples of the painter's work? But never mind. James Rorimer, the curator, and its trustees felt they needed it.

The purchase marked a landmark in the history of museum curatorship, and thus of the whole art market. If the Metropolitan Museum was not satisfied with its already stupendous collection of Rembrandts, then there was no reason why any other museum should feel adequately supplied with anything. The Rembrandt proved the biggest draw in the Metropolitan's history, justifying PCW's cynical remark that 'there's nothing so fascinating as a work of art to which a price is attached. People go into a museum to see a picture which has been sold for a large sum of money – they won't go to see a picture which is far finer which has come there by bequest. And the interest in pictures is not a vulgar thing of today – it's always been there.'

He was closer to the general public than to the tradition of his own institution. The essence of the 'Old Sotheby's' point of view had been brilliantly stated by Geoffrey Hobson in a short book typically entitled *Some Thoughts on the Organisation of the Art Market after the War*, published in 1946. He had concentrated his attacks on museums, asserting that they were dead and that they sacrificed 'noble pleasure to knowledge'. Above all, he wrote, they were too big: 'one or two fine things of a kind are delightful, but fifty or a hundred are just a bore ... masterpieces are best enjoyed singly ... although museums show far more than can be enjoyed, they do not show more than a comparatively small fraction of what they possess.'

Despite the enormous prestige and publicity generated by the Erickson sale, Leslie Hyam, the head of Parke-Bernet, was too old, too gentlemanly and old-fashioned a figure to cope with the competition. In September 1963 an unhappy love-affair tipped the balance and he committed suicide. After his death, Parke-Bernet suddenly seemed vulnerable to a bid, for the remaining directors controlled only a fraction of the shares.

This was only one of the ways in which the two houses differed. To the outsider no two institutions could have been more alike. In fact the gulf between the two markets was deep enough to be reflected both in the institutions which served them and the habits of the clientele which used them. Where Sotheby's capital invariably came from its partners, Parke-Bernet and its predecessors had been financed by members of the collecting classes. This was part of the traditionally direct participation by the 'working plutocracy', mostly from New York, in the auction business. For whereas in London most sales were impersonal and professional, largely confined to dealers acting for clients as well as for themselves, in New York the rich, and the not so rich, joined in directly. Saarinen tells how Mrs David Rockefeller, an 'amiable young woman without an ounce of pretension', successfully bid $31,000 for a Signac at the Lurcy sale. 'A friend asked her if it had not been an extraordinary experience bidding in that excitement-packed auction. "Not at all", Mrs David Rockefeller replied blandly, "I just raised my hand and kept it up until I reached my top price. Fortunately, the other bidding had stopped and the painting was mine."'

With the participative element went an overwhelming concentration on 'association', which traditionally mattered far more than authenticity – the crowds fighting for a 'Hearst piece' at Gimbels' were aping their richer brethren who continued to hunger after a 'Morgan piece'. Except in a few specialized categories, there was no real pretence at expertise, no systematic attempt to guarantee provenance or authenticity. (The casualness continued. As late as 1970 an English journalist, Bevis Hillier, found that 'Californian dealers have an odd habit of describing anything before 1800, short of a mastodon bone, a "Queen Anne" in one case "Queen Ann")'.

Not surprisingly, Parke-Bernet and its predecessors had enjoyed a history far shorter, far more troubled – and infinitely more interesting – than the stately progress of the London auction houses, especially Sotheby's, which had specialized for so long in the most scholarly end of the trade. The contrast extends to the histories of the two houses. Where Frank Herrmann wrote a scholarly tome about Sotheby's, the late Wesley Towner's history of Parke-Bernet, *The Elegant Auctioneers*, is a delightful, if rather discursive, slice of social history.

The American auction houses had to fight an even fiercer battle than their English counterparts against the disreputable aura that hung over their trade. Their traditional creed was put succinctly by one Colonel J. P. Gutelius, 'the converted auctioneer', 'Oh Lord', he would roar, raising his eyes to heaven in the middle of a disappointing sale, 'if I could only turn this sale into a revival.' Even after he had Seen the Light his motto was: 'Put in a few real good ones so nobody can say you're selling only the cheap ones.' The natural reaction to such huckstering was organizations like the New York Anti-Auction Committee, formed to battle against the 'death, dissipation and bankruptcy' allegedly embodied in 'sales at auction, which are fashionable machines of polite and licensed swindling, producing all the pernicious effects of gambling'.

The first successful attempt to legitimize this disreputable trade was made by Thomas Kirby, an auctioneer who had migrated to New York from Philadelphia. He saw the potential when another 'Knight of the Hammer' secured $327,792, an immense sum in 1876, for the possessions of John Taylor Johnston, the first President of the Metropolitan Museum. Kirby went into partnership with James F. Sutton, son-in-law of the founder of Macy's, who had set up an art gallery with the pretentious name of the American Art Gallery. Kirby's chance to change the status of the auction business came nine years later when a well-known banker, George I. Seney, fell on hard times. Kirby persuaded Seney's creditors that an auction relying on private buyers was the best (if not the only) way to dispose of Seney's collection of 285 paintings. There would be no reserves, but the sale would be lavishly promoted and previewed, the gallery would guarantee that the pictures were the property of the supposed owner, would pay the vendors within thirty days, and would not add anything to the collection, all novel elements in the ruffianly world of auctioneering.

The success of the Seney sale – which realised $405,821 – confirmed Kirby's beliefs, set a seal on the respectability of auctions – provided that they were conducted by the American Art Association* and confirmed a pattern which was to last eighty years. A few well publicized major sales of the possessions of well-known figures would leaven a mass of smaller, unspecialized sales, both types appealing mainly to a range of private buyers far wider than those attracted to London's major auction houses.

The following year Kirby refined the formula by producing a sumptuous catalogue at a cost of over $40,000 for the collection of Mary Jane Morgan, the little-known widow of a steamship tycoon. Only 500 numbered copies were sold (for a mere $10 a copy), hand-delivered to the most exclusive doorsteps in New York. The promotional expense was justified when Mary Jane's 240 paintings fetched $885,800 and catalogues like this became the norm. They were vitally important in the history of American taste. Tom Norton noted that sophisticated readers today might well be amused by the long descriptions, critical comments and detailed articles in these early catalogues, which were often printed in elaborate typefaces. But there was not then the abundance of publications on art, ranging from coffee table books to magazines and museum catalogues, that we have now, so the sale-room catalogue was more than just a means of selling, it educated as well (and continues to do so).

* The Galleries were renamed after Sutton and Kirby had stopped dealing in art. This had not proved a success, although in 1886 they had mounted New York's first exhibition of Impressionists.

But Kirby was a salesman, not a teacher. The row over the origins of Mrs Morgan's prize possession, the famous Chinese Peachbloom Vase, did not hurt him at all. It was all good publicity, and he was not concerned with certifying the origins of the older objects he sold. Although he boasted that only eight of the more than 1500 Barbizon pictures that passed through his hands were of doubtful origins, where Old Masters were concerned he would simply copy out the most grandiose attributions attached by the vendors.

Kirby's talents were reinforced by those of his alter ego, the formidable Rose Lorenz. She was a real tyrant, 'Miss Potsdam' she was called, instantly dismissing any flirtatious member of the staff in accordance with her belief that 'sex was a synonym for inefficiency'. But she contributed a crucial and unexpected flair for showmanship. No one disagreed with Kirby's belief that she was 'an acknowledged genius in the arrangement of objects of art', although he suffered from the fortnight of expensive chaos which preceded any major sale as she completely redecorated and rearranged the sale-rooms.

Their most influential sale before 1914 was of the contents of the veritable palace owned by Stanford White, the architect and arbiter of taste, after he had been shot by a jealous husband, the millionaire Harry Thaw. *Le tout* New York, the Whitneys, the Vanderbilts, as well as the theatrical crowd led by David Belasco, fought for every lot, from threadbare velvet tapestries to seventeenth-century rapiers. White's posthumous influence was assured when innumerable antique shops were established from the leftovers after the tycoons had taken their pick.

If Kirby's AAA could be compared with Christie's, a rival house had been modelled directly on Sotheby's. It was named after its founder, John Anderson, who was financed by a well-known collector of manuscripts from St Louis, William Bixby. Kirby's cavalier disregard for the niceties of cataloguing gave the newcomer its chance especially in the book trade, the most scholarly of markets. So it was the Anderson Gallery which sold the collection of books and manuscripts assembled by Robert Hoe, who had developed the family's printing machinery firm into the most famous and innovative in the world. The magnificent hoard – including a Gutenberg Bible which went for $50,000 – fetched nearly $2 million, a third more than the total reached by the four most valuable libraries ever sold in London. The record was not surpassed for fifty-seven years until the Streeter sales between 1966 and 1969 which raised $3.1 million, in real terms less than half the Hoe total.

For both before and after the First World War, the major sales held in New York were almost invariably bigger than their London counterparts, and the top prices fetched, particularly by pictures, higher. This was partly because the American sales generally came from executors selling all the possessions of some deceased tycoon or his widow, whereas the London sales included only part of such collections, while traditional British 'country-house' sales were on an altogether smaller scale than their American equivalents.

Kirby's son, Gustavus, universally known as GT, was a business-like fellow. But in reorganizing the firm he nearly broke his father's heart by following his fashion-conscious clients up-town, moving from Madison Square to a simple and dignified orange brick building – an 'elegant Renaissance style palazzo' – which occupied a whole block on Madison Avenue on the corner of 57th Street. In 1923, a year later, he sold the firm to an eccentric multi-millionaire, Cortlandt Field Bishop, a short impatient fellow in a coonskin coat, an American version of Toad of Toad Hall, eternally rushing around in the latest, fastest motor car, scattering instructions typed out on elderly typewriters in the finest suites of the world's best hotels.

Kirby's successors, who had to suffer Bishop's abruptly inconsequential whims for over a decade, were an ill-matched pair. Hiram Hanley Parke – whose military bearing, complete with trim moustache, encouraged the use of his rank in the Pennsylvania National Guard – had learnt his trade in Philadelphia. GT Kirby had lured him to New York by paying the expenses of his divorce from his first wife. Despite this – at the time unusual – lapse, he had greater moral authority in the rostrum than any American auctioneer before or since. No one disagrees with the famous description given by an old art dealer:

> Few people understand the exquisite artistry of Hiram Parke's performance . . . the grace, breeding and hidden force which molds a pack of rapacious wolves into a pliable audience. And it is all done in such a charming way. With his judicial eye fixed upon them, those cold-face harpies back down, ashamed of the paltry prices they have come prepared to pay. For how can you steal in front of the Lord Chief Justice, especially when he has such a good opinion of you?

This was a rather more authoritarian version of PCW's combination of charm and confidence. Like him, or indeed any other great auctioneer, he had an excellent memory and stretched it to the full in the weeks before a major sale. Like PCW, he 'knew who was going to buy' some great prize, 'I don't know how I knew, but I could tell – a look, a kind of tension, a sort of vibration, a brain wave maybe, something that was a dead giveaway. I knew but I never took advantage' – by carrying the bidding up beyond the price at which the bidder had secured the lot. Unlike PCW he was dignified and

102

aloof, but they shared a common inner coldness. 'If he used the word friend', wrote Towner, 'he meant a contact well-disposed to him in the politics of art selling.' Perhaps great auctioneers always have to keep their distance from their audience, as conductors do from their musicians.

By contrast Otto Bernet, affectionately known as OB, was a character straight out of the works of Ludwig Bemelmans, an ineffectually rushing, bumbling, bouncy German-Swiss\*, eternally, gushingly garrulous in his always-imperfect English: 'Put in a few mistakes', he would tell his secretary when he was writing to Bishop, 'so he'll think I wrote it myself.' 'Little Otto' had been recruited as a fourteen-year-old office boy in 1896. He was a hard worker, a great self-improver, without any particular aptitude for auctioneering. 'It was Bernet's fate', wrote Towner, 'to conduct the people's auctions, to disperse the endless pictures of grazing cows, the second-hand virgins, saints and martyrs, the furniture in reproduction, the objects of art unworthy to be labelled *objets d'art*. Meanwhile Parke sold the masterpieces.'

But the Anderson Galleries still provided stiff competition. They had been refinanced by John F. Stetson, the hatter's son, and had acquired one Mitchell Kennerley, a brilliant publisher (of everyone from Frank Harris to Walter Lippmann, from Upton Sinclair to D. H. Lawrence), bibliophile and self-promoter. His biggest coup came when he acquired one of the few English collections sold in New York, which had been assembled by Lord Leverhulme, creator of Lever Bros, – although in the early 1930s Parke-Bernet staged a major coup by selling some extremely valuable manuscripts former-ly owned by the Marquis of Lothian.

Kennerley was an eternal optimist and hatched a plot to sell the Anderson Gallery to Cortlandt Bishop and buy both firms from him with money he hoped to get from a rich divorcee he was pursuing. In 1929 Bishop did indeed merge his two properties (in the meantime poor Kennerley's divorcee had ditched him for someone younger, more handsome, more honest). Bishop appointed Kennerley's former treasurer Milton Michill, to run both sale-rooms – clumsily renamed the AAA-Anderson Galleries. Parke and Bernet were forced to accept a subordinate status. But Michill could not cope with the strains of the slump, took to drink, concealed the grim financial realities, was dismissed and later, his beloved wife dead and his finances in dire straits, shot himself in a hotel room.

Bishop died in 1935. A couple of years later Kennerley attempted a come-back through Bishop's widow. But by this time Parke had

<hr>

\* So 'Bernay', the way his name is usualy pronounced, is wholly inappropriate.

had enough. Pausing only to collect forty loyalists including Bernet, allegedly with the immortal remark: 'You're a stone around my neck but you're coming', he sought shelter in the hospitable offices of Messrs French and Co, New York's leading antique dealers, and soon found financial backing from former clients. With admirable timing a prominent Wall Street millionaire, Jay F Carlisle, had the grace to die a few months later and the executors were persuaded to allow the new firm of Parke-Bernet to handle the sale. Within a few years their old firm was bankrupt, Kennerley disgraced (later he, too, committed suicide), his successor was busy defrauding the clients, and Parke-Bernet was cosily ensconced in their old head-quarters.

They flourished even during the war years when many records were set, though barely noticed at the time. Poor OB died in 1945 and the Major retired in 1950. The previous year his firm had moved further up-town. They could have bought their 57th Street palazzo for a mere $500,000, but preferred to move to 980 Madison Avenue at 77th Street, where an art-conscious developer, Robert Dowling, had provided them with a splendid purpose-built new headquarters, a dignified, utilitarian building with a plain façade relieved only by bronze statues representing 'Venus bringing the arts to Manhattan'. The move was so far north that they even provided free telephones for the dealers to report prices to their galleries in mid-town. But they need not have worried: within a few years the new premises had become the focus for a new hive-full of galleries.

Parke left a trimvirate, dominated by one of his protégés, Leslie Hyam, born in England and with a Cambridge degree in physics. He had given himself a six-week crash course at the Metropolitan Museum where he filled three notebooks with an amazing synthesis of the world's artistic heritage. He was then appointed one of the two assistants to the chief cataloguer, who was on piece-work rates, but spent most of the proceeds on bootleg liquor, which soon killed him. The other assistant left soon after and Hyam took over. He promptly clashed with one of the firm's prize clients, the great carpet dealer, Vitall Benguiat – 'the Pasha' – who relied entirely on instinct, 'he had eyes in his fingers' as they say. Hyam painstakingly refuted most of Benguiat's sweepingly generous attributions and was violently attacked. 'I tell you dear', the Pasha shouted, 'a writing has never done anything except harm ... the day you do not see any more paper and ink, that is the day your eyes will be opened.' The Pasha owed the firm so much money that his view prevailed and Hyam learnt an early lesson in the realities of the auction business, New York style.

The second member of the triumvirate, Lou Marion, was a total contrast: compact, pugnacious, from a working-class background. He had been hired as a post-boy, had made his way in the firm by cheek and flair and become Parke's alter ego in the rostrum after his only rival had also drunk himself to death. The third, Mary Vandegrift, was small, blonde, tactful, married to an army officer when she joined in the early 1920s. Devotion to the firm led to divorce and a lifetime of loyal service.

Until Jake Carter's arrival, the trio had everything their own way. But Hyam couldn't cope: he hated the new money-soaked atmosphere, in the words of a friend, 'he was an old-time honest auctioneer. He didn't believe in open reserves, still less in hidden reserves. He felt that strongly, though in later years he had to have them.' But his death should not, in theory, have been fatal for the firm's independence. He had been something of an autocrat, so Marion and Vandegrift felt that with his death they could implement some of their own ideas. But they were never given a chance.

# 3  TAKEOVER

Hyam's death was clearly going to lead to a takeover bid. Even before his suicide a well-known American businessman-collector, Alex Hillman, had proposed a joint bid to PCW, but he was unwilling to agree to any sort of partnership. By early 1964 Hyam's estate needed the cash, and his executors also controlled the shares of two of the other dozen or so shareholders. Others, like the banker André Meyer, were perfectly happy to get out. The new team at Christie's had decided not to compete: they had made a loss in 1963, they had no real transatlantic links, no spare staff, no funds. Maurice Rheims, greatest of French wheeler-dealers, was soon on the scene, but his offer was too vague. By contrast, Peregrine Pollen had phoned PCW (who was in Tokyo) immediately after Hyam's death and Jesse Wolff promptly agreed to act for them.

Nevertheless, the idea of a bid was so daring that it could have been proposed only by an arrogant young man like Pollen, supported by a gambler like PCW. At the time few, if any, foreign companies, even those far larger than Sotheby's, dared contemplate setting up in the United States, let alone taking over their major American competitor. Moreover, Sotheby's faced a seemingly insuperable problem: the lease on 980 Madison Avenue. In essence, the landlord, Robert Dowling, was a silent partner in Parke-Bernet. He received only a tiny basic rental, but was entitled to 2 per cent of the gross income once this exceeded $6 million. What had seemed a magnificent deal in 1949 had become a nightmare fifteen years later. Sales had soared and margins had been cut to the bone by the competition from Sotheby's, and Dowling was taking a fifth of the income actually received by Parke-Bernet. So any bid – by Sotheby's or anybody else – had to be based on the assumption that Dowling would renegotiate the lease.

This suited the opposition on both boards. In New York it was led by a recent shareholder, a distinguished expert on aeronautical history, Colonel Gimbel, and an even more distinguished collector, Ralph Colin, who felt that Gimbel 'was a difficult human being, a gung-ho kind of fellow, whose happiest days had been in the Air Force'. Colin was a tough, pugnacious Manhattan lawyer and an early collector of modern art: 'In the 1930s', he says, 'I knew everyone who was buying modern art and most of them personally.' He had started his collection in 1933 with a Soutine, which cost himn $200. By 1960 his collection, including Klees, Rouaults and Juan Gris, 'with not a lemon among them', he told me proudly, was distinguished enough to be exhibited by Knoedler's, complete with extensive catalogue. He had helped the Art Dealers' Association purge some of their grosser elements, and organized the system by which the Internal Revenue Service called on the appropriate ADA member to advise on valuation for estate duty purposes. Where Gimbel, fundamentally, was interested only in making the most out of his shareholding, Colin stood for the whole New York system challenged by the arrival of Sotheby's. Although he played only a minor role at the time, he was ready to defend the system as and when Sotheby's introduced its own ideas.

In London, PCW, Carmen Gronau and Peregrine Pollen faced equally daunting problems. The bid for Parke-Bernet clearly represented a clean break with the past. Anthony Hobson was already in the middle of selling his shares, and was naturally opposed to the move. So were two respected specialists, Richard Timewell and Fred Rose. John Rickett and Tim Clarke professed themselves neutral – and thus, effectively, hostile. As usual Jim Kiddell was loyal to PCW and, in the end, Peregrine Pollen's eloquence won the day. PCW was entirely unperturbed. He told Godfrey Barker of the *Daily Telegraph* that half the board were not with him: 'it would have been most alarming if they had been. There was a very strong element in Sotheby's which absolutely did not want to go forward' – an early example of PCW's ability to divide and rule.

In the meantime Alex Hillman had made a bid which forced Sotheby's to increase their offer, but Robert Dowling had agreed to a new and acceptable lease (though only after another of PCW's well-staged tantrums). Gimbel was still being obstructive, and had forced PCW really to lose his cool, after which he returned to his office, spent an hour with his head in his hands, furious at this rare loss of control, before plotting a move to outwit Gimbel. In the end, the deadlock was broken by Stanley Clark who suggested a planned leak, an idea greeted by PCW with the admiring cry: 'You wicked swine.' The story duly appeared on 5 July in the *Sunday Telegraph*. In it a well-known art journalist, Edwin Mullins, reported that the value of the art works sent from the United States to be sold at Sotheby's in London exceeded Parke-Bernet's whole turnover. Sotheby's could, wrote Mullins, obtain control of the New York house but it might not want to, indeed was considering setting up its own sale-room in New York in time for the next auction season in the autumn. The scare tactics worked. Within eleven days Jesse Wolff was able to cable PCW with the news that 78 per cent of the shareholders had accepted.

Their 3,003 shares were going to cost Sotheby's $1.525 million and that meant raising finance on a scale unprecedented in the firm's history. So the deal inevitably led to the introduction of outside finance, from Barro Equities, a well-known venture capital outfit run by Clifford Barclay and Hermann Melchior Robinow, a friend of PCW's. Robinow came from a distinguished German banking family. One of his uncles had owned the Van Gogh *Usines à Clichy*, which had been one of the stars of the Weinberg sale, and a cousin had arranged for him to attend the private view. He fell under PCW's spell and worked closely with him for a decade after he had left S. G. Warburg, the well known merchant bank, and teamed up with Barclay. Peregrine Pollen's wife was friendly with the wife of a senior official at the Morgan Guaranty Trust, and Robinow soon arranged a $1.5 million eighteen month loan.

But finance was the least of Sotheby's problems. The first was Colonel Gimbel. He had beaten the nationalist drum for all it was worth, inspiring at least one major article in *The New York Times*. Within three months he had been bought off at a price which gave him a profit of over $200,000 (and a wide variety of free sales catalogues), but he had triggered off an investigation by the Antitrust division of the Department of Justice into the possible monopoly created by the merger. The government's lawyers went round interviewing everyone in sight, which threw a shadow over the purchase for the first few months. It took all Wolff's powers of persuasion to convince the investigators that the art market was so big that a single auction house was never going to take more than a small share of the action.

At the time this seemed reasonable enough. The takeover had far less immediate impact than the opening the previous year of a New York branch of the Marlborough Galleries. In the long run the presence of the two most powerful institutions in the art world confirmed New Yorks' importance, but it was Marlborough's arrival that was immediately perceived as the biggest threat. Their London gallery had already monopolized the work of the majority of the most famous English artists and they clearly aimed to do the same in a country which, in the words of the leading New York dealer Eugene Thaw, 'was always fascinated with having the last word in modern painting and sculpture' – a fascination heightened by Robert Rauschenberg's recent prize at the Venice Biennale. In the words of John Bernard Myers, one of New York's most respected dealers:

108

The Marlborough Galleries brought with them heavy capitalization, a large stock of nineteenth- and twentieth-century master works and high-powered methods of promoting them to rich collectors. All the important Abstract Expressionists except de Kooning joined to create the first large-scale international market for American painting and sculpture. And of course the taste for such art was immediately encouraged and made alluring to the richest collectors at home and abroad. Marlborough's success during the next ten years set up a new style of competition.

Marlborough's arrival was immediately recognised as a threat to the existing order; Sotheby's arrival was initially warmly greeted by the trade, although the dealers soon learned the extent of PCW's ambitions. These were nearly foiled by internal problems within the newly-acquired Parke-Bernet. The finances were in a mess, so the treasurer had to leave and Robinow was flown over to help. But worse was the general atmosphere: 'Sotheby's was the enemy', says one insider; 'the fear at Parke-Bernet was like that at *The Times* when Rupert Murdoch took over', says Tom Norton, one of the only four cataloguers employed at the time. The fear was not only personal, but institutional, that the new owners would bleed Parke-Bernet by sending the best lots to be sold in London. The fears were not dispelled by the *Annual Review* of the year of the takeover, which stated that 'New York will remain the obvious centre for the large range of goods of American rather than wide interest', a remark not likely to dispel the fear that Parke-Bernet would be reduced to a secondary role.

The fears proved largely groundless. According to David Nash, one of the only three Englishmen employed in New York, 'PCW was pretty cold-blooded about it, he took a straightforward commercial decision in each case'. Norton, like most of the staff, stayed, helped by the way they were treated (the purchase contract eventually included an immediate $100,000 bonus to the Parke-Bernet staff). Mary Vandegrift was soothed by PCW (and by Carmen Gronau), but Lou Marion was clearly never going to stay long: 'he was a staunch Irishman', recalls one sympathetic insider, 'so he didn't like the British upper classes, and he didn't want to work for anyone, particularly as he had become president of the company just before the takeover', and indeed had called in Ralph Colin to try and prevent it.

PCW's greatest achievement was to persuade Marion's son John to stay. 'Tom Norton and I had been at college together and we were the entire youth movement in the firm', he remembers. Originally trained to be a naval officer, he still retains the four-square openness associated with the breed. Initially he had not wanted to follow his father into the firm, but had been persuaded by Leslie Hyam with an appeal to tradition – you can feel the continuity he represents as he fingers a large green ring that formerly belonged to Otto Bernet. PCW had doubled his salary and whisked him off to London after the takeover: 'He opened my eyes', says Marion, 'I had lunch with people who had previously just been legends, like Carmen Gronau and Jim Kiddell. I took an auction and there was the headline: "A Yank comes to Sotheby's".'

Marion had hit on Parke-Bernet's greatest weakness, its sheer lack of expertise. The firm's four cataloguers dealt with everything that came in, apart from books and jewellery. One man was responsible for cataloguing most of the pictures. 'He was pale, a diabetic', David Nash remembers, 'he had no enthusiasm, no energy, he was simply a hack who could churn out catalogues fast.' Not surprisingly Peregrine Pollen found that the porters were the main source of knowledge. But then they always had been. Fifty years earlier, Kirby and Lorenz had relied for their valuations of Chinese porcelain on a 'heavy-set, laconic Negro' porter, Tom Clarke – best known as the resplendent doorman in charge of allotting the seats at important sales. He would take each piece (not dropping a single one during thirty busy years), fondle it, commune with it and then either grunt with disapproval or give it a muttered benediction. He was usually right (his son later became a book cataloguer for the firm).

So Pollen – and his two assistants, David Nash and Hugh Hildesley – had to tread carefully. 'Peregrine was very tactful', says Nash, 'he didn't try and Sothebyize everything.' But he did set one standard at the merged firm's first sale. The most important picture was a Vuillard, and the owner, a Mrs Ross, wanted to withdraw it at the very last minute, after the catalogue had been printed. Usually an auction house, desperate to avoid the loss of face inevitable when a major item is withdrawn at the last minute, raises the reserve to an absurd figure and buys the picture in (this once happened with a Degas racing painting sent in by Baron Thyssen. There had been a reserve of a mere $2 million, which was raised to an absurd $3.5 million. The picture nearly reached the new reserve anyway). But in the Ross case Pollen was determined to be ultra-honest and had the Vuillard pulled out of the sale.

The biggest test of the new firm came on 14 April 1965, six months after the takeover. The evening started with a sale of carefully-chosen Impressionists. John Marion took the opening lots. In theory he was supposed to hand over to his father, but proved so effective that in the middle father tapped son on the shoulder and handed

110

over the torch. Young Marion sold the eighty-seven lots for $2.345 million, far in excess of the estimates.

Dinner was then served in a miraculously witty recreation of the Monmartre café where Degas and Manet had drunk together and Degas had painted one of his most famous canvasses, *L'Absinthe* – the broadest of hints that SPB was in eternal communion with the Impressionists. After dinner it was PCW's turn; he had brought from Brussels the Philippe Dotremont collection of forty-three works by modern painters, including only the second picture by Robert Rauschenberg ever to be sold at auction. PCW had already had problems getting a New York auctioneer's licence. These were supposedly confined to American citizens, but Jesse Wolff successfully contended that refusal would have constituted interference with international trade. In the event PCW's first sale turned out to be his last. 'He couldn't dominate the audience', says David Nash, 'the room was too big and too poorly-shaped.' Other spectators were less sympathetic: private collectors – who of course dominated the audience in New York – thought his style a bore.

The sale proved that Sotheby's English image had reinforced, rather than undermined, the valuable snob appeal of sales at Parke-Bernet. Pollen and his assistants gradually improved the standards of expertise, and thus of cataloguing. This in itself caused trouble. In England auctioneers employed a simple code to indicate the degree of confidence they felt in the attribution of a picture. The classic example is of works by Rubens, most prolific of Old Masters, and the one with the biggest studio. Richard Rush felt he had to explain the code to his (American) readers: 'If a painting appears to be authentic ... it is designated Sir Peter Paul Rubens. If it is less certain it is labelled "P.P.Rubens" and if it very doubtful that it had anything to do with Rubens it is simply "Rubens".'

Such niceties were anathema to the New Yorkers and naturally irritated buyers. But Pollen made matters worse because he was also determined to introduce the system of secret reserves that was Sotheby's main weapon against rings (which Rush, like everyone else, assumed were 'prevalent in the art world'). But Americans were accustomed to the idea that auctions were principally designed to sell up the contents of homes left ownerless by death (or, increasingly, divorce or a change of life-style). They expected everything to be sold, without reserve, and if the auctioneer did put up a reserve it would be an open one. Colin was typical in believing that the use of secret reserves was a manipulative, un-American device, one that had been foisted on Leslie Hyam in his last years in order to compete with Sotheby's, but one which should be fought on legal grounds if possible. The occasion did not arise for some years, and in the meantime the improbable alliance of Pollen, the slim young English aristocrat, and John Marion, the bluff, golf-playing salesman, was working surprisingly well.

Their double act was particularly effective in dealing with the crucial class of executors. For, like Parke and Bernet, they recognised the importance of 'coffin power'. When they appeared at the 'mansion of some deceased Maecenas', Parke and Bernet reminded Towner of: 'nothing so much as the pastor and the undertaker . . . the portly Bernet would rub his hand in a gesture combining eagerness and unction, while Parke, handsome and magnificently composed, would assume the superior role of family counselor. Wry observers used to say that Bernet, who was stronger on the homely virtues, would present the flowers while Parke carried the sales contract ready to be signed.'

The business was serious enough – it had been Robert Hoe's executors whose critical appraisal of the AAA's cataloguing techniques had cost them the sale fifty years earlier. But most of the executors with whom Pollen and Marion came into contact were small-town bankers who 'wouldn't have known a picture if it bit them', according to Pollen. The twosome appealed to both sides. They remember fondly how in the early days they faced two executors in Indianapolis. One was a fanatical Anglophile and immediately took to Pollen, the other a hearty, suspicious, parochial soul who warmed to Marion. But these expeditions were the exception. Most of the action, then as now, was concentrated in New York, for a single auction house could never hope to cover the whole continent.

112

# 4 SPREADING THE GOSPEL

A month after the inaugural splash in New York the two sale-rooms were linked in the first Transatlantic auction ever conducted using a television satellite, a truly newsworthy event in the 1960s. The idea was the brainwave of the late Richard Dimbleby, dean of British television commentators. Before the war he had worked as Stanley Clark's assistant on a magazine serving the advertising business. Much to Clark's amazement he had left to become one of the first reporters employed by the BBC. When Panorama, the BBC's flagship public affairs programme of which Dimbleby was anchorman, was given a short slot on the Early Bird satellite he naturally thought of his old boss – a tribute to Sotheby's high profile. Wilson and Clark leapt at the chance. In deference to the BBC's staunch anti-commercialism, the sale was to be held in aid of the restoration of Florence after the recent floods. But the notice was short, and they had problems finding lots suitable for the first truly transatlantic sale – previous sales had indeed been conducted simultaneously, but the links had been only telephonic. They came up with some Audubon Birds, together with a mishmash of other lots that would appeal on both sides of the Atlantic. The star of the show was not, artistically, the most important: it was the first painting by Sir Winston Churchill, who had died a month earlier, ever to be sold at auction.

As so often with pioneering events, there was terrible technical trouble, Dimbleby had to use all his experience to cover the awkward minutes during which the pictures were not coming through from New York to the gigantic television screen in the sale-room in Bond Street. Eventually the satellite link worked and the sale was duly acclaimed a great success, although most of the prices were not enormously exciting – pictures by Degas and Mary Cassatt, for instance, went for sums plumb in the middle of the estimates. But Dimbleby's showmanship ensured that his programme ended with the sale of the Churchill painting for £14,000 ($39,200).

The price was paid by an interior decorator buying on behalf of an oilman from Dallas. The purchase emphasized that Marion and Pollen's efforts effectively reached only the inhabitants of mid-town Manhattan, and the many people (like the oilman from Dallas) in cultural thrall to its influences. In business terms this did not matter too much: there were plenty of buyers and sellers within thirty blocks of their galleries – by far the single biggest concentration of liquid cash in the world. The situation was completely different in Britain, where the traditional art-buying classes could, in most cases afford only minor artefacts; the professional classes bought prints not pictures.

The limitations were obvious. In early 1985 Anthony Thorncroft noted how 'both the strength and the weakness' of the market in British contemporary ceramics 'is that it is governed by private (British) collectors who probably paid a few pounds for their first pot, who have profited by the steady appreciation in price in the last ten years, but who cannot afford, or make the psychological jump, to pay £30,000 for an undoubted masterpiece'.

In the United States, especially in New York, such limitations did not apply. During the mid-1960s, as Wall Street boomed, thousands of upwardly-mobile investors had plenty of spare cash available for everything supposedly buyable through art: beauty and prestige as well as profit. In the words of Fred Hirsch, the money available had outrun the supply of 'positional goods' designed to impress the world with the purchaser's status. This produced that unprecedented phenomenon, a simultaneous boom in the works of both living and dead artists. The market was never going to lack for material. 'We don't have the same attachment to the family home as you do in Britain', says John Marion, and because Americans change homes (and spouses) more frequently, a mass of older material was guaranteed, not only through death, but through removal and divorce as well.

The takeover had been splendidly timed. Robert Rauschenberg's success at the Venice Biennale had ensured that he and his less talented contemporaries suddenly became the hottest properties in the international art world. The Metropolitan's purchase of the Erickson Rembrandt had triggered off an ever-increasing popular interest in art; a new generation of museum curators, led by Thomas Hoving at the Metropolitan Museum, were devoting their energies almost exclusively to increasing attendances.

In the general boom there appeared to be room for both sides, or rather for a duopoly, with Marlborough (and a handful of other dealers like Sidney Janis) dominating the sale of the works of living artists, and Sotheby Parke-Bernet doing the same for those no longer producing. Sotheby Parke-Bernet was not – yet – a serious competitor when selling modern art. Of course, given the haphazard nature of Parke-Bernet's acquisition techniques, its sales had often included some modern art. As early as 1918, the AAA had sold the first Cubist

114

paintings ever seen in the sale-room when the collection of Leonce Alexander Rosenberg (son of a well-known dealer) was dispersed – nothing fetched very much, a Signac went for $300, a seated woman carved by Jacques Lipchitz for a mere $10. And in October 1963 the first de Kooning ever seen in a sale-room fetched $27,000 (£9,643). But the artist was then nearly sixty; in the 1960s, as forty years earlier, the market in the work of living artists was made by dealers, not auction houses. Although Parke-Bernet held a major sale of modern art – collected by Robert Scull, king of the New York taxi business – in 1965, the old rules still applied. They had been enunciated in 1926 by H. C. Marillier in his history of Christie's: 'The work of the younger man active at the time does not come onto the market, but remains with the original purchaser on an average for twenty or twenty-five years ... such pictures as do come up in a sporadic way are as a rule minor ones, which pass unnoticed and have no effect'. Marillier's 'twenty-year rule' was to be broken in the subsequent fifteen years: the tastes, like the fortunes, of many of the buyers of modern art in the 1960s was subject to investment fashion. Ten years on they could sell at a profit; many of them needed the cash; others were updating their image.

The battle for the buyers' dollars was not between dealers and sale-room so much as between the desire to be thoroughly modern and the need to have a home in which you could actually live, and this gave Parke-Bernet a decided advantage. Modern American art was growing steadily less 'homely', to put it mildly. As Tom Wolfe pointed out, an increasing percentage of the works of art deemed to be 'important' by the authorities was, in most people's eyes (including those of the rich) inhuman, ugly or incomprehensible, or all three. Better a cosy, sexy Renoir or some amusing 'conversation-piece' than the downright ugliness of modern art.

The increasing shrillness and didacticism of the dominant voices in art criticism reduced their role as arbiters of taste in general, however great their power in defining the relative importance of new works. This was a comparatively new phenomenon. Hitherto, most well-heeled Americans had accepted the decisions of arbiters who decided who was In and who Out in art as in society. They could be great hostesses like Mrs Astor or Mrs Vanderbilt, or even an architect like Stanford White. The atmosphere in the 1960s was much freer, you could choose the way you were going to impress and this tended to change season by season.

So Pollen could use Sotheby's imported expertise to ensure that, as in London, sales grew increasingly specialized. 'We divided the sales', says John Marion, 'there were Marionized sales, which were general, and Pollenized sales which were specialized. And we tried to group these special sales in the same week.' There had always been a few specialized sales. At the turn of the century Kirby's AAA had encourged a Japanese firm to stage a series of sales of Japanese artefacts; there were regular sales of fine lace and household textiles – which also, of course, featured in sales of great houses. In the past, buyers had been looking for lace and linen to use or to decorate their homes, but the appeal of similar items in the 1960s was purely as curiosities, totally detached from their original purpose. Similarly the Benguiats had organized dozens of sales of carpets, tapestries, textiles and 'antiquities' – although, as Leslie Hyam found out to his cost, these had more in common with the mock auctions held in country towns by peripatetic rug salesmen than with Sotheby's scrupulously catalogued events.

The breakthrough into specialist sales came as a by-product of Parke-Bernet's traditional business, the disposal of the belongings of distinguished people, some of whom just happened to have accumulated specialized collections. Helena Rubinstein (generally known as 'Madam') left enough jewels, and, less predictably, enough African art to justify separate sales. The sale of her African art heralded an increasing interest in the artefacts of supposedly 'primitive' societies, which was to bring Sotheby Parke-Bernet, like everyone else in the trade, equal shares of criticism and profits in the following years. Madam's jewels were of more immediate interest. Elizabeth Taylor, then married to the late Richard Burton, was in full diamond-buying swing, which helped publicity. And in the next couple of years, although Europeans bought and sold largely through Christie's in Geneva, the American glitterati preferred to buy their well-publicized stones at Sotheby Parke-Bernet, where the sales included a tiara worn at their weddings by two Tsarinas and subsequently owned by one Helen M. de Kay.

Other early specialized sales included the collection of boxes and cases given to Cole Porter by his wife whenever one of his shows opened. (Sadly, Porter had to pay for the last one himself. His wife died before the first night of *High Society* in 1954.) The sale, on 17 May 1967, was a typical New York combination of glitter, nostalgia and charity – to benefit the New York Public Library's Theater Collection, to which Porter had bequeathed the boxes.

But the Coats-Connelly sale of Tiffany glass on 21 October 1966 went one further. It created a new sale-room category. Tiffany glass, which had been out of fashion for a generation, was suddenly, emphatically, in again, and prices never looked back. London immediately seized the point, and the *Annual Review* for 1966–67 duly contained an essay on Tiffany glass and the new-found marketability of Tiffany objects attracted a continuing flow of them to the sale-

116

room. It proved that, in New York as in London, a single, well-publicized sale, based on a single specialized collection, could create a new category of desirable objects, and justify more ambitious specialized sales from a variety of owners.

Two sales on the same day, 16 May 1967, opened up further vistas. The 'Will Weissberg sale of Photographica' transformed 'snaps' into an art form. Dealers could already secure high prices for the work of well-known names like Julia Margaret Cameron and David Octavius Hill, but at the Weissberg sale a single daguerrotype of a young American working man, taken by an anonymous photographer about 1845, sold for $260 (£99). The *Annual Review* felt this was 'an extraordinary sum for a small portrait of an unknown subject by an unknown photographer . . . since the subject is entirely anonymous and of no particular documentary value, the photograph presumably was acquired for its qualities as a work of art'. Not surprisingly there have been regular sales of photographs since then, in London as well as New York.

Prices of photographs have not risen nearly as fast as those of the other class sold that fateful May day: Americana. In the early 1940s the Rigbys had already noted a growing interest in early American artefacts. Sotheby Parke-Bernet had already sold the Thomas Streeter collection of Americana, including a defence of New England's church-dominated government, published as early as 1649, which fetched $80,000. This was among the treasures uncovered by Tom Clarke, the son of the old Negro porter with the magic hands. He had started as a mail boy under Parke and Bernet and had graduated to book cataloguer with a particular interest in Americana. The interest culminated in the May sale, which included a number of letters and documents written by the signers of the Declaration of Independence. Seventy-one lots fetched $74,790 (£26,710). The top price, $20,000 (£7,143), was paid for a document of truly historic significance: a letter written by George Washington on the 4 July 1776. No one seemed to think it incongruous that such a significant part of the American national heritage was being sold by a foreign-owned sale-room. Sotheby's was truly at home.

Nothing Sotheby Parke-Bernet staged in the 1960s matched the sale of the décors and costumes formerly owned by the Diaghilev and de Basil Ballet companies. After a pilot sale at Bond Street, Sotheby's transferred the next show to the Scala Theatre. The catalogue was a major memento, with photographs of the original productions, the costumes modelled by students of the Royal Ballet School. The sale itself was performed – there is no other word – in front of an ever-changing series of back-drops, which included Picasso's design for Cocteau's *Le Train Bleu*. The second sale, at the

Theatre Royal, Drury Lane was even more dramatic, with the students dancing onto the stage as each lot was announced.

These were individual spectaculars, not trend-setters. But London, even more than New York, could rely on a few specialized collections to set trends. The sale of the John Mellor collection of Japanese prints in 1963, and of the Hindson collection of netsuke later in the decade both exemplified the way individual sales could broaden the appeal, and thus the prices, of a neglected market. But there were limits: in 1963 Sotheby's also sold the private collection of Chinese porcelain assembled by a well-known dealer, H. R. Norton. Prices of porcelain had risen spectacularly throughout the 1950s and early 1960s, more than doubling in the four years before the Norton sale. But even in the generally optimistic atmosphere it proved indigestible and stopped the upward surge – albeit only for a year.

By now in London specialized sales were routine, originating in the mass of material that gravitated naturally to Sotheby's: 'While Christie's was putting twenty-five lots of Chinese porcelain at the start of a furniture sale', remembers Anthony du Boulay, a former Christie's director, 'Jim Kiddell had enough material to organize, to orchestrate, specialist sales in specific periods of Chinese porcelain.' The strain was appalling: two senior and two junior sales clerks had to cope with sixteen sales a week, noting every price, identifying and notifying every buyer.

The sheer variety of objects which Sotheby's was trading on both sides of the Atlantic was increasing by the year. Some of the buying remained utilitarian. In the 1960s the most massive buying came from Europeans, looking in many cases for the sort of heavy old-fashioned furniture that was virtually unsaleable to British buyers at the time. Regular container loads of 'shipping goods' were transported from the London sale-rooms to towns all over Europe – especially to Italy.

With an increased number of buyers, some with relatively shallow pockets, the biggest rises were seen in the cheaper items within a category, or (netsuke is a typical case) categories in which each item was, at the time, easily within the reach of the more modest investor. A vast number of recognizably fine artefacts, which had been underpriced, were being revalued: at the same time a growing number of categories were being traded on the general, rather than the specialist market.

The 1967–68 edition of *Art at Auction*, another name for Sotheby's *Annual Review*, included learned articles on changing tastes in English drinking glasses, 'The American Bird Decoy', and that classic aeroplane 'The Sopwith Camel'. 'Within our lifetime', the Rigbys had written in 1944, 'Cinderella changes have taken place in

The von Hirsch sale. Characteristically, only Peter Wilson remains apparently relaxed as he sells the 'Mosan Medallion', a twelfth-century plaque for a record $2.2 million to the Staatliche Museum in Berlin. Everyone else, including von Hirsch's friend Dr Jorgen Wille (in bow tie) is clearly affected by the strain

Peter Wilson as his friends remember him, mimicking a bronze lion to be sold at a country house auction in Spain

The autocratic Sir Alec Martin (left), and his successor, the gentlemanly and ebullient Peter Chance (right)

A 1981 photograph of the Hon Patrick Lindsay, one of the architects of Christie's revival. He is selling a suit of armour made between 1610 and 1613 for King James I's son Prince Henry. It fetched a record price of £418,000 – finally beating the records set in the 1920s

The modest exterior of Sotheby's in Bond Street

Sotheby's was always uneasy with modern art even though this 1953
Francis Bacon, *Study for Portrait VIII*, fetched a record £26,000 as early as
1970

The foundation of Sotheby's success in the 1960s, a sale of Impressionists formerly owned by the film magnate Sir Alexander Korda. Peter Wilson is selling a Van Gogh

Star of the Mentmore Towers sale in 1977 was undoubtedly the 86-year-old Dowager Countess of Rosebery

Mentmore Towers. The building itself may have been a masterpiece of Victorian architecture, but most of the contents resembled the two racing trophies: the 1869 Goodwood Cup (left) and the 1885 Edinburgh Cup

"*People tell me how valuable it is, but I just bought it because I like it.*"

Jim Kiddell in 1975, one of the key men at Sotheby's

Peter Nahum, who epitomized the spirit of Sotheby's Belgravia

John Marion in 1984 taking bids for Corot's *La femme à la grande toque et à la mandoline*, which went for $3,850,000, a record for the artist

'Toboggan and Skid':
Marshall Cogan and
Stephen Swid, the New
York financiers whose bid
struck terror into the
Sotheby management

The winner: Alfred Taubman in
front of his new possession

numerous instances, and even as we have long collected (and paid high prices for) the earthy objects of early American days – cobblers' stools, pickle jars, mustache cups, bootjacks and many other things – so a smaller number have already started to collect the first typewriters, automobiles, phonographs, radio sets, and other products of the machine age.' This obsession occupied most of my first meeting with Peregrine Pollen. In 1970 I was writing a book on European direct investment in the United States and was naturally intrigued by the story of Sotheby Parke-Bernet. Pollen was more interested in discussing which artefacts would be the next stars of the showroom: early typewriters were an obvious choice, but a more intriguing outside bet was the glass balls, their fractures producing some delightful colours, originally used to insulate telephone lines – once-useful artefacts transformed into decorative baubles.

In the 1960s the interest in art could still be concerned as much with fun – or education – as with profit. In Britain two television programmes showed up its popular appeal. First was a long-running quiz game, *Going for a Song*, first shown nationally in 1965 (and produced by John Irving, an old school-friend of John Herbert). The panel of experts (which included PCW on a couple of occasions) vied with outsiders – including show-business 'personalities' – to guess the value of objects. The show was popular enough to make a star out of the late Arthur Negus, discovered by John Herbert in a provincial valuer's, who became a regular performer. An even more surprising star was Kenneth (subsequently Lord) Clark, the former Director of the National Gallery, who enchanted viewers with a series of programmes on art, and indeed on civilisation in general (Sotheby's subsequently sold cassettes of one of his series).

The programmes captured high ratings, but the viewers were not wealthy enough to support the upper end of the market. Since 1967 Agnew's reckons that less than a tenth of their turnover has been accounted for by sales to private British collectors. Nevertheless, an increasing number of wealthy Englishmen were playing the art market as they did the stock-market. As early as 1965 Robert Wraight could assume that the art world was dominated by investment-minded people: 'never before has art been such big business and never has big business attracted so many speculators who want to get in and out'. As he looked back on the first years of the decade, he was struck not so much by individual prices as by the quantity of pictures changing hands at high prices. He could have looked wider. As Terence Mullaly of the *Daily Telegraph* put it: 'All the time fashion is becoming less important. As more and more objects disappear into museums, never to come out again, and as the number of collectors increases, prices rise, records are inevitably broken every week, and equally inevitably, fashion embraces ever wider fields.'

There was surprisingly little opposition to the trend. Reitlinger was almost alone in attacking the hype that accompanied the increasing pace of the market. Every object, he complained, had to be 'exciting', 'superb', 'tremendously rare', 'ravishing' or 'magical': 'The deliberate and indoctrinated confusion of artistic appreciation with self-interest means ... the corrosion of what is left of civilized life.'

He was not heeded, nor were his repeated warnings that the price rises were still often merely compensating for the tenfold inflation since the glorious days before 1914. During the 1950s the market in works of art had not performed very much better than that in stocks and shares; because the publicity had been concentrated on such star categories as the Impressionists, observers tended to forget that prices of silver, glass, French furniture, English porcelain and a number of other widely-traded categories had not kept pace with the stock-market. But in the early 1960s, in Britain anyway, the stock-market stagnated, while the market in works of art continued to rise steadily, if unevenly. Statistically, there was an increasingly negative correlation between the two. When the stock-market suffered a shock, the art market received a fillip.

Robert Wraight described sitting next to the famous financier Charles Clore at the sale of the Sir Alexander Korda collection of Impressionists, a fortnight after a famous Black Tuesday on the stock-market in June 1962. Clore had been outbid for a Soutine and asked rhetorically: 'Who has got the money at a time like this?' Given the level of prices, thought Wraight:

> Mr Clore's reaction was the exception rather than the rule and it would probably take a month of Black Tuesdays to cause panic in the art market. This was demonstrated again in 1965 when, with the Labour government wielding the Capital-Gains-Tax stick, and with rumours of devaluation and forecasts of disaster emanating almost daily from the City, the art market registered no serious adverse effects ... The headlines on facing pages of an evening newspaper one day in July 1965 summed up the situation succinctly. 'Leading shares Slip Back Again' said the first, '£88,000 for a Turner' read the second ... As a hedge against the vagaries of the stock market, art seemed unbeatable. Tycoons with pretensions to culture were reminded that in the Great Depression of the 'Twenties and 'Thirties works of art held their values better than almost anything else, and they acted accordingly.

120

Stanley Clark put it even more pithily in the 1965–66 edition of *The Ivory Hammer* (the grandiose new name for Sotheby's *Annual Review*): 'On the very day of the excitement about the stability of the pound the market indicated that it preferred Munnings to money.' The introduction of Capital Gains Tax in 1965 and its extension to works of art costing more than £1,000, merely increased the number of participants: seeing that the government was taxing capital gains on works of art merely confirmed the middle-class punter in his growing belief that there were profits to be made out of them.

All these symptoms of a swing towards investment in an ever-widening variety of objects received a major boost in November 1967. Until sterling was devalued that month, most currencies had been relatively stable for nearly twenty years. Since then there has been barely a single year in which the relationship between the world's major currencies has been stable. Prices took the devaluation in their stride, more than adjusted to the lower value of the pound. To achieve the sort of boom seen in the art market in the subsequent fifteen years you needed a double conviction: that art would make you money, and that nothing else would. Devaluation was a major step in that direction. For the English rich the market in art, unlike that in shares, or property, or any of the other hedges against inflation, was international, and there were no constraints. The market in Impressionists had been made by refugees fleeing from persecution; the wider market of the 1970s owed a lot to the 'internal emigration' of the English rich turning their backs on investment in their own country.

Needless to say, PCW was ready for the new atmosphere. Eighteen months before devaluation he was already preaching the word, significantly on BBC TV's *Money Programme*: 'Works of art have proved to be the best investment, better than the majority of stocks and shares in the past thirty years. I think lack of security in the world encourages that trend.' The same year Howard Ricketts had edited a massive volume pretentiously entitled *Antiques International*, in essence a glossy tip-sheet. 'The aim of this collection', ran the introduction, nominally written by PCW, 'is to provide signposts to fields of antique collecting which are not at present fashionable, have temporarily fallen out of vogue or have hardly yet been explored ... In recent years the layman has been made increasingly aware of the value of works of art, chiefly through the spectacular rise in the price of Impressionist paintings.' But this had overshadowed the fact that other categories – like Renaissance bronzes, Chinese works of art and arms and armour – had moved faster. PCW and Ricketts had assembled a distinguished group of tipsters who discoursed learnedly on a variety of themes: icons, buttons, Persian pottery, prayer rugs, locks and keys, Bohemian glass, later ormolu clock cases, art nouveau jewellery (one of Ricketts's real loves) and early American painting. The volume was reprinted in 1973, by which time it was thoroughly misleading, partly because the prices of the works so enthusiastically puffed seven years earlier had risen so spectacularly.

We know how far they had risen, because of an initiative of Stanley Clark's. He was lunching one day in 1966 with the late George Pulay, then City editor of *The Times*, and they dreamt up the idea of an index on the prices of works of art, similar to those which charted the progress of the stock-market. Unlike many other lunch-time notions this one was soon translated into reality: the editor of *The Times*, the normally aloof and scholarly William Rees-Mogg, was himself interested in the book market – following his retirement he bought an antiquarian book business; and a young statistician, Geraldine Keen (now known under her married name of Geraldine Norman), who had worked for the paper in the early 1960s, had just returned from Rome in search of a job. Fascinated by both art and figures she eagerly took up the challenge and was soon producing 'The Times-Sotheby Index' divided into a dozen different sub-sectors. She admits to a sleepless night when she realized that because of the imperfections of the statistical base, the result was more of an indicator than a real index. Indeed, in presenting her findings, she was careful not to give precise figures, but merely rather vague multipliers. The figures looked impressive for the base year, 1951, was Year Zero for virtually everything in the art market (with the possible exception of French furniture and English porcelain).

There were few protests, but the most irritated spectator was, inevitably, the redoubtable Reitlinger. When his first volume of prices had appeared in 1961:

> More than one reviewer in those days implied that it was presumptuous to compare prices across the ages, as if these odd movements of money could have anything to do with matters so pure as currents of taste which just grow like daffodils ... Most reviewers, however, accepted the lists for what they were: illustrations of a particularly odd aspect of human behaviour or human folly as the case may be ... Within six years of the appearance of Volume One, graphs and indexes to help the *investor in art* (his italics) had become an accepted feature of the financial press, led by Granny herself. I do not recollect having seen a single letter protesting at their basic fallacy, though one or two writers may have accused their bad taste. But indexes, it seems, have come to stay. Index is a good word, respectable, almost pontifical like the index expurgatorius.

*Part V*

# GROWING PAINS

# I   COMPETITION

By the mid-1960s the new team installed at Christie's since 1958 was mounting an increasingly effective challenge. The resurgence started in 1962 when Bill Martin, Sir Alec's son, was replaced as head of the paintings department by Patrick Lindsay. He was reinforced by a newcomer, the late David Carritt, who had a widely-acclaimed flair for unearthing 'lost' masterpieces. These boosted Christie's sales and generated valuable publicity even when the finds were not sold at auction – a typical Carritt coup was the discovery of a lost Rogier van der Weyden at a country house near London. Eventually it was bought by the National Gallery for £800,000.

Inevitably, Christie's come-back started with a reaffirmation of its dominance in its historic speciality, Old Masters belonging to equally ancient English families. Carritt's first triumph was to persuade the Cook family to sell some of their better remaining Old Masters at Christie's, a breakthrough made possible by Vere Pilkington's disastrous performance in 1958. Nevertheless, PCW tried hard. One of Christie's team vividly remembers him phoning the Cooks' Jersey home while he was there; but Carritt had a fair share of the same daring and arrogance as PCW, promising the Cooks unheard-of prices for their masterpieces – and then getting them. One of Rembrandt's portraits of his son Titus was sold to Norton Simon for $798,000 (about £286,000). The sale of the Cook pictures and the Spencer-Churchill collection from Northwick Park in Gloucestershire, both in the 1964–65 season, marked the turning of the tide.

In the previous season Sotheby's sales, at over £13 million, had been three times its rival's. Although Christie's sales slipped for a year after the Cook and Spencer-Churchill sales, in the five years after the 1965–66 season their turnover multiplied more than three and a half times, from £7.25 million to £25.3 million. By 1970–71 their sales outside the United States were actually bigger than their rival's. Christie's stranglehold on the 'country-house market' meant that a handful of the Old Masters they contained fetched more than anything Sotheby's could muster: a Titian owned by Lord Harewood went for £1.68 million, and it was Christie's which sold – for £2.3 million to the Metropolitan Museum – a Velasquez owned by Lord Radnor, even though he was a close relation of Peregrine Pollen's wife. But the family was adamant: Christie's had been valuing the picture regularly for a century and a half, so they were entitled to sell it.

Christie's 200th anniversary in 1967 was a natural occasion to emphasize the extent of the recovery and to rub in the distinction of the pictures which traditionally passed through its doors. There was only one Rembrandt actually on show, but photographs of a hundred others, all sold by the firm. Corots jostled with Degas, Gainsborough with Cuyp, and Canaletto with Van Dyck. Even the portrait of the founder was something special, it was by Gainsborough, and owned by Paul Getty.

The aristocratic connection was symbolized by Patrick Lindsay, son of Lord Crawford, who sold – for £1 million – a Duccio Crucifixion which had hung in his night nursery when he was a child. PCW tried to match such tactics by persuading his cousin, the Earl of Westmorland – his mother was PCW's mother's much-loved younger sister – to join him in 1964. The new recruit – a close friend of the Queen and for a long time Master of the Queen's Horse – was a godsend in helping PCW (who hated administration of any sort) keep some sort of order within the firm. But both Westmorland, universally known as 'David' within Sotheby's in recognition of his sheer niceness and unpretentiousness, and Sir Philip Hay, the former Treasurer to the Queen Mother, who became a director in 1969, were unsuited to the tough business of touting for pictures. 'They wouldn't push to let me get at the people they went shooting with', said one young director.

If Sotheby's had its gentlemanly side, Christie's was no nest of Bertie Woosters. The firm maintained a splendid image, of 'gentlemen pretending to be auctioneers' as against their rivals, 'auctioneers pretending to be gentlemen': it helped business to encourage the fiction that they lunched together every day at one of the more exclusive clubs in St James's Street (White's, say, rather than the Carlton), never, of course, mentioning business at luncheon. In fact their elegant velvet gloves concealed some pretty iron hands. 'In the sixties we were always conscious of being number two,' recalls Anthony du Boulay, 'we were Avis, trying harder.' David Bathurst, who was largely responsible for Christie's eventual success in New York, is always spoken of as the 'son of Lord Bledisloe' which indeed he is, but he is also a tough, pushy, terrier of a man. He is not unique: Michael Broadbent, hired in 1966 to restart Christie's wine department, dormant for more than a century, is the very image of the tense, driven type generally associated with Sotheby's.

Christie's also had a group of high-flying youngsters. In October 1969 seven were elected directors. They included Noel Annesley, who was only twenty-seven (in the previous two years he had trebled the turnover of the prints and drawing department), and Christopher Wood became a director at the same age in recognition of his efforts in selling nineteenth-century English paintings.

Broadbent's appointment was particularly significant: Christie's was proposing, not only to set up a new specialist department before Sotheby's, which started its own wine sales in 1970 but has never caught up, but also to back its ideas with cash. Earlier that year the owner of a small City wine and spirits auction-rooms, Restell's, had died. Christie's persuaded his son, Alan Taylor-Restell, to merge his firm and join them (he is a brilliant auctioneer, but became a director only seven years latter).

This was one of the many deals throughout the world as both groups expanded their coverage. In 1960 Lord Montagu of Beaulieu had pioneered auctions of old motor-cars, helping to attract a new breed of buyers: 'no longer was he a man who wanted a Bentley, and would not be fobbed off with a Bean, or even a Bugatti', said Montagu. 'Instead he had a yen for a "vintage" car, any sort of vintage car, irrespective of make, type, or suitability.' Five years later Sotheby's joined Montagu to stage their first specialized sale of motors. Subsequently the disposal of the Sword collection provided the trigger for ensuing interest in the genre. By the mid-60s even the humble Austin Seven, one of Britain's best-selling cars of the 1930s, had begun to move up in price. But the real mania was either for thoroughbreds, like Bugattis or Rolls-Royces, or the true Veterans, cars made before 1904, and thus eligible for the famous Brighton Veteran Car run (prices were boosted by the film comedy, *Genevieve*, based on the event).

The link-ups also affected the smaller auction houses. When Knight, Frank & Rutley (which fifty years earlier had probably been a bigger firm than Sotheby's) stopped selling the contents of houses, it was Christie's which grabbed the business. Both major houses' NSV (No Sale Value) items now went to another small auctioneers, Phillips. The gifts soon got rather out of hand: Christopher Weston of Phillips remembers the arrival of a lot of fifteen tea chests full of silver. This was rather dangerous. Once trustees and executors saw Phillips' efficiency they would divert more valuable material to them, thus exposing an increasing gap in the armoury of the Big Two: they simply couldn't afford to deal with too many, too small-value items.

127

Yet competitive fury kept the Big Two bickering over the smallest thing. By the end of the decade the two houses, like two small boys, were squabbling over which had been the first to sell model railways. In April 1970 Sotheby's announced their first sale of what they called 'railwayana ... the items included ... are the best examples of their type and of great rarity value'. To which Christie's replied that they had been selling 'railway relics ... in our model train auctions' for three years.

But this was only the joky side of a deadly world-wide battle. Sotheby's first sale outside England had been at Gleneagles Hotel in late 1967 when eighteenth- and nineteenth-century pictures had fetched a mere £27,000, and the next year it opened an office in Edinburgh, a modest start for its search for world domination of the auction business. At the same time Christie's mounted an ambitious campaign to outflank Sotheby's by seeking out markets outside the United States, for a decade almost entirely Sotheby territory. In 1967–68 Sotheby's was boasting that it had sold items from sixty-five countries, and had attracted buyers from seventy-four. In three days at the end of May 1968 they demonstrated their world-wide tentacles by conducting thirteen sales spread over five international centres. Apart from sales in London and New York, vintage aircraft were sold in Los Angeles, veteran and vintage cars in Boston, and a number of more orthodox items at Simpson's department store in Toronto.

The Canadian initiative was a typical case of competitive scrambling. The *Annual Review* mentioned only the five sales totalling $767,475, the airlift of pictures by Air Canada, the 35,000 people who paid to see the items, the opening of a permanent office. That was the story as told by Stanley Clark. Insiders remember rather that Simpson's approached Sotheby's, that Stanley Clark saw it as the basis for the world-wide orchestrated event. It meant frantic rummaging to assemble some convincing sounding lots in the face of departments sceptical about the possibility of getting good prices in Toronto. 'We went to the dealers and found some Canadian material', remembers one director, 'Both the dealers and our own people tended to hive off their duds. But we were lucky enough to get a Gainsborough, of an Irish subject. By then the Irish had a lot of money to spend on art because they were benefiting from George Bernard Shaw's will, so the royalties from *My Fair Lady* ensured that we got a very good price for the Gainsborough.'

By the end of the decade Christie's had even raided the United States' market when they sold the possessions of one of the great Detroit motor heiresses, the 103-year-old Mrs Anna Thompson Dodge, who had lived in her own version of Versailles on Lake St

Clair on the outskirts of Detroit. She went in for the association game in a big way: she allowed herself to be painted as Madame de Pompadour (complete with plunging *décolleté* totally unsuitable for a sixty-year-old widow); her furniture consisted largely of pieces which had belonged to Marie Antoinette. Christie's launched a massive offensive, despatching seven directors headed by Jo Floyd to convince the executors that New York was not the ideal place to sell her Old Masters and French furniture. They completely outgunned Sotheby's, which sent only one director from New York to pitch. The sales, totalling £2.3 million ($5.52 million) were a considerable morale-booster for Christie's and confirmed Jo Floyd's reputation as someone who could compete with the dreaded rivals at the very top of the market.

The Dodge sale was merely a cheeky raid, it did not dent Sotheby's supremacy in North America. But Christie's saw that this one battle-front was absorbing all its rival's resources and concentrated their efforts on Europe. They lost out in Italy – a country with theoretically strict rules for the export of anything to do with the national heritage. These rules could be broken only through smuggling, not in a public auction, which put both houses at an enormous disadvantage. But Hans Gronau had bought a villa near Florence, so his widow's contacts were superb. She managed to get the rare and valuable permit to conduct sales anywhere in Italy, and was lucky enough to secure the sale of the contents of a house belonging to Prince Paul of Yugoslavia, which had once been the property of one of the fabled Demidoff family. Tim Clarke rose to the occasion, taking the sale mainly in Italian. By contrast Christie's had appalling trouble with its first sale in Rome. A group of Italian art dealers claimed the sale was illegal because of an obscure clause in a trade agreement between Italy and Switzerland (Christie's Rome office, was technically, a subsidiary of their Geneva sale-room). They were plagued with fires and mysterious phone calls, obstructive police – and some very disappointing prices.

But this was the exception. In most of Europe Sotheby's was faced with a newly rampant Christie's competing throughout Europe. By 1969 both firms had offices in key European cities like Paris, Munich and Florence, but the patent niceness and honesty of Peter Chance, his firm's reputation, and his ability to pick the right man, at first gave Christie's the edge. As in London they specialized in hard-driving aristocrats – like the Archduke Geza von Habsburg-Lothringen, Olga von Furstenberg, Princess Jeanne-Marie de Broglie, while in Austria the former dealer who represented them was also of course titled, Baron Martin von Koblitz.

Von Habsburg was based in Geneva, scene of Christie's greatest

European triumph, unmatched by its rivals at the time. It was essential to have a base in Switzerland, virtually the only country where it was possible to import and export both old and new jewellery without any restrictions.

The Geneva initiative was a happy accident. Anthony du Boulay had been at Geneva University with a scion of the Lombard Odier family, owners of one of Geneva's most powerful private banks. Through him he secured an introduction to Hans Nadelhofer, a genius in the narrow world of jewellery – it was crucial to have someone whose opinion on the purity of the stones was universally respected. But it was a bold step. Zurich, with better air services and a tradition of auctions that Geneva lacked, would have been a more logical choice, especially as Peter Chance spoke German, not French. Sotheby's opened an office there, which was profitable in itself and also used to keep an eye on one major collector, Robert von Hirsch, who lived in Basle, sixty miles away; their representative, Dr Jurgen Wille, was a friend of Hirsch's and helped ensure that Sotheby's continued to value his collection for insurance purposes – always an elementary precaution. But in 1978 they had to open up in Geneva as well – with a typical flourish, a fancy dress ball. Christie's were cautious, they opened their Geneva sale-room in association with Robson Lowe, the well-known stamp auctioneers, while Robson Lowe himself joined the Christie's board (his firm was absorbed in 1980).

Christie's first major jewellery sale in Geneva in May 1969 created the same sort of resentment as Sotheby's had found in New York. The Swiss porcelain dealers tried to boycott the sale, but were told not to be so silly. They started with the jewels belonging to the late Nina Dyer, the former wife of Baron Henri von Thyssen – and the next year the star attractions were the Dodge jewels. Every year since then Christie's has mounted an increasing number of sales of jewels and Continental silver at the Hotel Richemond. These are rather more exotic affairs than those in London. Many of the lots come from backwaters like Estoril, the seaside resort near Lisbon which is the home-in-exile for many of Europe's Royal families, and where Christie's had a particularly effective representative – the name Habsburg didn't hurt either. So the catalogues are full of references to jewels that had been 'the property of a European Royal family', or, more frequently, 'of a member of a princely family'.

The war spread to other fronts. While fully-fledged sale-rooms were expensive, offices were relatively cheap. So Sotheby's opened them as far afield as Beirut, Johannesburg and Melbourne. Guy Hannen of Christie's promptly counter-attacked. He 'drove up to Japan' from Christie's Australian base. 'I never realized it was so far.' This was a crucial step, not so much because of the possibility of regular sales, but because of increasing Japanese interest in buying Western works of art (including, at the time, second-rate Impressionists for which they were prepared to pay far higher prices than Westerners). In partnership with the local art dealers' association, he organized a Western-style auction. In deference to local custom, an embarrassed Peter Chance had to conduct the sale in his stockinged feet, but otherwise refused to follow the local conventions. For normal Japanese sales were open only to dealers, the lots were unknown until they were brought forward one by one, and after they had been described (in invariably glowing terms) there was a deluge of shouted bids, at which point the winner could refuse the lot. The sale was a triumphant success, totalling over £800,000 ($1.92 million). Prices were remarkable. A record price for any single piece of porcelain – £26,000 ($62,400) – was set for a Ming jar; a Renoir sold for the equivalent of £34,000 ($81,600), six times the price paid for the same picture at Sotheby's seven years earlier; and European firearms 'of no special distinction made very high prices compared with London'. Hannen, who was forming an increasingly effective partnership with Jo Floyd, consolidated Christie's position by hiring a former British Ambassador, Sir John Figgess, well-respected as such elder statesmen are in Japan, in time for the 1970 World's Fair at Osaka. Sotheby's had already teamed up with the Mitsukoshi department store to mount its own major sale during a 'British Week' the same year after a pioneering sale in October 1969. The battle was now world-wide.

## 2 CHERS ENNEMIS

PCW's aggressiveness was bound to get him into trouble. His cavalier disregard of the legal niceties of the ownership of lots created one set of problems, his desire to take over the dealer's role another – so that by the end of the decade the firm's finances were in a mess, and a number of his most promising recruits had left.

Problems of ownership were endemic in the auction business: families which owned precious objects were often quarrelsome, and their arguments generally centred round the trusts that controlled the bulk of their assets. PCW had the dealer's attitude to ownership: provided that something could be proved to be the legal property of the vendor, it was silly to enquire further – and sometimes it was unwise to delve too deeply into the owner's claims at all. He was not alone in his attitude. Vere Pilkington had obviously not enquired too closely about the ownership of '*The* Poussin' sold so triumphantly in July 1956. Immediately after the sale Sotheby's had been sued: the picture, it was said, was legally part of the 'settled furniture' and the vendor did not have the right to dispose of it. PCW remained calm throughout the tense months that followed, but the lawsuit dragged on for five years – surviving the deaths of both the original owner and his lawyer.

Much worse was the row over the Somerset Maugham collection. In April 1962, PCW had conducted an apparently triumphant sale of the author's pictures. A Picasso, *Death of a Harlequin*, fetched £80,000 ($224,000), the highest sum ever paid at auction for a painting by a living artist (it was also a clear demonstration of how far the market had still to catch up with the Golden Days before 1914 when, in real terms, paintings by a number of living artists had fetched far more).

Maugham's decision to sell the pictures was rational enough – he was afraid for their safety after a spate of burglaries near his home in the South of France. He intended some of the money to go to his daughter. Because their relations were strained he told his son-in-law, Lord John Hope (now Lord Glendevon), at the time the Minister of Works in the Macmillan administration. By the time of the sale itself Maugham's mind was wandering and he apparently instructed PCW to hand the proceeds over to a family trust. Alan Searle, Maugham's constant companion, warned PCW of Maugham's previous instructions but the opportunity was too good to miss and PCW charged ahead with the sale. The result was an untidy lawsuit: the money had to be paid into an escrow account, and Maugham was forced to sue the trustees of the trust on whose behalf Sotheby's had sold the pictures. The experience terribly upset Lady John Hope, and the episode established a first black mark for PCW in the 'right' quarters.

Cases like this were more embarrassing than stolen goods, which simply had to be returned to the rightful owner – items like a stolen Epstein bronze statuette (then valued at a mere £650 ($1,814) ) brought for sale in 1967. And in the 1970s a butler tried to sell a Canaletto he had purloined from his master's walls, thoughtfully substituting a copy, which deceived the owner. Much more embarrassing were lots associated with notorious owners. PCW's aggressiveness ensured that it was almost invariably Sotheby's which got into trouble; the prospective sales of the diaries of such disparate personalities as Hermann Goering and Che Guevara both provoked international incidents. And twice over the years Sotheby's enthusiasm for acquiring important material at any cost, and preferring not to enquire too hard into the bona fides of the consignor, led to well-publicized clashes with a religious establishment. In both cases the sale exposed dirty linen within that establishment, which didn't help either side.

In March 1967 Sotheby's was due to auction twenty-three manuscripts, including a 700-year-old New Testament, amounting to 'probably the most important sale of its nature' ever staged. The items were all early Armenian Gospels: 'many in this remarkable collection', enthused the catalogue, 'are encased in bindings of silver or silver gilt and are engraved or *repoussé* with Gospel scenes or studded with precious or semi-precious stones'.

Unfortunately, a few days before the sale, Archbishop Bessak Toumayan, the Special Delegate of All Armenians to Lambeth Palace, sent a telegram to *The Times*. In it he claimed that the manuscripts had been 'taken without the knowledge or consent of the Patriarch His Beatitude Archbishop Yeshige or any authorized body'. They were, apparently, some of the finest treasures from the Cathedral of Saint James in Jerusalem, and were brought out of the Treasury only on very special occasions. The Supreme Catholicos Vasgen I said flatly that they had been stolen, and the crisis brought together the normally warring factions of the world's Armenian community. Sotheby's promptly claimed that the credentials of the anonymous vendor were 'impeccable'. The police authorities in

Jerusalem took one look at the case, concluded that the material had been stolen some years previously, that the theft was obviously the work of an insider, and, in the words of *The Times*, 'obviously expect the matter to be thrashed out within the labyrinthine passages and tangled courtyards of the Armenian cathedral near the disused Zion gate of the old city'.

The Jerusalem police had realized that the theft was a result of earlier quarrels within the Armenian community, and were not going to get involved. The Gospels had apparently been stolen eight years before: 'an Armenian monk of American nationality and a Lebanese teacher' were questioned but in the end the thief or theives were dealt with 'privately'. The world's Armenian community raised the £50,000 ($140,000)* required to buy back the material – which might have gone for ten times the amount if it had ever been put up for sale. But Sotheby's managed to secure one vital condition: that the name of the person who had brought them the manuscripts should not be revealed. As journalists appreciate, protection of sources is a crucial element in guaranteeing a continuing business relationship.

There was an even more convoluted problem in 1984 when Sotheby Parke-Bernet – by that time owned by a leading Jewish industrialist – put up for sale fifty-nine rare Hebrew manuscripts, which had originally belonged to a rabbinical seminary in Berlin. They had been smuggled out of Nazi Germany by one of the teachers, William Guttmann, who subsequently taught at a similar College in Cincinnati. They were auctioned for $1.3 million (£1.1 million), but the New York State Attorney General promptly accused Sotheby's of 'persistent fraud and illegality'. In the subsequent rumpus Guttmann was eventually flushed out in to the open as the vendor, and claimed that he was selling them only to provide for his old age and his children. A complex legal row naturally ensued, involving the original rules of the Berlin Seminary and the post-war legislation governing the restoration of Jewish-owned property in Germany. A leading New York dealer in Judaica defended Sotheby's with the classic statement: 'Dealers usually assume that the seller is the legitimate owner, if there is any suspicion, you simply don't buy it ... If Dr Guttmann had come to me I wouldn't have doubted that he was the owner.'

In PCW's time dealers did not often defend Sotheby's. They felt that he was trying to reduce their role, although his frequent threats on the subject were largely psychological, war cries designed to keep

---

* Most of the money came from an Armenian industrialist from Detroit, Alex Monoogian, President of the Armenian General Benevolent Union.

the pressure up. Here, once again, he was at the opposite pole to Jim Kiddell, who worked so closely with dealers and trained a number of his 'pupils' to do the same. They knew that in specialized fields, the dealers' collective know-how was always going to swamp Sotheby's institutional memory. But disciples who owed more to PCW than to Kiddell were inevitably tempted to compete with the dealers, rather than co-operate with them.

In practice PCW's aggressiveness was tempered by his eagerness to do a deal. Even so the relationship would never have been an easy one. Traditionally auction houses and dealers are *chers ennemis*: they hate each other almost as much as they need each other. They are each other's best customers, yet their interests are bound to be fundamentally opposed, if only because their habits, their working methods are so different. Dealers prefer the dark, auction rooms are the lightest and most public of retail outlets. Dealing through auction rooms emasculates dealers, they become merely agents, everyone knows what they are paid and can calculate their margins.

Even more crucially they lose their most precious asset, their reputation as the only source for the most desirable objects. Duveen was quite happy to pay a substantial commission to the Agnews for introducing him to their aristocratic clients if it preserved his reputation as the sole source of the finest and showiest Old Masters. Indeed the mere fact that a work has passed through an auction room recently – even worse if it has been sold several times within a few years – greatly reduces its value compared with what Jeremy Cooper, an auctioneer-turned-dealer describes as, 'the unseen item, the rarity which has not appeared in the market place for decades, perhaps for centuries'.

Brand Inglis, the silver dealer, describes how he was once offered a magnificent piece of church silver by a parochial council in a small English seaside resort. After some thought, he offered the council the then immense sum of £20,000. Greedily they refused the offer, thinking, as everyone does, that if a dealer (even one with Inglis's spotless reputation) offers a given price for an object, then it must infallibly be worth double. They sent it for auction, where it fetched just over £20,000 – thus netting the council rather less than Inglis had offered. He had dropped out of the bidding at £14,000, and they were furious with him, still incredulous when he explained that the additional £6,000 was the price for his potential monopoly power over the object, not to mention the boost to his professional reputation, the 'how on earth did you get that?' factor. Commercially, a dealer can add only a small percentage to the auction price: he is free to charge what he feels the market will bear for something bought privately. It makes matters worse if an object has been bought in.

135

'It's easy to tell if the final bid came from the chandelier. Then the painting's tainted', says Sir Geoffrey Agnew flatly, 'whereas if it's left on commission at a dealer's it's much easier to wait, to adjust prices.'

The dealers are pitiless in the auction room. A Sotheby auctioneer once got into trouble over a telephone bid that went wrong. 'There is some trouble with this lot', he announced. 'The trouble is yours, the lot is mine', said the bidder in the room. But then they are also ruthless with each other. 'It was a dangerous game for any rival to "trot" Duveen in the auction room', wrote the sale-room veteran, A. C. R. Carter. 'By this term I mean the risky business of bidding for bidding's sake, and inviting a rival to continue.' He cited one case where Duveen 'dropped it on the toes' of some unfortunate rival, left with the final bid of £5,900 on a totally unwanted vase.

In such an atmosphere, dealers were not going to sympathize too vocally with their brethren who had lost business to the auction rooms. It is fellow-dealers who will recount how a highly reputable furniture dealer found that PCW had snatched the famous Hochshild collection from them. Even the dealer's muttered comment: 'If one of our best clients chooses to sell the furniture he bought from us at auction that is none of our business', arouses only derision.

Paradoxically the dealers benefited enormously from PCW's hype and they knew it. As the Sotheby spotlight shone on so many new categories, so the dealers, who held the majority of the stocks, found their value soaring. In the 1960s prices were rising so fast that they could never be sure that a single price was not a freak. This posed considerable problems of timing as well as valuation. Robert Wraight observed:

> In November 1963 Christie's sold a picture by the eighteenth-century English marine painter Charles Brooking for a new record price of 5,200 guineas. At the same time a St James's Gallery was offering a comparable picture for £3,000. Four months later, at Sotheby's, an identical picture fetched £14,500 and a similar one made £15,500! Early in 1964 a painting by L. S. Lowry sold at Sotheby's for the then surprisingly high figure of £1,000. A minute's walk away the artist's own agents, the Lefevre Gallery, were selling comparable pictures for three or four hundred pounds less, and continued to do so for several weeks until another picture, again comparable in size, quality and subject, fetched 1,100 guineas at Christie's. Then the artist's agents raised all his prices in accordance with the sale-room prices. And they have been going up ever since. There was an amusing incident at Sotheby's in the summer of 1964 when a Henry Moore Bronze

Family Group was sold for £6,500. In the middle of the bidding a well-known dealer suddenly got up and hurried from the room. Afterward he explained that he had an identical bronze in his gallery priced at £900 and he had been phoning his partner to hide it quickly! There was a sequel a few months later when a third example of the same Family Group fetched £7,350 at Christie's.

It was equally traditional for dubious dealers to validate their goods through the sale-rooms. The great forger, Thomas James Wise, used Sotheby's to establish a high price for his fakes by getting two dealers to bid for the same lot. This was costly, but he more than compensated for the additional expense by using the newly-established price as a base to sell other copies to unsuspecting collectors.

The dealers' traditional weapon against the auction houses was the ring, the agreement not to bid against each other for particularly desirable lots, and then agree afterwards how the profits should be split. This was largely a British practice, for there were too many private collectors in most New York auctions for them to flourish as freely there. The classic British provincial ring was exposed in 1964 when a brilliant investigative journalist (himself a former dealer) Colin Simpson, smuggled a microphone into the 'knock-out', the real auction after a sale, at which a Chippendale commode from the Spencer-Churchill collection at Northwick Park was put up for resale. The resulting scandal involved several senior members of the trade and dealt a temporary blow to the practice.

Such obvious rings flourished mainly in the country, so the spotlight on them helped attract business to the London houses, supposedly too big to be subject to rings. Of course they weren't. Indeed the law itself supported the informal agreements between dealers which were far more frequent than overt rings. In the late 1970s the Agnews were prosecuted for having agreed in advance with Eugene Thaw and another dealer not to bid. Although the law stated that auctioneers had to be notified of agreements in advance of the sale, the prosecution failed because the defendants could show that none of them would have bid separately.

The sale-rooms had to balance the convenience and predictability provided by the rings with their duty to the vendors. For rings could be useful where demand was small. Before the Second World War, William Sampson, known to the press as the 'professional champion of British art in the sale-room', was head of the ring that controlled Victorian and Edwardian pictures, then referred to as modern. But in return he helped Christie's by supplying a great deal of the material they required for their twice-weekly sales of pictures and drawings.

The sale-rooms' most effective weapons against the rings were the use of reserves, and, an essential element in the game of bluff, their refusal to reveal the lots that had been bought-in, rather than sold, or to admit their value. This kept the trade guessing. Sometimes they could rely on the dealers' traditional individualism. Over the past twenty years the book ring has been largely ineffective because the two biggest dealers, Quaritch and Dring, steer clear of it.

At the other extreme have always been the, largely Armenian, carpet-dealers. Before the war they used to conduct blatant post-sale knock-outs in a tearoom opposite Sotheby's. Barlow responded by allowing extended credit to a dealer named Benlian to enable him to bid against the ring on any lot which he felt was going too cheaply. In the resulting chaos, Barlow, by then a Conservative junior minister, had to preside over a fair imitation of a Levantine bazaar. In the 1970s Sotheby's found another solution, they hired as head of their carpet department Jack Franses, a member of one of the best-known families in the carpet trade.

PCW inevitably complicated matters. Not only was he dealing on his own behalf, but also used a well-known dealer, Richard Green, as a buyer of last resort even of major pictures. This, like the earlier relationship with Benlian, created the potential problem, in a falling market, of an 'art mountain' largely financed by Sotheby's. For the relationship between dealers and sale-rooms inevitably revolved round the question of payment. For a decade or more, Parke and Bernet's biggest problem was Vitall (the Pasha) Benguiat, the lordly carpet dealer. For much of the 1920s they were forever arranging sales to reduce the Pasha's permanent debt to the AAA. But fashions had changed, and Benguiat often had to buy in most of the lots, or lend them to an interior decorator who tried to sell them to help furnish stately homes.

Benguiat posed the basic financial problem faced by any major auction-house coping with a demanding, dominating debtor: if the dealer owed enough, he was in a very strong position, since his only assets were his stock, and this was valueless without him and the prices he could command in the sale-room.

The same applied even to Duveen. In 1928 Major Parke had been able to acquire the collection of Judge Elbert Gary, the former head of US Steel, by giving the executors a gigantic guarantee – $2 million – knowing that Duveen, who had sold him many of the works, and had himself offered $1.5 million for them, would be forced to support the prices of 'his' pictures in the sale-room. After his death prices crumbled: Hoppner's *The Tambourine Girl*, which he had sold to E. T.

Stotesbury for $350,000 in 1915 (£72,300) fetched a mere $10,000 (£2,500) in 1944, and a number of other portraits were quietly repurchased for minimal sums after the war by descendants of the painter's subjects.

Duveen was a special case. In time of trouble, the auctioneers traditionally shortened the lines of credit they habitually extended to their regular dealers: 'picture dealers are not just now in the best credit', wrote the dealer Thomas Rought to the collector Joseph Gillott during one mid nineteenth-century financial crisis, 'and auctioneers look sharp after them.' But they still depended on each other. In the late nineteenth century, Sotheby's preserved its dominant position in the book auction business by providing continuous financial support for Bernard Quaritch, the most important dealer. Characteristically, Christie's flatly refused to engage in a credit war and the other potential rival, Puttick & Simpson, did not have the same credit facilities as Sotheby's. Quaritch would arrange for six months' credit, or he would pay regular monthly sums. Without such support the book trade could never have coped with the flood of books from aristocratic houses released by the agricultural crisis.

The position did not greatly change after 1909. Montague Barlow swiftly realized that 'the book trade is our life blood. Sotheby's has been financing it for generations. We cannot stop doing so now.' Even his attempts at putting the relationship on a more business-like basis came up against the booksellers, who knew well how dependent the auction rooms were on the purchases they made for stock. In 1918 Barlow threatened to charge interest on long-overdue accounts and was stopped in his tracks by the famous bookseller E. H. Dring:

> Had we been aware [he wrote] that it was your intention to charge interest on our purchases at the Vernon and Huth sales we should simply have ignored those sales so far as buying for stock was concerned, and should have confined our purchases to the commissions we held for which we should have paid cash. It is not of paramount importance to our policy to prevent books from fetching less than their value, especially when we have to pay five per cent for the privilege.

So the auction houses were liable to find themselves financing both sides. The sellers often wanted some form of advance and certainly wanted their cash before the trade was prepared to pay. Barlow was particularly caught by the Yates Thompson sale. This was a superb collection of books and manuscripts, and he had cut his commission to a mere 5 per cent to get it. He had the greatest difficulty in getting the second half of the collection: Yates Thompson was furious that he had still not been paid several months after

139

the first sale; while the commission had been so small, the sums involved so large – a record £52,360 for a mere thirty items – and payments so slow, that Barlow simply could not afford to take out a bridging loan to pay the irate Yates Thompson.

Sometimes, too, the borrower slipped away. Barlow lent a great deal of money to Charles Fairfax Murray, a leading dealer in German incunabula. But he had a long-standing relationship with the Agnews, who naturally steered him to their cousins at Christie's (Barlow's fury was something to behold).

# 3   WATERSHED

The devaluation of sterling in November 1967, the first of a series of disturbances which have dominated the financial world ever since, was a crucial event in determining attitudes towards art-as-investment. Prices in the London sale-rooms immediately leapt by more than the 14 per cent required to compensate for the devaluation. The devaluation of the French franc eighteen months later produced a similar swing towards investment in art. But sheer uncertainty was the motive that triggered the interest – the revaluation of the German mark merely encouraged German collectors to increase their purchases.

Even before devaluation the Antiques Collectors Club had been formed, geared to the needs of the professional collector. In due course it produced regular indices similar to those published by *The Times*. Two bright young property developers, Benny Gray and Douglas Villiers, dreamed up the idea of Antique Supermarkets (which soon became Hypermarkets) with room for dozens of stalls for smaller dealers. The smallest English town or village was not complete without its antique shop – often financed by husbands anxious to find something for their wives to do, anxious, too, to cash in on what seemed like a permanent boom.

Not surprisingly, Sotheby's grew over-confident. Both major houses had long been expert in advising their clients over their tax problems, but in 1967 Sotheby's went one further. They helped form a 'Capital Protection Consortium', which included stockbrokers, a merchant bank, and Knight, Frank & Rutley, by then purely estate agents. The desire to minimize death duties helped precipitate Sotheby's first major financial crisis, for a market that depended on tax loopholes was inevitably going to be vulnerable.

The loophole was simple enough: works of art deemed to be 'of museum quality' were excluded when an estate was being valued for death duty; when they were sold duty was charged at the rate paid on the rest of the estate. Because rates of duty climbed so steeply, if a great deal of the estate consisted of works of art the overall level of duty was sharply reduced.

The Consortium had mentioned that 'possible purchases include forests and exempt works of art', but only truly rich millionaires could afford whole forests – which carried even greater tax benefits. Lesser mortals had to be content with 'exempt' works of art. These had to be easily available, of uniform quality and value, easily transportable, a generally accepted currency. Standard eighteenth-century English silver: tea and coffee pots, candlesticks and salvers fitted the bill admirably. They were hall-marked, so buyers knew who had made them and when and there were regular, weekly sales at which similar pieces came up. It was all rather more like the stock-market than most auctions.

Not surprisingly the value of these routine lots soared. But the boost given by duty-minimizers was never obvious, for it coincided with a simultaneous rise in the value of the metal itself. In 1968–69 the silver market suffered from one of its periodic panics that there would not be enough silver for the world's increasing demand for silver-based photographic film.

Naturally, prices boomed: a Sotheby's sale on 20 November 1968 set an auction record of £218,645 ($522,562) including £56,000 ($133,840) paid for the 'Brownlow tankards' made for Sir John in 1686, a record for an individual piece of English silver. By February *The Times* could report on an unprecedented boom: 'Normal price levels have almost ceased to exist ... some crazy prices have been recorded ... a substantial number of people have taken to purchasing old silver to be tucked away in bank vaults until times are safer ... Although real collectors perhaps still predominate, "investment" in silver is on a larger scale than pure investment in other works of art. This may well reflect a psychological link to the bullion value of the metal' – which had indeed doubled. Sotheby's was getting the fullest benefit of the boom: in the first four months of the auction season its silver sales had amounted to nearly £1.1 million, more than double the figure in the same four months the previous season, whereas Christie's sales were up a mere 40 per cent to just under £700,000. Prices at provincial sale-rooms – where much of the buying on behalf of the rich and dying was concentrated – 'were well above London levels'. Nor were sales confined to the sale-rooms. One buyer swept into Spink's, next door to Christie's, pointed to a row of gleaming silver and asked simply: 'How much is that top shelf?' One old habit remained. Even at the height of the boom, at a sale on 30 January 1969, which totalled over £1 million, the weights were still solemnly given with each lot: '£8,000 was paid for a George III Starr cooler, 448oz 17dwt ... an austerely worked tea caddy 11oz £2,000 ... George I salver 54oz £5,000'.

Unfortunately for the market, one of the Labour government's Treasury ministers was Harold (now Lord) Lever, a financier popularly supposed to be able to find ways round Chancellors' clampdowns almost before they had finished speaking. But this particular poacher was now a gamekeeper, and on 15 April his superior, the Chancellor of the Exchequer, Roy Jenkins, introduced a budget that put an immediate and effective stop to this particular abuse. Works of art, even of 'museum quality', were to be included in the total value of the estate if they were sold within three years, and the allowance was greatly reduced even if they were sold much later. 'This will in no way make more difficult the position of a family which wishes to maintain intact an outstanding collection', Jenkins assured the House of Commons, and was roundly cheered by Labour back-benchers when he continued: 'the pursuit of art for loophole's sake will become less worthwhile'.

The market took a little time to absorb the shock and prices remained high at Sotheby's first big silver sale after the budget on 20 June. But by the summer dealers remember Arthur Grimwade, Christie's famous old silver expert, almost pleading for any bid at all on routine lots of eighteenth-century silver. A classic item – George II candlesticks weighing 35 ounces, chased at the angles with shells and with baluster stems – lost half its value between the Budget and the early autumn.

In 1973, after three years of general inflation, run-of-the-mill English silver was still a fifth or more below its high point of early 1969. Yet *The Times*-Sotheby index for silver in general went down a mere 14 per cent in 1969. Because the boom had been concentrated on routine items, 'rare and exceptional' pieces were not affected. In June 1969 a Charles I silver-gilt tankard from Lambourn fetched £15,000 ($36,000) – a similar piece had fetched a mere £1,040 ($2,486) six years earlier. Foreign silver, which had seemed relatively cheap, now moved up in price, rather to the disgust of traditional English collectors. Their views were reflected in a comment by the Antique Collectors Club. 'In the past year', said its bulletin, 'foreign buyers, Italians, South Americans and some Japanese' had moved in to flaunt their flamboyant taste, so 'centrepieces, candelabra and the fussier cake baskets have come into their own'.

Sotheby's problems were compounded by PCW's over-exploitation of the formula – the creation of an event – which had first brought him into prominence. The idea that a regular flow of such performances was essential is crippling: you can never predict when rich old men and women are going to die (or decide to part with their treasures), so you have to create events, 'discover' amazing collections to feed the appetite you yourself have created for newsworthy sales.

These came to a head in 1968–69 when Sotheby's started to make special arrangements to sell a number of 'collections' specially assembled by French dealers for auction purposes. By that time, it was assumed that even if regular buyers were uninterested, the Japanese would buy any and every painting, however feeble, by any Impressionist. 'Bought in pictures find their way' [to Tokyo], asserted Reitlinger, 'much as old horses used to end up in Belgium and old passenger liners in the Greek islands'. This was a bit unfair to Japanese buyers who were also interested in the better works: in 1970 Tokyo was included in the tour of the world arranged for the real Impressionist masterpieces collected by William Goetz.

Many of the collections were built up by the French wife of an English-born dealer, Stephen Higgins, who had changed his name to 'Higgons'. He was based in Paris and had been well-known in the 1950s for selling pictures to American collectors. PCW kept his efforts quiet: he used Michel Strauss, the French-born head of the Impressionist department, as go-between, but did not even tell Hermann Robinow of the risks he was taking in making substantial advances to Madame Higgons for the pictures she was accumulating. Strauss himself firmly denies that Sotheby's ever financed any specific collections to be sold at auction: 'you simply had a lot of private dealers who were better at finding good things than at selling them, in France people like to be paid immediately, and the higher prices themselves brought out a greater supply of pictures'. The most obvious source was Eugène Boudin, the minor Impressionist who mass-produced easy, undemanding vistas of the sky, sea and beaches near his home in Normandy. The scheme was vintage PCW, and more sensitive directors, notably Tim Clarke and Howard Ricketts, were even more shocked by the devious way PCW had acted than by the Higgons' and the other mass purchases. So serious was the resulting row that all concerned swore never to mention it in public, an oath they have kept to this day in a display of taciturnity rare in such a gossipy business.

Manoeuvres like this depended on an eternally rising market. During 1969 Wall Street suffered a major decline and an even more profound crisis of confidence. Initially this sparked off an increased interest in 'art-as-investment', culminating in the first Art Funds to be quoted on the stock-market. 'At a time when many people are hesitant about putting their money into conventional shares' these funds could offer 'a maximum of capital growth with the minimum of speculative risk'. The promoters talked of a 'balanced portfolio' composed exclusively of artists 'represented in major museums'.

These were amateur efforts, offering weekly revaluations and hopes of cash dividends. They were not themselves significant, but they exemplified the increasing importance of relatively amateur buyers liable to unload more readily than traditional collectors. And in 1970 the market, especially in New York, turned sour. The price of Impressionists, which had been rising for nearly two decades, suddenly started to falter. Inevitably Parke-Bernet suffered worst, buyers were ever-slower in paying, but even the home sale-room had its problems – up to a quarter of lots in both London and New York went unsold and at one time Madame Higgons owed Sotheby's a considerable amount of money. Christie's was virtually unaffected: in the 1969–70 season its sales increased by a third to £20 million while Sotheby's sales in London had risen only a couple of hundred thousand pounds, to £25.4 million.

The relative collapse in New York brought to the surface the problem over 'Buy-Ins', which had been simmering ever since the take-over. For many Americans, especially museum curators, were still naive enough to believe that the 'Final Bids Received' in the sales records had actually been paid by an outside buyer. The problems came to a head in May 1970. On two successive days there were a number of unreported, but important, Buy-Ins at major sales. The first included Impressionists and Post-Impressionists; the second was even more newsworthy since it was of Contemporary Art. *Soupcan with Peeling Label*, the first painting by Andy Warhol ever sold at auction, supposedly fetched a sensational $60,000 (£25,000), whereas the highest price previously paid had been a mere $50,000. The new figure turned out to be a Buy-In, a case of absurd greed because the biggest real bid, $55,000 (£22,917), was itself a record. In November there were more Buy-Ins, rumoured and actual, at a highly fashionable sale of Contemporary Art. At this point the Art Dealers' Association, led by Ralph Colin, rebelled, and Parke-Bernet began to separate Buy-Ins from Final Bids Received. New York had finally forced Sotheby's to change its ways, not surprisingly because of Sotheby's invasion of a field – Contemporary Art – in which sale-rooms had, historically, not been involved.

The row over Buy-Ins had one major casualty: *The Times*-Sotheby Index. In the summer of 1970 Geraldine Norman proposed to write a major article on the subject. In a rare display of unanimity, PCW and Peter Chance jointly tried to dissuade her – proof of the importance they attached to secrecy as a weapon against the dealers. (Publicly Christie's kept its cool. Patrick Lindsay stated that he would always separate Buy-Ins if asked and was merely keeping them secret to protect the interests of the vendors.) Nevertheless she went ahead and PCW was furious. Apart from personal abuse his main weapon of revenge was to try and set up an alternative Index with the help of the *Financial Times*. Geraldine Norman and her editor, William Rees-Mogg, terminated the arrangement with a dignified letter saying, reasonably enough, 'I do not think you would have liked it if *The Times* had moved by two steps from working with you to working with Christie's'. (In any case the Index's inherent problems had grown more obvious with the years. 'It was comparing similarities rather than actualities', says one expert. As a result the dealers had ceased to treat it as a totally reliable indicator.)

The 'artificial events' had damaged morale, and, financially, they compounded the problems created by the crash in silver and the 'pause' in New York. In normal times dealers got three months' credit – and paid less commission than normal sellers. But there were no real credit controls, and the whole London silver trade seemed to be in debt to the house – a marked contrast to Christie's, which had kept its habitually tight credit controls. The shock wave ran through the entire antique business; Phillips, which was in closer touch with small country dealers than any other firm, reported that between five and ten had gone out of business in nearly every field in which it dealt.

Within Sotheby's, still a small firm, the financial impact was appalling. The overdraft soared five-fold to over £1 million, and, although Robinow professed himself unworried, the other directors were shattered: 'We all sat around wondering who to phone up for money', says one former director, 'we squeezed every single client we could.' When one of them saw the drawn face of Tony Holloway, the financial controller brought in by Robinow, he offered him his life savings, which were gratefully accepted. The psychological impact was even more severe: it was the first time Sotheby's apparently irresistible progress had been checked, and naturally led to a continuing, rumbling series of boardroom rows. Even some of the youngsters dared stand up and criticize a 'headmaster' who had been found wanting. The board was split into factions, which were to last longer than the crisis which sparked off the rifts.

The losses inevitably led to a much harder commercial attitude. Historically, the book trade had depended on the firm to allow them up to three months' credit. The sudden clamp-down changed all that: for the first time in several generations the whole book trade had suddenly to find new sources of finance. In late 1969 Sotheby's tried to increase their profits through increased commission rates: the size of lot on which an increased commission of 12.5 per cent rather than the normal 10 per cent had to be paid was increased from its historic £100 to £500. Tony Holloway left and David Westmorland insisted that a controller be attached to each department, a sort of financial commissar checking on the commitments made by the experts. PCW, eternally loyal to the idea of a firm run by experts, found the idea most unappealing but had to go along with it.

The problem was intensified because of the ways Robinow had tried to help the partners to avoid at least part of the high taxes – amounting to over 90 per cent – then paid by the owners of a firm like Sotheby's. Until the early 1950s it had been a partnership, and in the subsequent two decades had moved to be an unlimited company. Robinow had tried to 'strip out' the surplus profits, first through a complicated share exchange scheme with his own company, Barro Equities, and then through a company, George Street Properties, set up specially to own the firm's only major assets, its buildings in Bond Street.

The problem came to a head in early 1966, at the expiry of the eighteen-month loan used to purchase Parke-Bernet. Robinow devised a complicated scheme with three objects: to provide the wherewithal to refinance the loan taken out to buy Parke-Bernet; to enable the existing directors – mainly Hobson and Clarke – to sell their shares; and to allow the younger new directors to buy shares, which they otherwise could not afford to take up.

At the time Robinow was very close to Jacob Rothschild, whose family bank (together with the Anglo-Israel bank) subscribed £250,000 in first preferred shares. These received a fixed 10 per cent return and were to be repaid five years later. In return for the relatively high yield, the two banks provided their invaluable guarantees to the New York banks so that Robinow could finance the purchase on a longer-term basis. This imposed a colossal strain on Peregrine Pollen and John Marion, who had to guarantee profits of $300,000 a year for five years. They succeeded, so that, in the end, Parke-Bernet paid for itself.

The older directors received some of the firm's £100,000 ordinary shares (of which PCW had 27 per cent), which paid little or no dividend. The younger directors were allocated some of another class of shares, the £24,700 worth of 'second-preferred' shares. They could be paid very high dividends without fear of attracting too much tax and the high dividend yield enabled them to borrow enough from their banks to pay for their new shares.

The Inland Revenue had never been happy with the original 'Barro scheme' and in 1971, a decade after it had been set up, ruled against it – although the directors had had the use of the money for a decade. That year Robinow set up a more permanent arrangement. An investment trust run by Jacob Rothschild bought a fifth of the equity. Some of the shares were provided by Tim Clarke, who had grown steadily more nervous as to the firm's future over the previous few years (he now blames Robinow and PCW for causing him to sell his shares unprofitably early); many of the rest came from Robinow, who had given PCW *carte blanche* but did not expect all his shares to be sacrificed.

The relationship between PCW and Jacob Rothschild was never happy. PCW was a dealer, but nevertheless could never understand tha Rothschild thought of his stake in Sotheby's as merely a routine investment, not involving a commitment to the idea of auctioneering. So when Jacob Rothschild bought control of Colnaghi's soon afterwards, PCW was shocked, as though Rothschild had deserted the auctioneering cause. There was one direct casualty of the end of the 'Barro Scheme'. Robinow's family felt that he had been under too much strain, and insisted that he leave the board. He and Richard Day left the same day: 'Great minds think alike', they said to each other.

All these problems rumbled on in the background. The rows became public when Wills offered Sotheby's £100,000 so that it could launch a new cigarette, to be called Sotheby's Reserve. The cigarette deal posed a far bigger threat to PCW's leadership than had the acquisition of Parke-Bernet. The firm was bigger, and the opposition – including some important protégés, like Howard Ricketts and Marcus Linell – was wider, younger, more vociferous, and felt strongly that the firm's name was being dragged into the commercial gutter. Opponents did not hesitate to point out that Fred Rose, an old friend of PCW's had died of lung cancer only a few years earlier. But PCW felt the opposition was a major test of his leadership: he became obsessed with pushing the deal through.

To assert his dominance PCW had to exploit the company's peculiar voting structure. At the time every shareholder, whatever the size of his or her shareholding, had only one vote, and PCW even had to make a special trip to New York to cajole the American shareholders. He finally secured a narrow majority and Wills duly launched their cigarette at considerable cost. The external effect of the deal was minimal. Typically, Lord John Kerr had worried because of the large number of doctors interested in books. Nevertheless, shortly after the decision, he secured the sale of books from the library of the Royal College of Surgeons. He pointed out that his firm's name was attached to a cigarette. They didn't care.

Internally the effect was devastating. Howard Ricketts felt particularly hit: 'The gulf was very sad, Hobson and Clarke represented the academic tradition with Sotheby's. They had brought in the experts.' He had always assumed that he would remain with the firm until he retired, but he, Clarke, and Linell all resigned, albeit with one curious proviso. If the cigarette failed, then they would stay, since no permanent harm would have been done. If it was a success, they would leave. Eventually it did fail, and was withdrawn from the market four years later, but by then it was too late and the 'failure clause' did not operate. In the event Marcus Linell was so taken up with preparations for a new sale-room specializing only in Victorian material that he stayed with the firm. Tim Clarke remained merely as a 'consultant'. For Ricketts it was a 'large last straw', after the 'Higgons' and other episodes in which he felt that PCW in particular had been less than frank and that deals had been done behind the backs of the majority of the board. He was not alone in this feeling. When Michael Webb retired to Yorkshire to carve beautiful and highly valued netsuke some years later, his parting words were: 'When I became a director of Sotheby's I thought it meant something ... now I know better.' This sourness was invariably balanced by a residual loyalty to the firm. Ricketts agreed to stay on for a year to find replacements for the many areas he covered. It was an awful time, 'bad for the spirit', he says; so his resignation was not announced until October 1971.

But only one blow hit PCW personally. In April 1970 John Rickett died, a victim of the same nervous depression as his father before him. A dealer friend, Jeremy Maas, wrote a short obituary in *The Times*: 'To him art and life were indivisible ... his affectionate and generous nature, which, since his illness began, he did not always succeed in communicating, made him more friends than perhaps he realised'. The obituary was pinned onto a normally unused green-baize notice-board in PCW's office, where it remained for a long time, a yellowing reminder of the Brightest and Best, of the Golden Years.

*Part VI*

# REVOLUTION IN BELGRAVIA

# REVOLUTION IN BELGRAVIA

Rickett and Ricketts left behind a legacy: Sotheby's Belgravia, the most important innovation in the firm's history. The sale-room, opened in October 1971, devoted entirely to post-1840 paintings and objects, was more important for the history of taste than for the parent firm. For the first time an auction house was to play the dominant role in the reappraisal of the products of a period. The role had previously been played by a variety of people. Leaders of fashion often extended their influence to cover the world of art. The so-called 'Dame de Volupté' and Madame de Pompadour had successively dominated French taste for much of the first sixty-five years of the eighteenth-century. One man's crusade could have an effect: it was a nineteenth-century French art historian, Théophile Thore Burger, who first revealed Vermeer's genius to the world. Dealers like Duveen, Durand-Ruel and Vollard had exerted their own influence. Exhibitions – like the Armoury Show – often opened people's eyes, even if they would have preferred to keep them shut. An author could provide the market with the crucial scholarly apparatus to enable it to establish a proper scale of values. The four massive volumes devoted to English eighteenth-century furniture by Percy Maquoid, first published in 1904, provided an unprecedented certainty of attribution and set off a continuing rise in prices. The post-war boom in Chinese ceramics was solidly based on *The Ceramic Art of China*, the monumental work by W. B. Honey first published in 1944. (Honey acknowledged the help he had received from Jim Kiddell 'whose sales catalogues of Chinese and other pottery have set a new standard of accuracy and scholarship'.)

The Sotheby sales and publicity machine charged the whole idea of Victoriana with a mantle of fashionable glamour. It also posed a new challenge to the dealers: for it specialized in artefacts without an established network of dealers, thus increasing the sale-room's relative importance. The impetus provided by Belgravia also conferred a seal of respectability, not only on objects from the Victorian age, but also on later artefacts – as it had already started to do with Art Deco and Art Nouveau; and its experts greatly strengthened the previously inadequate scholarly scaffolding underpinning the period.

153

Ironically, this venture, Sotheby's most influential, went against PCW's own inclinations. Although he loved decorative objects, he was a man of his time and class and therefore not really interested in Victoriana – he rarely, if ever, visited the Belgravia sale-room a mere mile west of Bond Street. And he probably never dreamt that the firm could fulfill such a creative role. Nevertheless, the idea fitted in with his basic concepts. Just before Belgravia opened he told a radio interviewer, 'A friend of mine was in the Philippines and he saw written up on one of their general stores: "We specialize in everything" and that's Sotheby's.' For PCW recognised a neglected seam of gold when he saw one. 'Many of the pieces illustrated in the following pages', noted the Introduction to *Art At Auction* for 1970–71, 'would not have been considered worth selling ten years ago' – typically the survey included an article on the books and drawings of Kate Greenaway, always appreciated but hitherto a private rather than a public taste. No wonder the time was right 'to devote a sale-room to nineteenth-century art and by so doing, to demonstrate the tremendously rich and varied achievement of Victorian art as a whole', in a sale-room where 'pieces which are usually relegated in obscurity to poor sales, will receive the sympathy and critical attention they deserve'. As indeed they did: up to 80 per cent of the items sold at Belgravia were 'new' in the sense that they would never have gone through a major London sale-room before it was opened.

For the sale-room was more than just another piece of commercial opportunism. Like the rise of Laura Ashley, it was the outward expression of a revolt against functionalism, a populist reaction in favour of prettiness against the brutality foisted on people in the name of modernism. It was a revolt against the chilly simplicities of tower blocks, abstract art, even the Regency furniture of the post-war period. It marked a growing gap between the taste of the people – including the supposedly civilized middle classes – and that of the experts. The revolt itself harked back to the situation before the end of the nineteenth century: 'the heyday of the belief that work which was popular and easily intelligible was therefore great and good', in Reitlinger's words. Then came the parting of the ways: 'at the beginning of the present century a situation had been reached in which the most expensive form of private taste had almost completely parted company with the text-book teaching of art-history'. Gore Vidal detected a similarly-timed movement in fiction going back to Henry James, leaving the academics and their students on one side, and the mass of the reading public on the other. Somewhat later, Tom Wolfe's polemics against the Bauhaus school and the exclusive intolerance of the New York art world echoed the same feeling. This could easily be extended to objects of all kinds that were recognizably man-made: 'the mere mark of the human hand in an increasingly industrialised age', in Joseph Alsop's words.

But the prejudice against the Victorian era, in Britain anyway, was so strong that its return to fashion was inordinately delayed. In the United States the general gap had always been shorter. The Rigbys quoted an old collectors' saying that 'one should keep a thing seven years before throwing it away: seven times seven and there is a collector after it' – the fifty, or rather forty-nine year rule. In the 1940s they already detected a return to favour of Victoriana: 'as antiques and collectibles suitable for display and for use in moderation, since they are characteristic of a period that has already become historic and imbued with a degree of romance'. In Britain the pause before 'collectibility' was probably longer. The pioneering historian of taste, James Laver, told Wraight of 'Laver's Law', developed from a lifetime spent observing taste: 'It seems to be a law of our own minds that we find the art forms of our fathers hideous, the art forms of our grandfathers amusing and those of our great-grandfathers attractive and even beautiful.' This rule, enunciated in 1960, was to be spectacularly broken in the succeeding twenty years. It was Sotheby's which promoted 'grandparental' or even 'parental' art. In the late 1960s the interest in Art Deco and Art Nouveau helped to underpin the revival of an earlier period – a revival which, because of the depth of the prejudice against it, occurred later than for more recent artefacts. The 'fifty-year rule' was already being bent at the end of the 1960s, when Art Deco and Art Nouveau emerged as periods capable of sustaining specialist sales, some of them well-publicized major events, before sales of Victorian artefacts had entered the wider stage. But the Art Deco and Art Nouveau sales also broke another barrier: they included mass-produced items, normally excluded from the sale-room.

For the prejudice against Victoriana remained formidable throughout the 1960s. In 1961 Reitlinger could still write of the period after 1919; 'In reality it was only the most overrated of the Victorian paintings whose fall proved permanent.' 'The period was like a page torn from a history book and lost to view', wrote Jeremy Maas, a pioneer in promoting its virtues. 'Contempt for Victorian painting had created a vicious circle: no one wanted to sell pictures of that period if they were likely to fetch so little: the museums and galleries kept them locked away in basements.' Occasionally they sold them, albeit for a mere pittance. Typically the Lady Lever Gallery had sold a major Victorian painting, *In a Rose Garden*, for a mere £241 10s ($676) as late as 1967. Maas felt that the neglect was prolonged partly because 'scholars are a ripe load of snobs. The

155

eighteenth-century way of life seemed so infinitely agreeable to contemplate, whereas the nineteenth century meant ironmasters, textile kings and their kind of art'. It also meant their kind of architecture. In the 1960s dozens of solid, decent town centres, townscapes built on a human scale in the mid-nineteenth century, were wantonly destroyed. Preservationist pressure, was concentrated on earlier periods.

Even at the end of the 1960s the legacy of prejudice was formidable. In 1967, when Christie's held its 200th Anniversary Exhibition, the sale-room correspondent of *The Times* remarked how: 'only one painting, Holman Hunt's *The Scapegoat* from the Lady Lever Art Gallery Port Sunlight, is conspicuous for its sheer banality', and, in 1970–71 *Art At Auction* could still talk of 'the thoroughly unworthy equation of Victoriana with junk'.

The first sign of a rivival was in the works of the Pre-Raphaelites. According to Robert Wraight, by 1957: 'Everyone in the trade knew the Pre-Raphaelites were coming back and a scramble for their works began.' This gave an opening for the pioneering work of Jeremy Maas, who had conceived a life-long passion for Victorian pictures while at Oxford in the early 1950s. Himself of Dutch origins, he had admired 'the exact accurate and sharp description of every-day objects' he found in Dutch paintings. He sought the same in Oxford's rich selection of Victorian paintings, and 'because there was no art historical faculty, I wasn't talked out of my enthusiasm'. After a miserable couple of years in advertising, he bluffed his way into Bonham's, persuading Leonard Bonham that his gallery should have a separate prints and drawings department. In 1960 he founded his own gallery, and in late 1961 he mounted a Pre-Raphaelite exhibition – the first purely commercial show ever mounted of the Movement. It was well received, the pictures sold. But the habit did not spread, for the Pre-Raphaelites were still seen, as they would have wished, as apart from the mainstream. (By 1970, according to the critic Robert Melville: 'the young have discovered premonitions of the psychedelic experience in Pre-Raphaelite colour, and associated the introverted beauty of the feminine images with pure sexuality'.)

But Maas faced an uphill struggle in selling most Victorian art. The Americans were ahead of the game. In 1962 he sold a splendid Frederic Leighton, *Flaming June*, known as the 'Mona Lisa of the Western Hemisphere', to the Ponce Museum in Puerto Rico, and he was supported by a small band of enthusiasts – one of the earliest was the late Reginald Bosanquet a much loved television newscaster. Prices did rise: at Sotheby's during the 1963–64 season the collection of Victorian paintings assembled over the previous fifteen years by

Tom Laughton, a hotelier and brother of the actor Charles Laughton, had fetched £32,500 ($91,000), 'a remarkable sum when one learns that he had not paid more than £2,400 for them.'

Over the next few years prices rose gently from the abysmal level at which they had been stuck for a generation. But to push them back anywhere near the levels of seventy years before required the joint efforts of a group of arrogant young men, unable to remember, or self-confident enough to ignore, the neglect and scorn poured on the Victorians by their elders and betters. They were not all at Sotheby's: at Christie's a young enthusiast, Christopher Wood, was pushing Victorian paintings; and Phillips ran regular sales of Victorian artefacts. A big boost came in 1968 when *The Times* acquired a new sale-room correspondent, Bevis Hillier, a young man who could just as easily have been one of the gang at Sotheby's. He immediately broadened the paper's horizons, writing with great enthusiasm about previously neglected sale-room subjects. He was not specifically interested in Victorian works: his most important contribution was that he looked with enthusiasm at works from all periods. Like PCW, Hillier 'had an enormous amount of expertise in his head', in Linell's words. Like PCW, he found art fun and fun perfectly compatible with profit. Unlike previous sale-room correspondents, who had assumed that their audience was confined to aficionados concerned solely with prices and trends, he was primarily a journalist: 'I worked on the principle that people are interested in people, not things.' He conveyed his enthusiasm with enormous zest and readability: 'as the auction season gained momentum, schoolboy sketches executed at Charterhouse by Max Beerbohm fetched £480 ... a bronze figure of Juno at Sotheby's was recognised as a Cellini; letters of A. E. Housman were sold, giving new insight into his sex-life; and Sotheby's held a sale of instruments of torture, leaving not a rack behind ... there were people who found something shocking in my way of treating the world of antiques as a continuous source of entertainment.' (Although he also wrote books of the 'more-footnotes-than-text' description, which he sharply distinguished from his journalism.)

His enthusiasm forced people to look again at artefacts they had hitherto dismissed. Geraldine Keen, his successor on *The Times*, was typical in finding that: 'Victorian jewellery has a grace and charm far from the heavy and ornate styles we generally associate with the word Victorian, and although beginning to rise in price is still inexpensive. Much nineteenth-century pottery and porcelain have great charm.' John Rickett was an earlier enthusiast. As Jeremy Maas wrote in his obituary: 'few worked harder or more successfully in creating interest in the English national school'.

On 11 November 1968, the fiftieth anniversary of the Armistice – the moment when the British intelligentsia had turned their back on their Victorian heritage – Maas opened the first exhibition ever to use the word 'Victorian' in its title. He thus invited the British to return to their inheritance, as the Americans were doing at the same time to the great profit of Parke-Bernet. The exhibition galvanized Sotheby's into action: 'Hordes of directors turned up and crawled over the place', says Maas, 'PCW came several times.' The following year he published the first edition of his massive work on Victorian paintings, another important step in educating not just the public, but also the professionals – Maas noticed that Christopher Weston of Phillips came in the very first day to buy a copy.

It was Howard Ricketts who shaped the idea. He and his wife had always loved Art Deco and Art Nouveau: 'We collected Art Nouveau jewellery and what we liked we pushed.' He had been writing a book on *objets de vertu*, enamelled works of art. Previous books had stopped short at the 1830s and restarted with Fabergé in the 1880s. To fill in the gap Ricketts looked in the bound volumes of the *Art Journal* and the catalogues of contemporary exhibitions to try and separate objects that had previously all been lumped together as 'Victorian'. He immediately saw that here was a major source of information on a little known, but to him fascinating period and he cast around for help.

He found it as a by-product of the Sotheby's training scheme. This had just been started after pleas from Parke-Bernet, eternally hungry for additional expertise.* Ricketts was allowed to use the best trainees from the first year of the scheme as researchers to provide a foundation for a proper assessment of dates and designers' names. The more they worked, the wider the horizons he perceived for translating knowledge into trading possibilities. This was a revolutionary novelty: hitherto even Kiddell had never thought that auctioneers could blaze a scholastic trail. Eventually he came up with a fully worked-out scheme, which he sent to Marcus Linell in New York where he was running the works of art department. Linell wanted to come home for his children's education, but was intitially chary, not realizing how important Belgravia was to become: 'If you go to one of the out-stations for two years', he told Ricketts, 'you'll never get your old job back.'

Ricketts and Linell had to find a building, things to sell, and staff to sell them. They were lucky to discover the ideal site for the showroom. For a number of years Sotheby's had been using as a warehouse a curious building in Motcomb Street, Belgravia, sur-

* In recent years, especially since Caroline Kennedy became a pupil, it has become more of a select finishing school than a source of expertise.

rounded by the homes of likely customers. The Pantechnicon was built in the early nineteenth century as part of the development of the whole district. A dignified classical structure, blending externally with its neo-Grecian surroundings, it had been designed originally to house the horses and carriages belonging to the area's largely aristocratic inhabitants. It had subsequently been used to garage removal vans – which were later named after the building itself. It had then been used as a store-room 'and an informal club-house for the racing fraternity', in the words of Sir John Betjeman, the prophet of the whole Victorian revival, whom Stanley Clark had persuaded to write a short history of the building. In the 1960s it had been saved from the developers only after an almighty row and the new use made everyone happy (including the landlords round about; the Pantechnicon, like Parke-Bernet on Madison Avenue, soon attracted a cluster of dealers).

Getting material to sell was more of a problem. No one doubted that it was available, but would 'Bond Street' – and the former Belgravians still talk of their colleagues in Mayfair as of hereditary enemies – release it? Linell was firm: 'Whatever we were going to sell it had to be everything, including the plums.' Some very specialized departments, like coins and snuff boxes, were excluded anyway. Some departments – like Richard Day with drawings – were cooperation itself. Sometimes Linell found enthusiasts – like John Culme, whose passion for Victorian glass had previously been thwarted. Others again were only too glad to be rid of what had been regarded as merely 'shipping goods' to be shovelled into containers bound for Europe. The arguments came above all with British pictures, which were clearly rising in price and therefore worth keeping at Bond Street – there was a major row over a Burne-Jones that the paintings department naturally wanted to sell.

For his staff Linell had recruited only enthusiasts, he was trying to recreate a junior version of the Academy of the early 1960s: 'I was looking for people who believed in the subject, not on those who hoped for promotion . . . I found a good bunch of missionaries.' They return the compliment: 'He enthused us all', says Jeremy Cooper, a former trainee who ran the works of art department at Belgravia, 'he encouraged us to try new specialist sales, do experimental catalogues.' His two most important disciples were David Batty, a former 'gentleman porter' who took over from him, and the extraordinary Peter Nahum, recruited as a sales clerk five years earlier and given Victorian pictures to sell. He stood out, not only because he was Manchester-Jewish rather than Home Counties middle class, but also because of a whip-crack impatience and intensity. He epitomized the Belgravia spirit: 'We were more commercial. Someone

159

like me couldn't have survived in the old Bond Street. I'd live and die by my ways in my department.' He and Linell, the intolerant, driven, perfectionist and the polite organization man, had a tense relationship. But in their first years at Belgravia the sparks struck by the 'creative tension' between them set the whole art world on fire.

Linell followed Ricketts' lead, by using the new auction room to expand the still-minimal fund of scholarship on Victorian subjects. 'If we were going to succeed it had to be serious', he says. 'Using the full weight of scholarly apparatus, we had to change the general perception of the period' – before Maas opened his gallery virtually the only dealer handling Victorian paintings, Charlotte Frank, sold exclusively small, decorative ones: 'They were decoration rather than art', says Maas, 'rather like pretty little mistresses.'

Despite pioneer studies, like Maas's, and some by staff of the Victoria and Albert Museum, yet, as Ricketts had perceived, further boosts in prices required more specialist studies. Geraldine Keen noted, 'Finely-made Victorian furniture is still much cheaper than its contemporary counterpart. For a similar reason Edwardian furniture has been climbing notably in value recently ... Little up-to-date documentation is as yet available on the designers, styles and trends of the period 1820 to 1880. Most collectors are daunted by the difficulty of finding their way among the plethora of goods available without a guide.'

The researchers found startling gaps in the coverage: the latest book on Japanese cloisonné ware, for example, was dated 1870. But Linell had not spent a decade working for Jim Kiddell for nothing. He insisted on pinning everything down: 'We kept refining things. I wasn't satisfied with an entry saying something was made between 1875 and 1880, it had to be precise.' The training ensured that most of the department heads within Belgravia wrote monographs: Peter Nahum on the monograms of Victorian painters, John Culme, naturally enough, on nineteenth-century silver, Philippe Garner on Art Nouveau.

The sale-room got off to a marvellous start, not surprisingly since its first few years coincided with a general boom, the likes of which had not been seen since 1914, but it soon became possible to distinguish three themes which dominated the sale-room throughout its ten year life: the effect it had on widening the areas of 'marketable collectibles', its effect on Sotheby's itself, and, narrowest and most glamorously, the transformation it effected on the value of Victorian pictures.

From the first season, it became clear that Belgravia would break all the previous rules. Objects would be sold even if they had been mass-produced, even if they were of relatively recent origin. The bigger the supply, the greater the apparent demand. By the end of the decade auction prices – not just in Belgravia – were built into the financial plans of such disparate classes as professional musicians and wine merchants. In 1971–72 the *Annual Review* had devoted an article to the Kirckman family of harpsichord makers, but this interest deepened during the decade. For professional string players the instrument they play 'is the second most important purchase after a house' in Anthony Thorncroft's words. Since 1970, when Phillips dominated the field, both the major houses have taken up the challenge: Sotheby's turnover of musical instruments as a whole has multiplied literally a hundred times – to over £2.5 million – in the past fifteen years. As a result, says Thorncroft, 'for many musicians their violin is their nest-egg, to be sold on retirement to finance their declining years'. Similarly, wine-merchants learnt during the Great Slump of 1974–75 that the sale-rooms – in this case primarily Christie's – were capable of dispersing to the well-heeled private buyer the surplus stocks they had accumulated in times of apparently endless boom, like the early 1970s. A whole new market, composed mostly of syndicates of knowledgeable laymen, restocked their cellars at absurdly cheap prices with everything from fine hocks in abundance to hundreds of dozens of Lafite and Mouton Rothschild.

Belgravia's specific contribution was to widen the categories sold. They culminated in 'Collectors Sales' of items which even the increasing ingenuity of the cataloguers could not categorize. The assumption was simple: anything was bound to interest someone even if it had never before attracted a group of buyers or collectors. By no coincidence the Ephemera Society was formed in the middle of the decade. There are a few shops devoted to the oddities of the collecting world, and the Society runs a number of bazaars. But most of the turnover goes through sale-rooms. In 1984 a new auctioneer – Onslows of Winchester – was founded specializing in ephemera.

Of course satirists had a field-day, especially with the sales of 'Collectors' items'. The satirical magazine *Private Eye* was joking when it wrote of a sale of 'Highly important sausages' including 'highly important Polish garlic sausage by Topolski (slightly chewed) ... exceptionally fine pair of English hand-made cocktail sausages in perfect condition, uncooked by John Wells of Piccadilly, with matching carved oak sausage-sticks, both mounted on mint doily and disposable cardboard plate'. But what was the point of satire when real lots included: 'seventy titillating postcards including three mobiles of girls with elevating legs and various others with themes on sex and lust, also a view of the interior of Maison Frida', and 'A collection of thirty-three boxes of crackers ... including rare

Emancipation Movement Crackers'? In early 1985 the sale of a collection of early teddy bears rated an item on the radio, a short appreciation from a Sotheby's expert explaining the extent to which the prize lot had been restored.

Behind the jokes was an increasingly efficient sales machine. One of Linell's most important discoveries was his administrator, John Cann, the first director to be promoted 'from the floor'; as a non-expert sales clerk, he had been quite distinct from the 'gentleman porters' who did manual work, but like 'gentleman cadets' in the Army, were destined for promotion to officer rank. Within Sotheby's he was enormously respected for the way he made everyone's life easier by improving the administrative systems. Under him Belgravia developed its own booking systems: thanks to him, after every twenty lots the figures were sent to the accounts office, so that the new owners could collect their purchases at the end of the sale – a major factor in making private buyers feel they were shopping at a department store. (He even pursued them to their homes, offering to photograph their collections of silver, ostensibly to help with insurance and security problems, but also, of course, tying them closer to Belgravia.) For the atmosphere at the Pantechnicon was highly business-like: nothing went into the catalogue without a form signed by the owners authorizing the reserve price: costs were closely scrutinized. So Belgravia not only made a major direct contribution to profits, but many of its innovations found their way back to Bond Street, and helped the Group cope with the enormous expansion of the 1970s.

But none of this would have been any use without a touch of glamour, and this was generated by Peter Nahum's arrogance and missionary zeal. He brought the world of pictures to Belgravia and forced it to take Victorian pictures seriously, as he kept piling on the reserves to seemingly ridiculous heights. The leading Victorian artists played the same role for Belgravia as a whole as the Impressionists had done for Bond Street fifteen years earlier. At first, according to Linell anyway, Nahum did not want illustrations in his catalogues because he was relying on dealers who didn't want to pay for them. But he fell in with Linell's practice and could soon boast that every one of his precious offerings would be illustrated. He became particularly expert in producing magnificent catalogues which were not too costly. He tried to 'take the mystery out of cataloguing ... each catalogue explained itself, each picture related to the one before and after, we arranged them by schools or laid out spreads all of seascapes or of girls' heads. As early as 1972, within a few months of opening, we were making them accessible. At the same time I was always aware of the costs. I always felt I must recover so much per page of catalogue while still keeping charges down.' Vendors of lesser items sometimes have cause to regret this tradition, finding that a substantial percentage of their gross receipts may have been absorbed by the costs of providing the photograph. But Nahum was not primarily concerned with cheaper pictures. His 'well-researched, highly descriptive, fully illustrated hard-cover catalogues' were designed to enable private buyers to send in a bid for even the finest picture judging by the description alone.

The first major test of what Maas describes as a 'very fragile edifice which never collapsed' came with the curious sale of the pictures by Sir Lawrence Alma-Tadema owned by Allen Funt. Even many defenders of Victorian art considered Alma-Tadema to be merely a meticulous, but totally uninspired, painter of frigid reconstructions of an implausible Classical Age. Funt was an even more improbable collector. His fame and fortune came from his invention of the television programme *Candid Camera*; he had been introduced to the painter by a dealer who 'asked if I wanted to see a picture by the worst painter who ever lived'. Funt took this description as a challenge. As he told Russell Ash: 'I jumped to the defence. I swore I'd find someone worse no matter how long it took me. Soon I found myself with a homeful of Alma-Tadema paintings and a warm feeling of sympathy for this painter who received rather critical treatment. I have now discovered many better painters in his time, and many worse. Because I have received my share of brickbats from the critics, I enjoyed sympathising with Alma-Tadema.'

He was buying on a rising market. Back in 1960 two of the painter's most important works had been offered at Christie's, and deemed unworthy of illustration. One was bought in at £105 (less than $300), the other sold for £252 (just over $700). But in 1962 twenty-six of his paintings were shown at the Robert Isaacson Gallery in New York and prices rose so fast that the thirty-five superb specimens Funt assembled probably cost him $250,000. Then in 1972, Funt discovered that his accountant had embezzled $1.2 million, leaving him with 'everything a rich man has – except cash'. Virtually his only assets were his Alma-Tademas, and the only place to dispose of them was at Belgravia. On their way they were exhibited at the Metropolitan Museum, where they were described as 'refreshing camp' and 'the best of the worst'.

Although the painter's finest work, *Spring*, had fetched $55,000 (£22,900) at Sotheby's in Los Angeles the previous year, no one was sure that this mass disposal would not depress prices, especially as the sale took place on 6 November 1973, just as the full impact of the oil shock was reaching London. For the first five or six lots, says Maas, 'we were all looking at each other, wondering what prices would be, so the first few lots were relative bargains, but then it began to take off'. In the event Funt made a profit, walking away with $425,000 (£177,800). The best prices – well above the estimates – were made by historical and sentimental pictures from his middle period, with early works going for relatively little, proving that the market was still relatively selective. But it was clearly hungry enough to absorb the biggest collection ever likely to be assembled of any major Victorian painter.

The Funt sale came before the crash of 1973–74 removed most English private buyers from the scene. And naturally Alma-Tadema in particular suffered badly in the short slump of 1974–75 – although this was partly greed – *The Woman of Amphissa* was bought in for £11,550 in January 1975, but then the estimate was twice the figure it would have been a year earlier. With the help of his lavish catalogues, Nahum soon attracted massive foreign interest, originally from Germany, over the whole range of Victorian pictures. This was to be expected: as Marcus Linell points out, artistically the 'Victorian' period is badly named because the word is too insular, the era was the first in which taste was truly international – taste spread by the continuing flow of international exhibitions after Britain had led the way in 1851. 'They internationalized taste', says Linell, 'they made style more internationally homogenous than it had ever been before.'

Later in the decade the Americans joined in, but before that Nahum was setting reserves no one had ever dared dream of – and regularly topping them. 'They said I was mad to quote £500,000 for a Victorian picture.' A Richard Dadd made £550,000. A few months later a Tissot made £520,000. This was soon topped by a Millais that made £750,000. (Duveen would have been happy. 'Millais was my God in those days', he once told A. C. R. Carter when reminiscing about his early life, 'and he may yet become a real old Master.')

The lucky few who held on to their pictures throughout the slump made a fortune. In the late 1960s a financier based in Jersey had bought Sir Edward Poynter's famous painting *Cave of the Storm Nymphs* for £6,500. His family thought this piece of Victorian soft-porn was indecent, so he sold it again for a couple of thousand pounds profit. Later in the decade it was sold at Belgravia for £180,000.

Nahum's friends would say that he is enthusiastic, his enemies that he hypes things. In this he is the very opposite of the careful, scholarly Maas, and in 1980 the two clashed publicly, in an incident which emphasized the importance – and the prices – attached by that time to Victorian paintings. The star of an evening sale was to be no less than a version of William Frith's famous epic *The Railway*

*Station*. But Jeremy Maas had done some detective work – he had been wary of attributions since he had once bought a number of Sargents, apparently from a highly reputable source, which were subsequently found to be forgeries. He had concluded that the picture was in fact a copy, made by a young pupil of Frith's, Marcus Stone – indeed the then assistant secretary of the Royal Society had visited Frith's studio at the time and described Stone at work. He took the opinion round to Nahum but the doubts were made public only the day before the sale. After what he described as 'this mind-boggling piece of historical evidence', Nahum concluded that the picture was 'if not entirely from the hand of Frith, at the very least finished and polished by the artist'. Frith had done enough to sanction and sign the painting, for it was far superior to anything Stone was producing unaided at the time. The row resembled earlier disputes about other busy painters with many assistants, like Rubens and Reynolds – a compliment, albeit a back-handed one, to the status now enjoyed by the Victorians. The picture was originally estimated to fetch over £200,000: after Maas's evidence it was bought in for £45,000; more recently Nahum, who is now a dealer, sold it – as a Marcus Stone – for a much higher price.

The best price at the sale was paid for Alma-Tadema's famous *Caracalla and Gaeta at the Coliseum*, described in *The Times* as 'a remarkable piece of archaeological painting in which the artist claimed that he had depicted about 2,500 spectators.' Estimated to fetch between £50,000 and £100,000, in the end it went to a German dealer for £145,000. At long, very long, last, this most lifeless of all Victorian painters had returned to prices above those he fetched in his lifetime – but only in sterling terms. Unlucky American buyers, who had paid $30,000 in 1903 for *A Reading of Homer*, or £15,880 (then $79,400) the same year for *Dedication to Bacchus* were still out of pocket.

*Part VII*

# IN ALL DIRECTIONS

# I   THE RESILIENCE OF A MARKET

By the early 1970s, even quite ordinary criminals had realized that there was money in art, an unwelcome compliment to the success of the incessant propaganda on its ever-increasing value. In Belgium, France and, above all, Italy masterpieces were hacked from their frames, purloined from museums and churches to swell the regular and increasing flow from private homes.

For the first three years of the decade saw an unparalleled boom, in art as in prices for everything else. There were still bargains to be had: for all the well-publicized boom of the 1960s, whole sectors had still not recovered to their pre-1914 levels. Apart from minor areas like German Medieval sculpture, these laggards were often the work of artists who had been immensely fashionable in their own lifetime and had thus commanded enormous fees – like the 2,500 guineas paid to Canova by the Duke of Wellington in 1816 for a statue of Napoleon in the nude. Canova was typical: in 1970 the highest price ever paid for a modern sculpture remained the £10,000 paid in 1913 for Carpeaux's *La Danse*.

The rise in the price of art in general by no means matched the sudden surge in the price of gold, that other refuge in times of uncertainty. On both sides of the Atlantic, art handsomely out-performed the stock market, and the return to investors was well above even the increased rates of inflation. But the tables do not show that the rise in the early years of the decade was concentrated on two particular categories, nineteenth-century European paint-ings – dominated by Peter Nahum's beloved Victorians – which rose 60 per cent faster than inflation, and Chinese ceramics, which quadrupled in price on the same basis.

These peaks were a reminder of the concentrated nature of the buying: from Japan and from speculatively-minded British finan-ciers. But there was a contrast between the two. Even though the flow was interrupted for a short time after the first oil shock of 1973, the Japanese and the 'Overseas Chinese', mainly from Hong Kong, continued to buy back their cultural heritage throughout the decade: and because their free-market economies weathered the storm so well, they were able to afford the erratically-increasing prices.

169

It was inevitable that the whiz-kids of the City of London should join in. The first outward sign that something was afoot came in July 1970 with a short news item that twenty paintings by the nineteenth-century British artist, George Frederick Watts, then worth £150,000, had been stolen from the offices of Slater Walker. Jim Slater was at the heart of the speculative boom which swept the City at the time, so it was not surprising that he should have been investing in a newly-fashionable artistic field. In the late 1960s John Rickett had lectured to City audiences about investment in art, and he would naturally mention Victorian pictures as a promising field. For, despite the efforts of Maas and others, a great many Victorian painters had virtually disappeared from the sale-rooms – Reitlinger omitted a dozen or more, including such once-famous names as Meissonier, Rosa Bonheur and Ford Madox Brown from his volume of 1960s prices.

Until Christopher Wood left Christie's in the early 1970s to set up his own specialized firm Jeremy Maas was virtually alone in the field and derived a great deal of business from the City, remembering in despair how speculators would phone up and order pictures 'off the shelf' without even looking at them. The pictures were also a favourite of the many art 'consultants' who sprang up at the time. For City buyers were accustomed to dealing through middlemen like stockbrokers and estate agents. It was relatively easy to persuade Slater to 'punt' on Watts: he was a respectable painter of good lineage – a pupil of Constable's. But Slater, normally highly sophisticated in dealing with middlemen, did not appreciate how different the world of art was from the stockmarket. He would ask a number of dealers to acquire pictures, as he would have asked stockbrokers to find shares in a company. But whereas brokers would be looking for different parcels of shares, the dealers instructed by Slater quickly found themselves bidding for the same pictures at auction. This was a situation tailor-made for the sort of 'arrangements' at which dealers are so expert. Nothing so vulgar as a ring, just a cosy understanding by which the price of Wattses rose steadily, so far as Slater was concerned.

But no one seems to have mentioned to Slater that Watts painted a very large number of pictures, as did Williams and the other Victorian landscapists bought by other City slickers. These had lurked unconsidered for generations in the backrooms of coutnry houses, and the flow became unquenchable. Without any non-speculative demand the biggest hype, the best-financed corner, was bound to fail. It did. When the collections accumulated in the late 1960s and early 1970s had to be sold a few years later prices never recovered, although the German dealers moved in to snap up some of the better pictures and prevent a total collapse.

For by the early 1970s the market was so internationalized that Britain's entry into the Common Market made virtually no difference. One of the fond delusions raised at the time was that France and Italy might relax their control over their art markets. Of course they haven't, but at least PCW managed to limit the damage from the introduction of Value Added Tax, the new tax which accompanied Britain's entry in the EEC. 'He buried it with four phone calls', says an admiring insider, 'he and Christie's got a better scheme altogether.' He and Christie's threatened to move big sales to New York if VAT was imposed on the movement of art within the EEC. This was not idle talk. The distinction between the two was getting blurred, Sotheby's was holding even Old Master sales in New York. Within Britain the art world largely escaped VAT: it was to be charged not on the value of the objects being sold, but on the margins taken by the auctioneers and dealers, and then only if they were British. Foreign buyers escaped tax entirely. This has cost the British Treasury dear: despite increased rates and a colossal rise in turnover, it still collects a mere £15.9 million from the trade, although this is three times the money received in 1975–75.

But VAT was a minor annoyance within an incredible boom. The figures tell only part of the story, for Sotheby's had started to lump together its sales in London and New York – a natural response to the disaster in 1970–71 when its sales in London had dropped behind Christie's. At the same time both houses separated the lots actually sold from total 'announced' sales. In the first couple of years the revelations were not that startling: only between 10 and 15 per cent of Christie's total turned out to be Bought-Ins. At Sotheby's the tighter financial controls introduced after the traumas of 1969–70 meant that the following year less than 10 per cent of the lots were unsold.

Not surprisingly, Sotheby's got a bad attack of over-confidence. Its general lavishness was most openly demonstrated by an ingenious development scheme for overcoming its increasingly desperate shortage of space in Bond Street – which the expansion in Belgravia had done little to alleviate. Grandiose plans were drawn up to rebuild the whole complex warren of buildings owned by the firm: during the rebuilding they would be housed in the spacious galleries owned by the Royal Academy (PCW even offered to relieve the Academy's cash shortage by selling some of its treasures). The Academy was confused because Jacob Rothschild pre-empted PCW and presented his own rebuilding plan – a piece of opportunism that led to a terminal row between him and PCW. In the end the Academy declined both offers.

171

Both firms seemed to be diversifying for the sake of it, simply to find somewhere to put their excess profits. Some of the initiatives have lasted. Christie's still sells contemporary prints by mail order. Sotheby's increased the flow of books from its own publishing house. Then as now, this is run by Philip Wilson, PCW's second son. Its financial links with the parent house (and with PCW personally) were always complicated and it is now largely independent, and the purchase of James Bourlet, a firm of packagers, worked out well enough. But most of Sotheby's initiatives were either unimportant or gimmicky. They produced a series of cassettes on Romantic and Classical Art, compèred by Lord Clark, whose BBC Television series *Civilisation* had been an enormous success in the late 1960s. Its insurance venture had found few takers, as did the expensive cultural tours run by Heritage Tours, jointly organized with the ill-fated form of Clarkson's (which went spectacularly bankrupt in 1974).

When Peregrine Pollen returned to Bond Street in 1972 everyone hoped that he would impose some sense into the sprawl. He came back as joint deputy chairman with Lord Westmorland, but very much the heir apparent, without any specific department to run. Unfortunately for Sotheby's, in the next seven years his position grew steadily less secure. He admits to having been arrogant, stand-offish (he was also under a certain amount of personal strain at the time). But his basic problem was PCW: loyal to individual departmental heads, and above all unwilling to admit that there was a successor at all. So Pollen was left with PCW's dirty work to do: it was he who had to break gently to long-serving directors, such as Carmen Gronau, that perhaps it was time for them to retire; he was getting the blame, while PCW retained the power. Possibly he remained too loyal to the firm as a whole: other senior directors had a solid base in their own departments, and, significantly, they all sold their shares at the earliest opportunity. Pollen alone retained most of his massive stake until very late in the day.

Pollen's first task was to try and impose some form of order on the chaos of advances and guarantees that the firm was providing. This was not because of the competition. Peter Chance had set Christie's face firmly against any form of advance, and even their guarantees were guarded, taking the form of carefully drafted letters of comfort to the client's bank rather than outright support. Sotheby's should have been warned by historical experience. As early as 1914 Barlow had been caught by two Italian gentlemen, Signor Avvocato Marcioni and Cavaliere Capitano Lucatelli who brought in a magnificent collection of maiolica. Unfortunately it was so fragmented that it proved to be virtually unsaleable and Sotheby's lost £3,000. They were not alone. In the 1920s the eccentric Cortlandt Bishop advanced $1 million for the Chiesa collection from Milan, a jumble of stuff ranging from ivories, enamels, and, again maiolica, to a great many alleged 'Old Masters'. Unfortunately an eternally suspicious Italian government refused to allow any of the genuine ones out of the country, and Bishop had to support the market when the more dubious ones were sold through his own sale-room, thus, effectively, paying twice over for the lots. In the end he lost most of the money he had invested.

Less historically-minded people could remember how they had lent £55,000 in the late 1960s to the executors of the estate of the late Captain George Pitt-Rivers, whose unequalled family collection of European bronze-age artefacts and African art was mysteriously dissipated after his death. But very little of the collection found its way into the sale-room – where its appearance would have set off a rumpus regarding the export of a part of Britain's national heritage.

Pollen was undeterred; he refined and systematized the ideas he had developed in New York. Sotheby's would guarantee a collection, charging an additional 7.5 per cent for the privilege. If necessary Sotheby's would even buy a collection. Of course rumour had it that the firm was going round with an open cheque book: in fact they were reluctant buyers, even though purchases could be extremely profitable – a classic case was the Renwick collection of arms and armour. But, inevitably, the firm was tempted to set low estimates and reserves on lots in which they had a financial interest through guarantees, advances, or outright ownership, simply in order to reduce the financial burden on what was still not a big firm, a stark contrast with their primary duty, to extract the maximum price for the vendors, their clients.

Sotheby's made matters worse by not acknowledging that they owned the works, and in April 1973 they were forced to admit in their catalogues that they 'might have an interest' in some of the items, although they would not say which, and strongly denied that their ownership conflicted with their role as an independent agent. In financial language, they would say that a 'Chinese Wall' separated the two roles.

The rumbling discontent came to a head with the sales of the pictures originally owned by Jack Dick. He was a rather dubious New England businessman, involved 'in the transport business' – a delicate New England way of hinting that he had business links with the Mafia. He had also bought stock and stud farms and gravitated to an interest in English sporting pictures. Apart from Paul Mellon, there was not an inordinate amount of competition and he soon accumulated a group as good as Mellon's. He was advised by Hugh

173

Hildesley, one of the original trio of English executives sent to New York to help run Parke-Bernet. In advising a major collector, Hildesley, and thus Sotheby's, was usurping one of the dealers' most cherished and profitable functions, thus increasing the trade's hostility when the pictures were sold.

In 1973 Dick was in all sorts of trouble: under indictment for forgery and grand larceny, some of his pictures mortgaged to his creditors, the Internal Revenue Service trying to get its hands on others, and allegations floating around that invoices relating to some of the pictures had been forged (in one case, a painting by R. B. Davis, the value on the invoice had been upgraded from a purchase price of £400 to £60,000). None of this deterred PCW from devising a highly complicated arrangement to sell the pictures. Sotheby's effectively acted as an agent collecting on behalf of the IRS. He advanced $5.6 million to help start the payment process and paid $30,000 a month to Mr Dick himself – and to his widow when Dick died soon after the first sale. The dealers claimed to be worried that the title for the pictures could be challenged by any of the numerous parties involved. Although Sotheby's had not actually bought the Dick collection, the publicity surrounding the sale triggered off questions in Parliament over the ramifications, most notably the foreign exchange costs, involved in Sotheby's purchases and guarantees. By the time of the sale, Sotheby's was forced to issue a convoluted statement that: 'in conjunction with its lawyers in New York and London' the company 'had made extensive enquiries as to the rights of the sellers to offer the Dick collection for sale at auction and as to the sellers' title and interest in the pictures'. They were being offered on behalf of 'Mr and Mrs Jack Dick, the United States Government and other parties having an interest in the collection ... Sotheby & Co is satisfied as to the sellers' rights and warrant that all buyers at the above sale will have good title to their purchases.'

The Dick collection was caught up in the traumas of the oil shock – although the first sale in October 1973 was a triumphant success, the remaining pictures had to be disposed of – often at low prices – during the bad eighteen months that followed. For the oil shock had a curiously delayed and muffled impact on the art market. In the sale-rooms, the 1 October 1973, when the crisis broke, was remarkable for the first time a gramophone had reached over £1,000. (Mark you, it was no ordinary phonograph. It had been 'consigned for sale at Christie's by the late Lord Torphichen, whose elder brother received it as a gift two weeks before going away to prep school. It had been little used' and went for £1,050 ($2,552)). On the same day Geraldine Norman reported that at 'an auction which broke many price records ... an extraordinary and, to my mind, hideous mahog-

174

any cabinet became yesterday the most expensive piece of English nineteenth-century furniture ever sold at auction.' The first sign of trouble was the absence of Japanese buyers at a sale of Chinese wares the next day. 'More than half' the lots were sold, not a good sign. The market, it seemed, was flooded: Sotheby's 'was receiving jade for sale on an unprecedented scale: the publicity attaching to the jade princess at the Chinese exhibition at Burlington House seems to be sending people rummaging to their trinket boxes.'

Nevertheless, much of the market was not affected by the Japanese retreat. On the 5th a Tissot fetched a record £16,800 ($40,824); on the 8th a baton in silver, ivory and malachite once presented to Hermann Goering fetched £2,400 ($5,832), and Howard Ricketts paid £13,500 ($32,800) for an English flint-lock fowling piece – proof that it was sometimes useful for Sotheby's to lose even its brightest people because they were then transformed into its best (albeit most demanding) clients. On the 9th Sotheby's sold a Hausmaler bowl for £6,000 ($14,580), a record for any piece of Viennese porcelain.

But the ground was shifting slightly: on the 16th, while high prices were paid for top-quality netsuke, there was only 'modest competition for middle-quality items.' And the next day came the first major test of the autumn season, when seventeen modern pictures were sold at Parke-Bernet for $2.578 million (£1,060,900) , including a record $720,000 (£292,296) paid for a pink period Picasso. 'The new shape of the art market', reported *The Times*, 'was perhaps indicated by the nationality of the purchasers. Nine went to Switzerland, four to Japan, and four stayed in America ... with the Japanese in muted form and much of the spare cash being channelled to the Middle Eastern War prices were quite strong.'

On the 29th a sale of French porcelain at Christie's 'saw price levels unknown to the London auction room ... Christie's had secured from South Africa a large collection totally unknown to scholars' – how different from the sale of routine paintings at the same sale-room a few days later when the 'bidding on some too-familiar work did not in many instances match the ambitious reserves', although, classically, an exceptional work, a water scene 'of really beautiful quality' by R. M. Kruseman fetched a record price.

On the 30th Christie's showed the value of creative cataloguing. In May 1972 Sotheby's had sold a Russian ikon of Saint Matthew for £1,750 ($4,568). They did not bother with a photograph, referring to it in the catalogue as 'early seventeenth century, North Provincial'. Christie's put the ikon on the cover of its catalogue and went to town with the description. Where Sotheby's had referred to the evangelist 'seated holding a closed book against a classical Byzantine setting',

Christie's claimed he was 'seated at his desk in the act of writing the Gospel' and continued with a long lyrical description, referring to the 'rhythmic colour reflexes' and the like. They got £6,090 ($14,799) for it on the 30th.

So ended the most traumatic month since the end of the Second World War, four weeks which saw another Middle Eastern War, the quadrulpling of oil prices, the resignation of the Vice-President of the United States, the dismissal of the Watergate prosecutor, and the first rumblings of the crisis which was to topple Edward Heath.

The same pattern – in the sale-rooms anyway – continued for the rest of the autumn season. 'The competition for rare pieces was intense' at a sale of English porcelain held on November 14, the day Princess Anne was married to Captain Mark Phillips, 'but some of the minor items could scarcely raise a bid.' And during the month the market for routine items grew steadily softer. But the pattern of the next few years was emerging. On 15 November Sotheby's held its first sale in Hong Kong. It was a sensational success. A Ch'eng Hua blue and white silver dish ('brought in to Sotheby's representative in Hong Kong wrapped in old newspaper with a few other oddments from a family cupboard') fetched £160,000 ($372,800). The two-session sale raised £982,610. ($2,289,481). Among the bigger buyers, it was noted, was Hugh Moss, whose firm, Lampa Investments, backed by Jim Slater, and due to collapse, like the rest of the Slater empire, in the next few months. At the end of November an Iranian private collector living in Paris bought a little ormolu-mounted table with a Sèvres porcelain top for £115,500 ($269,115). 'Love has no price', he said. A new wave of buyers-for-love-and-show was taking over from the investors.

That same month Christie's successfully sold some of its shares on a generally shaky stock-market. The issue was deliberately structured so that the directors firmly retained control. It was typical of Peter Chance. He was coming up to retirement age and wanted to leave a proper management structure. His predecessors had stayed on long after they should. He was determined not to repeat the mistake. The two senior members of the 'Gang of '58', Jo Floyd, the auctioneer and business-getter, was to be chairman, Guy Hannen, the tough businessman, was to be managing director, a partnership Sotheby's never enjoyed. 'I go to see Guy Hannen only when I've got a problem', says one departmental head. 'He cuts through the crap and tells me the truth, even if it's sometimes unwelcome.' The partnership, and the quotation, provided Christie's with an essential internal discipline during the hard years that followed: they simply had to analyse their business and ensure that they were not pursuing prestige at the expense of profit. The issue was ten times over-subscribed, the shares opening 9.5p above the issue price of 70p – the last success before the London market completely lost its head in the face of the oil shock and the miners' strike, which eventually brought down the Heath government.

When the stock-market caught pneumonia, the art market merely caught a belated cold, albeit a bad one. Where financial confidence had collapsed in October 1973, not to recover for a couple of years, the art market was affected for only a relatively brief period. 'From a dealer's point of view,' says Julian Agnew, 'the market simply ground to a halt in '74–'75.' The figures support his contention: average prices fell by a mere 15 per cent in the traumatic two years after September 1973, and were still over a tenth above their level of September 1972; they had lost only the extra gloss given by the hyper-boom year of 1972–73. Unlike the owners of stocks, shares and property, buyers of art generally had no need to liquidate their holdings. The market simply froze, as it had done in face of worse disasters like the Slump. So the two houses' turnover dropped, but not too drastically: Sotheby's sales in 1974–75, £75 million, although £15 million below the previous year's record, were still marginally above those for 1972–73; Christie's suffered a similarly-sized fall, from £44.3 to £33.7 million.

But there was one exception, the market in Oriental porcelain. The market had been so run up by speculative City buying combined with Oriental enthusiasm that it was vulnerable. But it was an apparently irrelevant event, the Portuguese revolution of April 1974, which burst the bubble. All through the previous winter prices of Chinese ceramics had soared, and in every sale the name of one London dealer, Mrs Glatz, was prominent. That revolutionary month all records were broken at a ceramic sale. An early Ming bottle decorated with a single dragon went for £420,000 ($1,008,000), two other lots fetched £160,000 ($382,400) and £170,000 ($406,300), a Ch'ing famille rose bowl went for £95,000 ($227,050), all going to Mrs Glatz. She was not bidding for herself but for a Portuguese buyer, Manoel Ricardo Spirito Santo. He was the nephew of Ricardo Spirito Santo, a leading banker who had formed a highly important collection of Chinese porcelain. The nephew was naturally tempted to outdo his uncle (although his purchases were of a different type and period). After the revolution he simply could not remit funds abroad, although the family's bank was not nationalized for a year and the family had enough assets abroad to emerge controlling banks in Brazil and Florida. But Sotheby's had to put many of his purchases back on sale in their July auction when prices dropped dramatically. This was only the start of the panic. Average prices of Chinese ceramics, which (even allowing for inflation) had quadrupled in the three years to September 1973, dropped by a mere 40 per cent in the following year (because they had been so run up in the first six months of the season), before plummeting from 277 to 100 in the Sotheby Index in the following year.

Even before the slump PCW appeared to have lost his nerve when he resurrected that old chestnut, merger with Christie's. So he approached Earl Jellicoe, whose daughter Alexandra had married Philip Wilson in 1970. 'George Jellicoe' had been a well-regarded Minister in the Heath administration until he lost his job in the wake of the sex scandal involving Lord Lambton. Although he went onto the Sotheby's board after his resignation he took care never to get too close to PCW, whom he regarded charily, albeit with enormous amusement. But PCW dropped the proposal when Jellicoe refused a tentative offer to be chairman of a proposed joint holding company (PCW was possibly already looking for a means of cashing his shares, which he could do through merger with a quoted company like Christie's).

PCW compounded Sotheby's problems by a typically impetuous gesture. In April 1974 he bought Mak van Waay, the biggest auctioneers in the Low Countries. In theory the purchase was a major coup. In fact he exceeded his instructions from the board, paid too much, and, worse, did not realize that the vendor kept not only the premises, but also the rights to two of the best future sales as well. By that time Sotheby's extravagances – and the porcelain crisis – had taken their toll of the balance sheet. Debtors had jumped from a mere £1.6 million at the end of September 1972 to £3.8 million a year later, and a terrifying £7.5 million in September 1974.

During the same two years advances had doubled to over £2.2 million. But by that time Pollen's short-lived experiment was being wound up. In July 1974 Sotheby's agreed to indicate with a G the items where they had provided guarantees, and property they owned was to be sold either as their own or as 'property from the estate of John Smith sold by order of Sotheby Parke Bernet'. This was rather shutting the stable door after the horse had decided that straying wasn't such a good thing after all. Despite pressure from New York they were not prepared to reveal reserves. But Sotheby's promised not to put reserves up at the last minute – they would not exceed estimates available twenty-four hours before the sale.

The most important changes were organizational. Marcus Linell was brought in from Belgravia to liaise between the management and the experts. He had a delicate job. PCW instinctively sided with the experts, but they soon had a new enemy, Peter Spira, the financial director appointed that summer. So Linell's job became one of the most 'political' in what was becoming a highly politicized institution.

The man chosen to save Sotheby's from its financial and administrative tangle was an improbable one, a merchant banker with no apparent interest in art. Peter Spira, the small bouncy workaholic son of an unorthodox gastro-enterologist, Jacques Spira, had been educated at Eton and Cambridge, qualified as a chartered accountant, and had been one of the small band of bright young disciples of Sir Sigmund Warburg, who made S. G. Warburg into the single most important new banking star in the post-war City of London. But by 1974 Spira had given up the hope of becoming chairman after two decades of overwork, which had already cost him one marriage, so he was looking for new fields to conquer; nevertheless Earl Jellicoe, a fellow-director of both bank and auction house, was surprised that someone so senior should have approached him. PCW himself was only too happy to take on someone with Spira's reputation.

Spira himself 'never realized what a bad shape Sotheby's was in. It was never going to make the £5 million profits they had forecast'. Initially he endeared himself to PCW: three days after his arrival he retrieved a crucial letter which enabled Sotheby's to escape from an embarrasing guarantee. But within a few months relations between 'Big Peter and Little Peter' had deteriorated to the point where, says Spira, 'I felt like Thomas à Becket, with PCW going round saying who will rid me of this turbulent priest?'

Their initial break came over a sensational guarantee PCW had given: that the vendor could be sure of getting his money in dollars at the then-prevailing rate of $2.40 to £1 at any time in the three years after the sale. Spira's natural reaction was to clamp down on any such speculation in a firm as exposed to currency fluctuations as Sotheby's. But PCW would have a different reaction. He remembered how in the 1930s, when currencies were also fluctuating 'any delayed settlement after an auction sale could mean an unknown loss to the vendor, who therefore made every effort to avoid the saleroom'. The two were bound to conflict. Spira was a banker, looking first last and all the time at the figures, PCW was concerned only with the next sale, confident that he could save the day by pulling yet another rabbit out of the hat – unluckily for him there were few major sales during the mid-1970s.

The two naturally formed factions. At a board meeting eighteen months after his arrival, Spira announced that he was ready to become managing director. Derek Johns, always one of PCW's most loyal supporters, was heard to mutter, 'That's the most depressing thing I've ever heard.' But PCW knew how crucial Spira was: he may have been the man his supporters loved to hate, but the disciplines he imposed enabled the company to be floated on the stock market a mere three years after he arrived.

179

Nevertheless, Spira's first season was described by Frank Herrmann as: 'The most dramatic for generations. It seemed to start reasonably well in the early autumn; then went into a short decline reminiscent of the worst pre-war doldrums on either side of Christmas' – a period when the London stock market collapsed completely to levels not seen since before the war – 'it staged a slow recovery in the spring and bounced back to near record-breaking form in June and July 1975. In the crucial autumn three months of 1974 Sotheby's sales were down by a third to £27.4 million. Christie's suffered less, its sales were down by £3.75 million to £16.5 million. Departmental figures showed that paintings were badly hit, as was Oriental porcelain, naturally enough: jewellery, that traditional refuge, was stable, and such marginal departments as coins and arms and armour healthy, as, of course, were sales of wine as the trade unloaded. Sotheby's tried to conceal the fall, mentioning the sale of a Dubuffet for £145,300 in a Parke-Bernet sale which totalled £980,000. 'They do not mention', wrote Geraldine Norman, 'that the gross total of the sale, including unsold lots, was £2.045 million. Failure to sell more than half the goods on offer is not exactly a bull point.'

(Frank Herrmann pointed out that a number of lots unsold at the beginning of the sale included some pretty familiar Impressionist pictures. Their owners, clearly speculating on a continuing rise in prices, were having to offload pictures they had acquired relatively recently, thus breaking 'the old rule that five to ten years is a minimum level of safety'. Herrmann added that, if the quality was right, such pictures often subsequently proved to be bargains.)

The slump was relatively short-lived. Even the Chinese ceramic crisis lasted only a year. In late March 1975 Sotheby's offered a major collection assembled by Alfred Clark, a former chairman of the record company, His Master's Voice. Thanks to buying from the Far East, £442,700 ($1,071,334) was paid for 145 pieces with only six minor items unsold. The pattern was confirmed in a major sale in early July when the 192 lots fetched £681,000, ($1,491,390), with only 7 per cent bought in (the highest price was £100,000 ($230,000) for a Ming blue and white bowl sold for a mere £32 in the Eumorfopoulos sale during the dark days of Dunkirk).

But the recovery came too late to save the twenty-six junior staff sacked by Sotheby's and the twenty-five junior staff (and six porters) dismissed by Christie's that winter. Christie's successfully reassured the City by cutting costs by a quarter. Within the firm, however, there was something approaching panic, which led to the epoch-making decision in April 1975 to impose a buyers' premium of 10 per cent on every lot it sold. For Christie's relied on sales in Switzerland for over a fifth of its total turnover, and its European rivals were using their more flexible premium system to attract clients. They all charged the buyer 10 per cent, and, relying on this solid base, could shave margins to major vendors to the bone. Christie's couldn't persuade Continental vendors to sell in London, they were too worried about the state of sterling, so they had no alternative but to copy their rivals.

Although the Christie's board did not officially discuss the premium with their rivals the debate within Christie's was well-enough known. Sotheby's were not, of course, under the same pressure because their major overseas sales were centred on New York, where there was no buyers' premium. Although American buyers were regaining their confidence Sotheby's had to follow Christie's lead – they simply couldn't afford to do without the same weapons as their rivals.

On the Friday before the announcement Jo Floyd told Sotheby's and Phillips that his firm was going to impose the premium on the Monday. Christie's softened the blow to the dealers by increasing the commission paid when they introduced lots. Traditionally it had been a fifth of the commission received by the auction house – 2 per cent or less. This was doubled to 4 per cent. PCW was furious: he knew that the dealers would take it out on him, convinced that the premium was merely another invasion of their territory on his way to world domination. They both knew that the real threat was to the dealers' relationships with private buyers, for whom they bid on a commission basis, a cosy and relatively undemanding slice of their incomes: and private buyers were unlikely to countenance two 10 per cent premiums, one for the bidder and another for the auction house. PCW tried to soften the blow by providing buyers with a five-year guarantee of authenticity. But nothing was going to dampen the dealers' anger. 'The last straw', says Julian Agnew. 'It was so arrogant, we felt it was sprung on the trade. To us it was more a matter of their getting things for sale by offering to sell without any commission. It gave them the advantage of the concealed percentage, the basic, irreducible 10 per cent.'* Privately, PCW was convinced that he could have soothed the dealers by talking to them in advance if Christie's had not presented them with a brutal *fait accompli*.

The premium – together with an announcement that Christie's was to abandon the use of the guinea – was announced in June, to

---

* Three years later the tax authorities added insult to injury by ruling that the buyers had to pay VAT on the premium.

take effect from the start of the next auction season.* The London dealers attempted direct action: at the first silver sale at Sotheby's a group of them walked out just as Richard Came had reached lot 50 (a pair of George II sugar nips). At Belgravia the auctioneer was asked whether he would accept bids without the premium. He wouldn't. The dealers walked out again, as they did at a book sale conducted by Lord John Kerr. Unfortunately individual greed sabotaged the gesture. They simply couldn't bear the idea of all those lots going cheap, or, even worse, to foreign competitors not involved in the argument, so enough bids were left with the house or with runners for the sales to fetch reasonable sums.

At Phillips, Christopher Weston took a deep breath and didn't follow suit – but then it was easier for him, he didn't really face any competition from the Continent, his overheads were markedly lower, and his controls were tighter. His debtors' ledger, for instance, was run by a former bookie's settler 'who could sniff out trouble at a hundred yards'. Whereas Christie's reckoned it needed £17 commission a lot to cover its overheads, he needed only £5.50. (His premium structure was always rather different. It had been 12.5 per cent, with a fifth off for larger consignments.) He was forced to stay competitive and cut his basic premium to 10 per cent, while retaining the discount for large lots. He reckoned, rightly, that the goodwill he would gain by not imposing the buyers' premium would compensate for the tight margins. It did. In the season before he fell into line his sales rose disproportionately.

The dealers soon abandoned their boycott, but had created enough waves for the possible collusion to be referred to the Prices Commission under a former taxman, Sir Arthur Cockfield. In New York the dealers went one further. They had helped finance their London colleagues in their fight against the auction houses, but were also involved in a local attempt to legislate against secret reserves. Colin helped persuade the New York State Department of Consumer Affairs to put forward a bill outlawing them as a restraint of trade. Martin Stansfeld, Stanley Clark's partner in New York, organized a lobby at the state capital, Albany. The final blow was delivered by John Marion. He wrote to thousands of Parke-Bernet's well-connected clients. The hapless consumerists were soon deluged with an unprecedented barrage of letters and abandoned their investigations. But they were always ready to renew their attacks, and in July 1985 they latched on to the hapless David Bathurst of

* The natural time of year to announce any changes in commissions because the auction houses had already accepted and priced virtually all the goods they were going to sell that season.

Christie's following the revelations that he had given false information about an Impressionist sale four years earlier (see page 235).

In Britain the investigations rumbled on, but business recovered so fast that the dealers' did not suffer too badly. In retrospect the buyers' premium can be traced back to Christie's share issue and the subsequent need to protect its margins. If Christie's had been a private company it could probably have waited for increased sales to compensate for reduced margins. Indeed, the directors now admit that 'a year later we wouldn't have had to do it'. The lessons – that slumps in the market are temporary, and that a stock-market quotation brings its own disciplines were, however, ignored by the directors of Sotheby's.

# 2   OUT OF CONTROL

Judging by the figures, the couple of years after the crisis were triumphant: by 1975–76 the Sotheby Group's sales were 10 per cent above the record £90 million achieved before the slump, and they increased a further 20 per cent the following year. In percentage terms, Christie's moved even faster, with sales of £73 million in 1976–77. But the figures, as always, do not tell the whole story. Within Sotheby's there was perpetual politicking – 'they were all empire-building to show they were worthy successors to PCW', says one former director. He encouraged them, using what Souren Melikian of the *International Herald Tribune* describes as his: 'natural inclination to steer people where he wanted them and to build up precarious pyramids of power easily controlled ... he was not so much a leader, adept at organizing teamwork as a grand master in the human chess game. People were deemed adequate in a given position rather than in absolute terms. He enjoyed the strategy as much as the poker game of the auction world.'

Peregrine Pollen suffered worst from the unhealthy atmosphere. 'He was the messenger bringing the bad tidings of what had to be done, and that helped PCW pull the rug from under his feet', says one sympathetic insider. 'The contracts with clients, all the departmental business, the relationship with the banks. Peregrine was too proud to duck.' He was also aloof, spending a lot of time in his office, away from the tougher departmental heads who would have been his natural allies. Everyone else kept their heads down. Julian Thompson, the ceramics expert, was best placed, away for four months each year running the increasingly successful Hong Kong sale-room.

Even without the desire to embarrass the natural heir, PCW was not involved in administration, and operated on a 'divide and rule' basis when dealing with his directors, for decisions had never been made at Board meetings. 'He was weak, not devious', says a close associate, 'he hated telling anyone anything that would offend. But he still had tremendous authority. People would still do what he so much as suggested.' His diabetes grew steadily worse during the 1970s and although it was kept firmly under control through regular injections, part of the game of office politics meant avoiding him when he was tired and irritable just before the next injection was due. (He also needed food regularly. Friends recall the efforts made to find something for him to eat in the early evening in countries like Iran or Greece where the evening meal was going to be delayed).

PCW had always been an early riser and hard worker, habitually phoning his colleagues at any time between 7.00 am and 2.00 am. As he grew older the strain increased. The bleakness of his office was matched by that of the small impersonal company flat he occupied in Mayfair. This was merely a refuge for a quick nap between coming in from the office and going out to dinner, and for a few hours' sleep. His only respites during the sales season were a few weekends when protective lady friends whisked him off for a complete rest. But he was increasingly restless, 'he needed something to amuse him every five minutes', said one associate.

In the office the Byzantine atmosphere created appalling problems for Katherine Maclean, his long-serving, even longer-suffering personal assistant. She was inevitably protective towards PCW and many directors felt that she prevented the tellers-of-home-truths from getting through to him. But this may have been simply because he had so many calls on his time – most of the afternoons were spent with the many clients who would talk only to him. A devout Catholic, she had her own emotional problems at the time. Her worries were no concern of PCW: he grew increasingly irritable and her colleagues were sympathetically appalled at her evident misery. Eventually she moved to take charge of liaison with the Monte Carlo office.

The strained relationship with Katherine Maclean symbolized PCW's unnatural position. Despite its growth, Sotheby's was still small enough to be run by one man, if that man had been interested in running a business. PCW wasn't and yet he wanted total control. 'He had the art market in his head, and he thought it was a business that could be played only by ear . . . he was always so involved in the next sale', remembers one director. So the quarrelling intensified, and, with no one exercising any real discipline, the numbers of employees jumped: they had risen by only a couple of hundred in the decade until 1976. But the staff in London nearly doubled in the next couple of years. Yet, because they were so badly organized 'they were always more over-stretched than we were', says a Christie's director, 'throughout the 1970s our profitability was greater. We had one person, they had three or four doing the same job, it was counterproductive. They were all over-promoted.' (In 1975–76 Christie's profits were a tenth more than its rivals, even though its sales were less than two-thirds Sotheby's. To be fair to the bigger house, it did depend greatly on sales in New York, where the buyers' premium had not yet been introduced.)

The departmental heads had to cope with growing sales and improve their instant mental arithmetic when negotiating with the dealers, increasingly anxious to squeeze Sotheby's commissions. Outsiders were more severe on the apparent slackening in the standards: 'It was the Nescafé era, instant expertise' was one typical summary. Earlier in the decade Robert Wraight had provided a more judicious summing-up: 'their expertise is less valuable than it was in the days when a few scholars came and a few clever dealers. They have a mass of stuff, they can't possibly vet it all.' They even abandoned the informal no-poaching agreement that had formerly operated between Sotheby's, Christie's and Phillips. 'In the mid '70s, they were so desperate for people who could run a department that they were offering my people the earth', says Christopher Weston, 'they tried to use us as a training ground.' Even so salaries could not keep up with inflation, and departmental heads who found themselves earning less than £20,000 after twenty years service suddenly realized they were underpaid, which didn't help morale.

They had to run hard just to keep up with the increasing flow. 'By the 1970s it was so big it didn't depend on individuals', says Howard Ricketts, 'they were getting the collections relying simply on the name.' But the aggressive attitude did not let up. An 'intelligence department' was created, with eight people under a director, George Hughes Hartman, for the fuller exploitation of 'coffin power'. Lines were established into nursing homes so that Sotheby's could have an early indication of potentially valuable estates. More attempts were made to insert the telling phrase 'In the event of my death I want Messrs Sotheby's to dispose . . .' into wills. The aggression went too far for many clients. 'The Sotheby's system of consistent bombardment of people with things to sell was a bit counter-productive', says Julian Agnew, 'only a relatively low percentage was sold, there was a complete abdication of responsibility. The sense of aggression meant that we got people on the rebound, asking us, "How do I sell this?"'

Sotheby's aggressiveness was crucial, however, in finding new markets, in the Far East, with the oil-rich Iranians and, nearer home, in Monte Carlo. The new buyers from the oil-rich Middle East were often grateful for the auction rooms, which provided a check on dealers' prices. The biggest collection of silver in the decade was assembled by Mehdi Tajir, a billionaire, close adviser of the Sultan of Dubai, and for a long time the Ambassador in Britain of the United Arab Emirates. He bought massive quantities – three or four complete ladies dressing-room toilet sets, one for each of his country houses, for example, and impressive quantities of the works of such luminaries as Lamerie and Storr. He relied largely on a single dealer, Jack Coupman, but insisted that his prices be validated by those achieved in the sale-rooms.

The Iranians, too, divided their loyalties between dealers and the sale-rooms. In January 1975 the Alexander Gallery was opened in Belgravia. Financed by Iranians, it was set up to buy and ship the land- and seascapes, flower pieces and 'decorative' nineteenth-century French furniture on which they were so keen – for the buyers were old-fashioned, they were looking for objects with which to decorate their homes. Like the Orientals they were also buying back their own national treasures. These had fallen out of fashion in the West. Before 1914 enlightened capitalists like Charles Freer has pushed prices up, and in the 1927–28 season three sixteenth-century carpets had fetched over £20,000 apiece. But by 1961 Reitlinger could say dismissively that Islamic Art was 'little heard of'.

PCW was determined to change all that. With David Westmorland and Lord Jellicoe he went out on an unsuccessful flying visit to Tehran. Then his personal assistant, Jeremy Cooper, tried a different tack. He approached the Iranian subscribers to Sotheby's catalogues, mostly carpet dealers who had never previously dreamed of coming to London. But he enticed them over with specialized sales – culminating in 'Islamic weeks'. He even infiltrated the court of the Shahbanou. As soon as Cooper had shown the way, PCW was out again in a flash, virtually commandeering the private jet owned by the sugar firm, Tate & Lyle, of which Jellicoe was chairman at the time.

He was much less involved in the single most successful new venture undertaken in the 1970s, the partnership with Lane Crawford, Hong Kong's equivalent to Harrods. The venture was the baby of Julian Thompson, one of Kiddell's protégés, who had joined Sotheby's straight from Cambridge in 1963. He had emerged as an outstanding expert on Oriental porcelain, almost as respected as his master – and, like Kiddell, he took care to stay close to the dealers. The firm had done other deals with department stores – notably in Canada and Japan – but these had not created any major, new auction centres. In Hong Kong the first sale in the dark days of 1974 resulted in others, leading to a formal joint venture in January 1977. Lane Crawford even took up 100,000 shares in the parent group.

The tens of thousands of Chinese families which had fled to Hong Kong since the Communist take-over in 1949 had mostly brought with them their precious porcelain. Twenty-five years later the children of these immigrants had grown wealthy and confident, willing to sell some of the parents' belongings, but had not lost their taste for their national treasures. They naturally welcomed the chance to buy back the mass of material bought cheap by Europeans in earlier centuries. The prices, however staggering, still did not seem ridiculous in comparison with the sums paid before 1914, when Pierpont Morgan had contrived to spend £2 million (then $10 million) on porcelain. Before 1914, in Reitlinger's words: 'Chinese porcelain in the most lavish eighteenth-century taste, such as *famille jaune* and *famille noire*, could make prices which approached £200,000 for a single vase in terms of today's money' – and he was writing in 1961, before inflation had more than doubled prices.

Hong Kong became a self-contained market, the first and only new auction-room centre created by Sotheby's. The locals had a free run because the London-based speculators had been eliminated by the financial crash of 1973–74, and the Japanese, for reasons of prestige, preferred to deal in London (which is why neither Sotheby's, nor Christie's, nor Spink's has ever managed to establish the same sort of permanent presence in partnership with department stores in Tokyo as Thompson did in Hong Kong). Thompson made his name with two regularly profitable weeks of sales a year, specializing in Ch'ing and Ming imperial porcelain.

Nearest PCW's heart was another successful new venture, the sale-room in Monte Carlo. Early in 1975 he was at last offered the opportunity to crack the single biggest gap in the Sotheby's network: its inability to tap the rich French market directly because of the monopoly enjoyed by France's state-controlled auctioneers. On the commuter train from Henley Stanley Clark had come across Prince Rainier's personal representative in Britain, who mentioned that His Highness was anxious for the Société des Bains de Mer to include regular sales as part of its attractions. PCW immediately seized on the hint, for Monaco was the only chink in the French defences against alien auctioneers. Moreover, in Souren Melikian's words, PCW 'had sensed what all experienced observers had questioned – the readiness of the very rich to have a flutter with the art game in their favourite gambling setting'.

The first sale in late May 1975 was a double landmark: it marked the end of the recession in the art market, and it established Sotheby's on the Riviera – PCW's natural habitat. The sale itself resulted from a complicated move of houses involving Baron Guy de Rothschild, the Chilean millionaire Arturo Lopez Wilshaw (Sotheby's had already sold his magnificent collection of Renaissance jewellery) and his great and good friend, the Baron de Redé. The French government blocked the sale of a number of items, including a suite of furniture made for Versailles, but this was only a minor blemish.

Monte Carlo, like Hong Kong, opened up a new, specialized and largely self-contained market. The sales in Monte Carlo were a throw-back to the years before 1914, reflecting the whims of the rich rather than the investment needs of the dealing and financial communities. Not surprisingly, the biggest percentage of fine items was of French furniture, which brought in some extraordinary new clients. The weirdest surfaced with the sale late in 1977 of the magnificent collection of furniture assembled by the Wildenstein family, not in Paris, but in their New York mansion in East 64th Street. The collection was sold privately just before the auction to an anonymous buyer who turned out to be a Saudi businessman, Akram Ojieh. He intended to use the SS *France*, the world's biggest passenger liner, which he had bought to act as a floating museum of French culture, only to discover that the salty sea air would ruin the furniture. Two years later it emerged into the daylight at a Monte Carlo sale, where, for the first time, allowing for inflation, French eighteenth-century furniture fetched more than it had just before and after the First World War.

The Monte Carlo operation was vintage PCW. He could conduct a few glamorous sales every year, and make some money on the side when the company needed proper offices. It also fitted in with his plans for retirement. With money provided by Robinow's first 'share strip' he had bought Clavary, a small château on the Riviera. Before the war it had been the home of a couple of rich American homosexuals, but had lain neglected for twenty years and was going cheap because the village garbage dump was at the edge of the park. This was moved but was replaced by a cemetery, a hospital – and a sewage works.

Nevertheless, the setting was magnificent and Clavary became the only real home PCW ever had, allowing him to exploit to the full his love of decoration and above all landscaping and gardening. He furnished it in his typical eclectic style, and kept there his special pride and joy, a collection of Renaissance bronzes, which he showed to only a handful of people (even when he did they tended to be wrapped in old newspapers). From the beginning he spent a long summer holiday there, although he could never keep away from the telephone for more than a couple of days even in mid-summer.

After the Monte Carlo partnership was established he started to shift towards Clavary as a permanent home. In 1976 he sold his country house in Kent, and spent most of his weekends at Leeds Castle, a magical medieval house in the same county. Earlier in the decade he had become a Trustee of the Foundation set up to run the castle after her death by Lady Baillie. She was one of the many older women enchanted by PCW and on whom he relied for physical and moral comfort. In his ten years as a trustee he exercised to the full his flair for decoration: he supervized the decoration of the Royal

Chapel, which dated from the thirteenth century, helped arrange the medieval furniture (some of it loaned by the trustees of the Burrell collection, so much of it bought through his old mentors, the Hunts), and, typically, urged his fellow-trustees to find ways of increasing the income from the house and its gardens. He forged a close partnership with the late Lord Geoffrey-Lloyd, the former Tory cabinet minister who was chairman of the trustees. But PCW was not being totally altruistic: as trustee of a charitable foundation he could escape from the restrictions that prevented Englishmen resident abroad from spending more than a few days each year in Britain without sacrificing their exemption from British taxes. In the mid-1970s his colleagues noticed his frequent absences abroad, but not the elaborate preparations he was making for his own retirement.

PCW's increased restlessness produced a rash of new ventures. Perhaps the most glamorous was an unsuccessful investment in a firm selling Irish bloodstock, a field in which Sotheby's had no specialist knowledge whatsoever. It lost money for a couple of years and was then resold to the same people who had sold it to Sotheby's in the first place.

The most successful diversification was into the house agency business. American clients – or, more often, their heirs or executors – usually sold houses at the same time as their contents. The contrast in prices became painfully apparent with the most glamorous sale of the mid-1970s, the disposal of over $7 million worth of pictures and furniture from the estate of Mrs Geraldine Marcellus Hartley Dodge. She was the niece of John D. Rockefeller and widow of the former chairman of Remington, who had inherited $50 million from his grandfather. Mrs Dodge had lived mostly at Giralda, her luxurious country estate at Madison, New Jersey, but, until she died, kept New York's biggest town house at the corner of Fifth Avenue and 64th Street. The mansion was built in 1922 on the site of ten brownstone houses, and was occupied only when Mrs Dodge came to New York for her weekly shopping expedition. John Marion was furious to discover that the house fetched far more than the contents and determined to get into the act. Hence the grandiosely named Sotheby Parke Bernet International Realty Corporation. The firm sensibly concentrated on 'dream homes at high prices'.

The idea of selling homes and contents together was by no means a new one: in Britain estate agents had fulfilled the dual role for centuries. This natural business diversification was an immediate success. Soon Marion could boast that he had fifty properties on his books and had sold ten properties – which had brought $4 million of fine art with them. Far more marginal was the joint venture with Algernon Asprey and a Saudi prince, Sheikh Abdulaziz Abdallah

190

al-Sulaiman, into the 'design building decorating and furnishing of private houses, art galleries, government institutions and museums'. This soon joined the trail of other amusing marginal ventures.

But there was another way to increase business, to open more ordinary sale-rooms. Sotheby's already had Belgravia and in New York 'PB 84' for cheaper lots, but it was Christie's which really scooped the pool. In 1975 it took over the long-established firm of Debenham and Coe and turned their premises in South Kensington into a sale-room specializing in cheaper lots. The directors were extremely worried that vendors would feel snubbed when relegated to the second division, the bargain basement. They weren't. To their surprise and relief they discovered a new market, one largely untapped even by Sotheby's at Belgravia. Like their rivals they could now offer a speedy service and handle even the bulkiest furniture. In its first year 'Christie's South Ken' achieved a turnover greater than Belgravia, established four years earlier (in 1983–84 its sales totalled £24 million). They even developed their own specialities: their costume specialist, Susie Mayor, is the acknowledged authority in the field (she once spotted a seventeenth-century embroidered cap bought for £10 at a car boot sale which eventually fetched £2,700); and South Ken has been the single most systematic seller of old photographs – relying partly on regular sales from a massive collection of photographs by the Victorian, Roger Fenton.

But both rivals were now aggressively looking for new customers. Parke-Bernet had shown the way with its Heirloom Weeks. These had started accidentally as a way of finding material to fill the gap in the auction schedules one bleak February. No one was doing any catalogues so they dreamt up the idea of 'Heirloom' Weeks, the name carefully chosen to discourage people from bringing in recent purchases, or new artefacts, or simply wanting a free appraisal. The first was written up in *The New York Times*, and queues of hopefuls formed around the block.

During Heirloom Weeks the experts 'were doing the same thing they normally did every day', says John Marion. More daring was to go out onto the road. Parke-Bernet added respectability to their sallies out of town by arranging joint occasions with museums, who would charge up to $20 for the first day's opportunity to meet the experts. Marion reckons: 'We were able to take a lot of the mystery out of auctioneering . . . but the collectors were already there.' But long, tiring trips to far-away places were never popular with the experts, and the system was never properly developed although the firm's customer base widened significantly during the 1970s.

But Britain is much smaller and the Big Two could aspire to national coverage. In 1975 Christie's sent a single expert to Hereford

191

(a county town in rich farming country 150 miles west of London). He was to give valuations and advice to anyone who came along to the estate agents Knight, Frank & Rutley. 'An hour after he set up shop, he was phoning South Ken for reinforcements', wrote Antony Thorncroft. 'The first antiques roadshow was proving an embarrassing success.' Two years later the BBC filmed a road show – at the smaller town of Tavistock – and launched another popular television programme, reinforcing the belief that everyone has an unconsidered fortune in their attic. Soon Sotheby's had its own roadshows, and Phillips its sober 'valuation days'. They were, basically, public relations exercises, with the fees going to charity and the houses not reckoning to make much profit – although they invariably produced a crop of surprise discoveries: the £14,000 violin wrapped in a pair of Edwardian bloomers, the Ming vase used as a dog bowl, the medieval diamond-pointed silver spoon found in the thatch of a Devon cottage.

But there was another way of getting out of London, by colonization. In the mid-70s Sotheby's moved, on a scale unmatched by any of its rivals, into the provinces to form 'loose trading arrangements' and then to take over local auctioneers in rich country towns like Torquay, Taunton and Chester. The moves, master-minded by the hapless Pollen, were far too costly and ambitious. Sotheby's had to pay enormous prices for the firms – three times the real value for King and Chasemore of Pulborough according to one well-placed observer. The moves were relatively small but absorbed a disproportionate amount of management time – especially the former Beresford Adams in Chester, whose losses became yet another internal political football.

The dealing fraternity inevitably saw the takeovers as yet another step towards the 'absolute domination' which they feared Peregrine Pollen was master-minding for PCW. They were also a sign of desperation, since the best items usually ended up in London anyway, although previously they had usually passed through the sticky fingers of the country furniture dealers, who were naturally alienated. 'It also increased the scope for mistakes and they didn't get a high enough percentage of the cream', says Julian Agnew.

Christie's and Phillips were altogether more cautious. Christie's took over only one sale-room outside London, Edmiston's of Glasgow. And in London they paid only £750,000 for the stamp auctioneers, Robson Lowe, whose profits that year – 1980 – were just over £200,000. Philips had owned the coin auctioneers, Glendining's, for some time but allowed it to operate independently, and its country activities were altogether more business-like.

These were peripheral battles. For a decade or more there had been sporadic rumours that Christie's was about to take over one of New York's second-line auction houses, but despite occasional talks Christie's preferred to wait until they could go it alone. In the meantime Christie's ran a small office in the ballroom of one of the few remaining town houses in New York, the Rhinelander-Waldo mansion. Jeremy Cooper remembers how the 'office succeeded in maintaining an overwhelming period quality and invariably looked as though Noël Coward was expected to tea at any moment, the atmosphere stylishly enervated. On Fridays the time difference meant that contact with London was unlikely after one o'clock and the office was then regularly transformed into an enormous luncheon party.' All this was to change when Christie's finally opened its New York sale-room in May 1977.

Typically, Christie's invaded New York only when they had the necessary resources in money and people. Their timing was superb. 'It was incredibly cheap to start up in New York in 1976', say the directors. The Big Apple was feeling particularly unloved at the time, so even Mayor Beame, anxious for some sign of affection, welcomed the newcomers (a decided contrast to the antagonism which had greeted Sotheby's thirteen years earlier). They were lucky, too, in acquiring a site bang in mid-town Manhattan, the old Delmonico's Ballroom (it was spare because the rest of the building was being transformed from a hotel to a block of apartments).

They sent over a group of keen young men anxious to make their name, together with Anthony du Boulay who had started Geneva so successfully. 'He was supposed to be a sort of father figure', says one of the pioneers, 'shepherding us, showing us how a new auction room worked.' They had to be prepared for a world in which the private collector, encouraged by Parke-Bernet, still made much of the running (even though the New York dealers were by far their single biggest block of customers).

They could not avoid one basic row: to secure their margins they had decided to bring the buyers' premium with them. Ralph Colin thundered that it was an outrage, 'an unjustified charge on someone for whom you are not performing a service'. John Marion naturally joined in, declaring it 'as welcome to 1970s America as the Stamp Act was to 1770s America', and made a public pledge that Parke-Bernet wouldn't follow suit. He held out for eighteen months, succumbing only ('over PCW's dead body') to Peter Spira's insistence.

Christie's first sale on 17 May was something of an anti-climax, in spite of the fact that they had assembled lots of Impressionists and the sale-room was packed, with people standing round the walls. Although they fetched $4.172 million (£2.458 million), twenty-seven pictures out of the sixty lots were withdrawn – and a Renoir, *Baigneuse Couchée*, went for a mere $660,000 (£383,720), against an estimate of between $750,000 and $1 million. Martin Stansfeld had mounted a 'spoiling' publicity campaign which culminated on the afternoon of the sale when he announced that Sotheby's was opening an office in Saudi Arabia.

Christie's unpromising debut lulled Parke-Bernet into an unjustified sense of security. But it also helped ensure the success of Sotheby's share issue a month later. Unlike Christie's, Sotheby's made no provision for special voting shares. The timing was lucky, the terms generous, the yield 1 per cent better than Christie's. The issue, of 3.85m shares at 150p represented just over a third of the capital and priced the whole firm at a relatively modest £16.35 million. The major motive was clearly to enable the existing shareholders to cash in, not to raise new finance – RIT were selling half their holding. Even including the 100,000 shares being issued to its Hong Kong associates Lane Crawford, the issue brought in only just over a million, £100,000 to add to working capital in the US, and £750,000 for improvements to the Bond Street warren. Eighteen months later £400,000 went to buy the Aeolian Hall, the former BBC studios opposite the offices.

The issue was as successful as Christie's four years earlier – the two neatly framed the great London stock-market slump, Christie's was the last before the deluge, Sotheby's one of the first after the floods had subsided – and it marked a crucial turning-point. PCW could now bail out at any time he chose and Christie's opening in New York removed the one unique advantage that had kept Sotheby's ahead – for they had been slugging it out more or less equally outside the United States in the previous few years. But before Sotheby's felt the full impact of Christie's invasion of New York two earlier time bombs had exploded. Both eruptions covered Sotheby's with money, neither with much glory. The sale at Mentmore Towers the month before the share issue and the firm's involvement with the British Rail Pension Fund showed just how far, and how far against Sotheby's, British public opinion had moved.

*Part VIII*

# DOWNFALL

# I  MENTMORE AND THE 'NATIONAL HERITAGE'

Sotheby's was a natural target for anyone concerned with that nebulous concept 'the British artistic heritage', or worried about that even vaguer notion 'cultural imperialism'. To the Victoria & Albert Museum, chief repository of historic artefacts, it was 'the knacker's yard of the national heritage'. Inevitably, as Sotheby's grew increasingly dominant, the pressure – not only from the British authorities – grew, culminating in the blazing row over the sale of the contents of Mentmore Towers in 1977.

'Art has shuffled round the countries of the world since the year dot', in the words of the Marquis of Northampton, whose Mantegna was sold for £8.1 million by Christie's in April 1985. The movement is by no means confined to 'cultural imperialism', loot from supposedly inferior civilizations. The systematic pillage of Italy's incomparable artistic inheritance began when the Stuart King Charles I of England bought the collection of the Gonzagas of Mantua, a family not culturally inferior to the Stuarts, simply poorer. Similarly Duveen's millionaire clients were simply richer (and often less artistically insensitive) than the noble vendors. King Charles's purchases were the first of the massive flow that subsequently became, by a process of cultural naturalization, the 'English inheritance' – a phrase which assumes that the British can appreciate other people's heritages better than their original owners, or anyone else for that matter. PCW naturally found this attitude absurd and parochial, paying too much attention to the recent history of the 'inheritance'.

Once Charles's collection had been dispersed throughout Europe the argument had already become thoroughly confused. Were his pictures part of the national inheritance of the British, or the Mantuans – or the Dutch who bought so many of them? For the argument is never clear-cut: the most unjustly-looted artefacts can evoke the most admirable responses. Nothing in history was bloodier than Cortés' conquest of Mexico, nothing more moving than Albrecht Dürer's response to the artefacts Cortés sent to the Emperor Charles V. Among other wonders he saw: 'a sun all of gold

197

a full fathom broad and a moon all of silver of the same size . . . all the days of my life I have seen nothing that has gladdened my heart so much as these things, for I saw amongst them wonderful works of art, and I marvelled at the subtle Ingenia of men in foreign lands. Indeed I cannot express all that I thought there.'

In an ideal world such responses, the origin of the works and their importance in the life of the countries involved, would be considered more important than their actual location at any one time. In real life the argument tends to polarize between an unappealing commercialism and a rather dishonest cultural nationalism.

Both were fully in evidence in the various arguments in which Sotheby's was involved. The most suspicious case was the dispersal of the mass of objects originally assembled by the great Victorian soldier-archaeologist-collector, General Augustus Henry Lane-Fox Pitt-Rivers. It included a great many Benin bronzes, English pottery, and a wide range of Bronze Age objects from all over Europe. It was considered so important that the Inland Revenue exempted it from duty on the death of his grandson, Captain George Pitt-Rivers. A piece of fiscal sleight-of-hand allowed the collection to be sold for a mere £50,000 to a 'charitable trust' run by the Captain's widow and a dealer, Kenelm Digby-Jones, who had previously been PCW's assistant. Because the value was apparently so low only a small sum had to be paid in death duties. The collection was then removed from its home in a local museum in a small country town and gradually sold for far more than the sum agreed by the Inland Revenue – Sotheby's advanced nearly £56,000 for some of the works. When the news of the dispersal broke in the *Sunday Times*\* PCW claimed that: 'nothing that was English had passed through this sale-room' and, indeed, Sotheby's did not benefit greatly from what insiders remember as 'an appalling mess'. But without the advance the trustees could not have gone ahead with the manoeuvres which dispersed the objects throughout Europe and North America before anyone knew what was happening.

Sales of 'ethnographic' material like so much of the Pitt-Rivers collection were relatively routine in New York in the 1960s and 1970s, for it was a booming market, and one where Sotheby's was anxious to break the dealers' stranglehold. The prevailing belief was that possession was ten points of the cultural law. The tone was set by Thomas Hoving at the Metropolitan Museum with his swashbuckling attitude that 'there is no right way to get a $5.5 million

---

\* In January 1973 in the Spectrum section, which I was then editing. Subsequent enquiries were blocked by the mysterious death of Captain Maumen, Mrs Pitt-Rivers' third husband, just before he was due to testify about the collection and its dispersal during a divorce hearing.

painting. You get it.' In such a moral climate it was refreshing to read the attitude of Norton Simon: 'If a thing is stolen, I want to know it. I won't buy it. But as far as anything else goes, you just can't tell what's true.' Like other collectors, he bought most of his major items from dealers, for sellers naturally shunned the sale-rooms where the provenance of their treasures would be publicly exposed. Moreover, the market was too narrow and specialized to attract a wide enough range of buyers to generate the competitive atmosphere required. Typical was a relatively unsuccessful sale of Indian, Tibetan and Nepalese bronzes in late 1973 when the top price was the £47,200 paid for an eleventh-century bronze of Siva Lord of the Dance – Norton Simon had just paid a dealer \$1 million for a much better example.

Inevitably Sotheby's attracted more blame than the dealers simply because its sales were so well publicized. In 1968 the government of Turkey – a country rich in relics, and even richer in smugglers – protested vigorously over a sale of archaeological finds and Sotheby's had to try and prove that the lots had been exported before a law passed by the old Ottoman government in 1906 banned their sale abroad (in the end two pieces of solid gold jewellery were taken out of the sale). But more important, and infinitely more contentious, were Parke-Bernet's sales of the increasingly fashionable pre-Columbian material – unfortunately their biggest auction coincided with a blazing row between the United States and Mexico over the possible restriction of the trade as part of a new treaty between the two countries.

The Mexicans were merely struggling to impose the sort of controls with which, in theory, the governments of developed countries have been armed for a long time. In practice, they often found the weapons were rusty or non-existent. In 1962, when the Spanish government prevented the sale in London of a Rubens equestrian portrait of the Duke of Lerma they had to improvise, using a law passed by their arch-enemies the pre-Franco Republican government. In its quarter of a century in power the Franco government itself had drawn up the necessary regulations but had not got round to promulgating them.

Other governments are better organized. The Italians have the strictest of regulations, mitigated by a great deal of smuggling, while the French have their famous law that any antique leaving the country must first be offered to the government at the market price. But such protection exacts its inevitable toll: despite its incomparable national heritage Italy has never had an active international art market; while the Paris market has slipped in importance – dealers do not even take very seriously the certificates of authenticity handed out to anyone buying at the Hôtel Drouot.

Other countries, like Britain, tend to muddle along. The magnificent Dutch Royal collection at the Mauritshuis at the Hague is based on a last-minute intervention by an eighteenth-century Prince of Orange, William V, to prevent an auction. He acquired the pictures for a mere 50,000 florins. But even the Dutch had their equivalent of Mentmore: in 1955 the heirs of Willem Dreesman offered his splendid collection to the city of Amsterdam at a price far below its true market value. The city claimed it had no funds available and the paintings were sold at auction, where the burghers bought a number of them for far more than they had been asked to pay for the entire collection.

In Britain the argument started immediately the aristocracy began to sell their possessions in the 1880s. As we saw on page 23 the first crisis came with the sale of the Duke of Marlborough's gallery of pictures at Blenheim Palace. As foreigners, particularly Americans, began to buy more and more British-owned masterpieces, the howls of protest naturally grew louder. The first major painting to be 'saved for the nation' was the *Rokeby Venus* by Velásquez, bought by the government in 1906 after a supposedly Puritanical public had vociferously claimed this unashamedly voluptuous picture for their own. During the First World War anti-American paranoia saved some able-bodied members of the antique trade from conscription. *The Connoisseur* magazine explained, 'unless we retain experts to handle the matter, American collectors are likely to secure bargains that the country can ill afford to part with'

In the 1920s Duveen set off another turmoil with his sales of family portraits to the Americans. In theory, the situation improved after 1945 when the government used £50 million from the sale of surplus war stores for a novel type of War Memorial, a National Land Fund in the form of a Trust to help buy up any of the national heritage that might be in danger. During the 1950s the Treasury decided that the Fund was merely a notional entry on the nation's balance-sheet, so any withdrawals counted as government expenditure. No one seemed to care very much at the time. In 1957 Mollie Panter-Downes heard the House of Lords debating a motion lamenting the departure of so many masterpieces (the Weinberg pictures, birds of passage, which had been in the country only a few weeks) when the British national collections were so deficient in Picassos, Braques and Matisses. But the debate was desultory, ending when the proposer, Lord Silkin, noted, 'most people have gone . . . and anyway the Chief Whip wants to get away and have his dinner. In these circumstances I can only, with regret, beg leave to withdraw the motion.' Modern Art was clearly not going to stir their Lordships.

In the twenty years after that inconclusive debate in the House of Lords objections to the loss of individual pictures steadily increased in volume. The logical consequence of successive furores seemed to be that any determined museum curator or pressure group could whip up a storm of righteous indignation over anything historic or valuable that had been in the country for more than a generation. The idea of 'heritage' had grown fuzzy, leaving the real national treasures, part of the very fabric of English life and history, vulnerable because 'wolf' had been cried so often and so unreasonably. The dispersal of the contents of Mentmore Towers, following the death of Lord Rosebery in 1974, finally crystallized the argument. It exposed the ramshackle inadequacy of the mechanism for protecting or even defining the British national heritage and, belatedly, led to a marked improvement in the situation.

Mentmore Towers was one of the many mansions in the Vale of Aylesbury, forty miles north of London, like Aston Clinton, Tring, Waddesdon, Ascott and Halton, built (or bought) by the Rothschilds in the third quarter of the nineteenth century, when the family was at the height of its fame and fortune. The house was designed by Joseph Paxton, the former gardener who designed the Crystal Palace housing the great exhibition of 1851, the year before work started on Mentmore. But the Rothschilds did not propose to live in a glass-house: Mentmore was basically a copy of the Elizabethan Wollaton Hall in Nottinghamshire, although the interior was thoroughly up-to-date with an early hot-water central heating system and rudimentary air conditioning.

For all the ingenuity that he lavished on the interior, Mentmore, unlike the Crystal Palace or the great glasshouse at Kew, did not display Paxton's real originality, his genius for 'functional scientific design, combined with extraordinary delicacy of vision', in the words of David Carritt, writing in the *Guardian*. If the fabric itself was no original masterpiece, the contents were never more than a fashionable hotch-podge. Originally, in Joseph Alsop's words, Mentmore was the 'house and collection which set what the French call le style Rothschild'. But this was more a matter of sheer money than inherent taste. For Baron Meyer was even more of a magpie than most of his family. He filled his palace with the recognized status symbols of the age, masses of Sèvres porcelain and French furniture, and the inevitable items with famous associations – lanterns from a barge made for the Doge of Venice and a marvellous marble fireplace originally designed by Rubens for his own house at Antwerp. (Mentmore's defenders never did explain how it had suddenly become part of the British national heritage: the Antwerp City Council had been pleading for its return for decades.)

Back in 1878 Baron Meyer's only daughter, Hannah, had married Lord Rosebery, and it was the death of their son ninety-six years later that precipitated the crisis. Originally the sheer gaudiness of the show must have been breath-taking. Even David Carritt had to admit that: 'Brimful of orchids and footmen it must have looked pretty stunning'. But by 1977 the house itself had grown shabby and most of the finest individual pieces – the Watteaus, the Greuzes, two marvellous Canaletto drawings, and three Titians, as well as a great deal of the best furniture – had already been removed. The new Lord Rosebery had decided to withdraw to his Scottish homes, taking with him many of the remaining treasures.

The family's feelings were reflected by Lady Jane Primrose, then a sixteen-year-old school girl, in a letter to *The Times*. She hoped that everyone else would see it as the family did, as a 'beautiful home rather than part of the national heritage or a large pile of "filthy lucre" ... but ... it is unsuitable for children accustomed to ponies and wellingtons.' Less clay would stick to his shoes, said the Earl, at Dalmeny, his Scottish home: the walks were better. 'After seeing the dilapidation of Mentmore', said *The Economist*, 'many who might have cried Philistine will be inclined to agree.'

The Earl offered the house and its contents to the government in lieu of death duties for a mere £2 million. The National Trust could not help: an enormous amount of land or other capital would have been required to repair and then maintain the property. The offer presented the Labour government with a difficult dilemma. If the National Land Fund was no longer a separate entity, itself a rather dubious assumption, no Labour government was going to find it easy to spend public money on such a vulgarly plutocratic ensemble. The politician who had to shoulder the burden was Alma, Lady Birk, then a junior minister at the Department of the Environment. She was an unusual Labour minister, a well-known journalist married to a wealthy solicitor, Ellis Birk. At the time they owned a delightful house in Regent's Park, containing a number of pieces of mainly English furniture. So she could cast a cold and expert eye on Mentmore's supposedly priceless contents. She, like the experts at Sotheby's, was relatively unimpressed. They were aghast at the cramped rooms above the ground floor level and at the general air of neglect. She, like them, was appalled at the way valuable cabinets had been cut about so as to fit washbasins, and other evidence of dereliction and neglect.

Her natural instincts were reinforced by the opinion of the late Lord Clark, the country's most famous expert on works of art. He

202

told her that the collection – unlike that at other Rothschild houses, such as Waddesdon – was artistically not worth saving. It was merely an interesting illustration of a very particular part of social history. But when he had said as much to his friends he had been so ferociously attacked that he was unwilling to declare his support in public.

Lady Birk then suggested to an inter-departmental meeting of officials that the government should buy Mentmore and then sell off a few of the finer pieces to pay for the purchase. An official from the Inland Revenue could scarcely believe his ears: 'You mean, minister', he gasped, 'you are suggesting that the government should make a profit from the transaction.' That was precisely what the lady did mean, but the idea was firmly squashed by the Treasury, arguing that a dangerous precedent would be set, that future donors would not be sure if the precious objects they were handing over would not be sold off.

To make matters worse, the original offer had been made at the depth of the slump in the art market, and Lord Rosebery's demands naturally escalated to £3 million as the argument came to a head. He needed a decision by early 1977: if the contents had been auctioned after June that year, they would have been valued for duty purposes at their sale value, rather than at the – much lower – price agreed by the Inland Revenue for probate purposes. The timing was unfortunate: in late 1976 the International Monetary Fund had clamped a stern disciplinary hand on British government spending, and through the spring there were strikes, especially in the motor industry, over the strict pay policy being imposed.

The government's final refusal to buy the whole estate came in April, so Sotheby's had only a few weeks to catalogue and prepare the 2,702 lots for the ten-day sale the following month. They were determined to do it in style: not a funeral so much as a superbly-organized village jumble sale. John Cann and Marcus Linell had already ordered a marquee to seat 2,000 as the centre for a temporary village at Mentmore. For it was clear that the British public was looking forward to a chance to pry into the lives of the rich and famous. The fascination is universal. When the possessions of Mlle Deschamps, the former mistress of the Duke of Orleans, was sold in mid-eighteenth century Paris, the whole city flocked to inspect the rewards of vice – the visitors including ladies of quality who would otherwise never have dreamed of being seen near the Deschamps residence. Similarly, New Yorkers were accustomed to peering into a succession of the houses sold up by Parke-Bernet over the years.

The closest British precedent for the Mentmore sale was in 1848, when Christie's* sold the contents of Stowe, the magnificent house owned by the splendidly-named Richard Plantagenet Temple Nugent Brydges Chandos Grenville, second Duke of Buckingham and Chandos, who had finally been driven into bankruptcy by the cost of entertaining Queen Victoria and Prince Albert. The Stowe collection itself was remarkable enough. In Reitlinger's words it was: 'formed strictly on late eighteenth-century lines, with a cabinet of natural curiosities, a gallery of classical statuary and Greek vases, and a number of Oriental novelties, including some bits of Indian sculpture'. But it was the grandeur and aristocratic associations that drew the masses. Although Stowe was fifty-five miles from London, omnibuses had to be hired to take hordes of Londoners out to gaze at the splendours. The outing was not cheap: the catalogue cost 15/-, a week's wages, and allowed only four people to view the house. Yet the Aubusson carpets were worn out days before the sale. The combination of aristocracy and decline was irresistible. As *The Times* thundered:

> Over the past week the British public has been admitted to a spectacle of painful interest and gravely historical import. One of the most splendid abodes of our almost regal aristocracy has thrown open its portals to an endless succession of visitors, who from morning to night have flowed in an uninterrupted stream from room to room and floor to floor – not to enjoy the hospitality of the lord or to congratulate him on his countless treasures of art, but to see an ancient family ruined, their palace marked for destruction, and its contents scattered to the four winds of heaven ... Stowe is no more.

Well, up to a point. Eighty years after the sale it became a thriving public school. With publicity like that the sale was naturally a success: the forty-day event raised £75,560.

At Mentmore the fuss over the supposedly irreplaceable contents fed the curiosity of a public sure that every lot would have the genuine Rothschild-Rosebery stamp on it. This was not always the case. In the nineteenth century auctioneers often slipped in 'introductions', oddments belonging to other owners, in the hope that the glamour of the sale would rub off on them. When Strawberry Hill, the former home of that voracious collector, Horace Walpole, was sold six years before Stowe, a contemporary satirist suggested that one of the auctioneer's assistants 'proposed to introduce a very ancient cradle that has been kicked about upstairs for years, as the very one Horace Walpole was rocked in'.

* As usual at the time, Sotheby's took the library and sold it separately.

There would be no such shenanigans at Mentmore. All the items in the astonishing five-volume catalogue were vouched for – and the 11,000 copies were sold weeks before the event at £30 a set. The family was obviously glad that the waiting was over. The 82-year-old Dowager Countess stayed in the Towers until two days before the sale and proved a journalist's dream, spunky, lively, sharp. The press also made much of Chadwick, his Lordship's former valet and now Her Ladyship's butler, how he chose a piece of Lord Rosebery's racing silver as his memento, and how he took Her Ladyship racing at Sandown Park the day after the sale.

The journalists' reactions to the house itself varied. Bevis Hillier imagined Fred Astaire and Ginger Rogers gliding down the main staircase. By contrast Peter Conrad in *The Times* thought 'the guestrooms are a wasteland of peeling paint and gilt tat: the pictures have been discoloured by generations of grandees' cigars ... it is difficult not to feel slightly exhilarated at the dispersal of this pile of geegaws and hideous rarities ... Most of the objects left in the house are coarse and unlovely embodiments of wealth.' He noted, too, that the house 'belies its own spaciousness by seeming merely an agglomeration of odd, misshapen small areas which, jumbled together, never manage to be imposing'. He naturally noted the false wall of the library containing books with imaginary titles, redolent of the crudest Victorian humour, like *Jewellery* by Goldsmith or *Sanitary Reform* by Washington.

The crowds, attracted partly by the fine weather and festive atmosphere, were immense (though, at the sale itself, they were serious: the bar was usually deserted). The hordes of foreign visitors included French dealers eager to buy the unprecedented quantities of French furniture on offer. They lived down to their reputation. In the eighteenth century they would systematically laud to the skies any piece of junk at the sale-room if it happened to be similar to something they had in stock, while simultaneously deprecating the worth of anything of real quality. At the sale of the Rothschilds' mansion in Piccadilly in 1937: 'their Gallic tactics of appraisal before the sale caused some consternation and much amusement', according to Frank Herrmann. 'Small huddles of them round every major piece noisily refuted the veracity of the catalogue descriptions. Every detail was minutely examined and condemned. To those not familiar with this technique, the effect was more than a little alarming' – the more so because some of the pieces were, indeed, nineteenth-century copies and not, as claimed eighteenth-century originals. At Mentmore, forty years later, Peter Conrad noticed one room in which 'a trio of gum-chewing French dealers scrambled on all fours beneath a sofa, probing its horse-hair innards with pocket torches like impudent obstetricians, or up-ended chairs and cast them aside with snorts of derision'.

The first viewing day saw them at their worst. The British Treasury had, belatedly and reluctantly, agreed to the purchase for the nation of four major items, including a Gainsborough and a magnificent piece of eighteenth-century German furniture. The agreement came so late that it was in fact telephoned through to the experts from the Victoria & Albert Museum, who had arrived with a plain, unmarked van in the hope that their pleas had been answered. They promptly carted the splendid bureau down the stairs, pursued by a horde of dealers virtually thrusting open cheque-books at them, offering any sort of price to deprive the unknown buyer of his treasure.

On the opening day of the sale itself the microphone refused to function for a tense twenty-five minutes. But the Earl, a theatrical lighting engineer by profession,* saved the day by repairing it. The sale-room correspondents concentrated on the – relatively few – important items, the Louis XIV ormolu secretaire, which was bought in despite a bid of £280,000 ($481,600), the highest for any single piece of furniture, the £900,000 ($1,548,000) paid for the French furniture as a whole, the porcelain milk-maid's bucket made for Marie-Antoinette, which went for £60,000 ($103,200), five times the estimate.

But, as the critics had insisted, most of the lots were valuable only because of the Mentmore label. So an ordinary armchair with a loose chintz cover would fetch £620 ($1,118), a dozen times its value in a lesser sale. The bidding for the minor lots was often accompanied by a sotto voce dialogue between the Dowager Countess and her daughter-in-law, overheard by Philip Norman:

'Together they frowned at a pair of lack-lustre candlesticks. "I found seven dozen like that," said young Lady Rosebery, "seven dozen pairs all wired for electricity" ... A venison dish made her wince. "Ugh, horrid stuff" ... there was a George II marrow scoop still to come. And the Portuguese toothpick-holder in the shape of a Red Indian.

' "Now where in the world did that come from?"

' "All I care is that it's going," said young Lady Rosebery.

' "Yes, thank God for that. It's going." '

Even the cradle (which really had been occupied by generations of Rothschilds and Roseberys) went for £400 ($688). The last lot, a George I chocolate pot (with a little label on it reading 'The End') went for £1,700 ($2,924), three times the estimate. It was that sort of sale, a giant clearance fetching £6.39 million ($10.99 million), much

* 'My son the electrician', was his mother's description.

of it spent by ordinary people buying for fun rather than profit. There was only one obvious bargain: *The Toilet of Venus*, a painting attributed to Carle van Loo. David Carritt bought it for a mere £8,800 ($15,136). After some high-grade detective work he proved to everyone's satisfaction that it was a Fragonard, which he graciously allowed the National Gallery to buy for £400,000 ($688,000).

Apart from that one error, it was all very satisfactory for Sotheby's, although its very success merely exacerbated the feeling that the state had missed a bargain. Fundamentally the battle had surely been lost when the Rosebery family decided to abandon it. In Geraldine Norman's words: 'As a family house open for the public reflecting the family's idiosyncracies, Mentmore and its contents would have formed a fascinating and significant whole. As a state-run museum it would not. Three dozen or so museum quality items, mostly of the eighteenth century or earlier, would have been rattling around in a supreme example of nineteenth-century architecture.'

The argument lingered on after the sale. PCW's nerve snapped and he tried to punish *The Connoisseur* because its editor had initiated criticism of Sotheby's in *The Times*. Two years after the sale the house itself was sold to an Eastern religious sect and became a centre for transcendental meditation – on the transitory nature of man's works among other things.

But the affair did have a more serious and worth-while result. Lady Birk set up a departmental committee to improve the mechanism for preserving Britain's heritage. Its report was followed up by a Parliamentary Select Committee and in 1980 an unusually united House of Commons established the National Heritage Memorial Fund. It was granted the remains of the old Land Fund, reckoned by a parsimonious Treasury to be worth a mere £12.4 million and over the following years became the first government body to concentrate on the preservation of the National Heritage, as understood by most people apart from museum curators. They bought occasional works of art – like a Rubens sketch. But most of the money went on more esoteric items: the papers of Admiral Beatty, the restoration of the pier at the small Welsh seaside resort of Bangor, raising a Wellington bomber from Loch Ness, reprocessing the nitrate films stored at the National Film Archive, the conservation of the eighteenth-century Old Furnace at Coalbrookdale; and early in 1985, during the miners' strike, the longest major industrial dispute in British history, the government found £25 million, the largest single investment ever made to preserve our inheritance, for two major country houses and their contents, as well as the furniture at Nostell Priory in Yorkshire, which had all been made by a former assistant to the estate carpenter, one Thomas Chippendale.

## 2  BRITISH RAIL AND THE NATIONAL CONSCIENCE

Mentmore had been fun: the Great British Public had greatly enjoyed the festivities, and Sotheby's was blamed only by the kill-joy preservationists. Its deep involvement with the British Rail Pension Fund in the only systematic institutional attempt to invest long-term in works of art was a different matter. British Rail is the most closely scrutinized of that heavily supervized band, Britain's nationalized industries. So the Fund's decision in 1974 to place a small proportion of its cash flow into works of art was bound to be contentious, the more so because Sotheby's acted as sole adviser to the scheme.

The idea seemed natural at the time. In mid-1974 all alternatives for combating inflation seemed to be broken reeds. The London stock-market had plumbed depths not seen for generations, the property market was littered with bankrupt companies and half-completed projects. Government stocks had been money-losers for a generation, and foreign investment was tightly controlled. Later in the decade, when the scheme was called into question, investment prospects had been transformed. But the publicity reminded the British public of their own feelings a few years earlier, when their nerves had been shot to pieces, they had assumed that double-digit inflation was here to stay and had looked to gold and works of art for protection. No one likes to be reminded of times of panic. Because the decision had seemed so sensible, because the majority of their fellow-countrymen would have agreed with the Pension Fund's trustees at the time, the backlash was particularly vicious. All the other arguments deployed against the scheme – that the money should have gone into British industry, that the investment was not itself sensible – were secondary. 'We were scapegoats for people's feelings ... we were doing no more than everyone else in the art market ... but somehow people were shocked that we were hoping to make money out of spiritual values', recalls one railway executive.

The man behind the idea was Christopher Lewin, a quiet, precise, mild-mannered actuary – one of the small band of mathematically-inclined experts who dominate the investment policies of Britain's insurance policies and pension funds. He had helped to devise a modern pensions scheme for the railwaymen, and was naturally conscious of inflationary pressures. He had always been a collector in a modest way of manuscripts and books, mostly on recent British social history. So investment in works of art was not an unthinkable prospect.

Looking around for alternatives to shares and property he dismissed commodities and investments in small companies not quoted on any stock-market, because of the problems of marketability. He then embarked on what remains the single most thorough analysis of trends in the art market ever undertaken. He used Reitlinger's figures and excluded exceptional prices (those ten or more times the average) so as not to distort the indices. He concluded that most categories of 'traded art' had proved sound investments in the long term – and a pension fund can afford to ride out slumps of up to a quarter of a century if the eventual return is sufficient. From his vantage point only tapestries and arms and armour had failed to keep up with inflation in the fifty years up to the end of the 1960s.

His conclusions seemed flat, trite, unexceptional: 'The risk element is not as great as you might think ...demand will increase, supply won't ... we could be international in buying goods without any problems of foreign exchange regulations ... I had very good reasons to suppose that works of art would be an excellent hedge.' He convinced the Fund's trustees, including the trades union representatives, and the chairman of the British Rail Board, Richard (now Lord) Marsh, an ebullient former Labour Cabinet Minister, who urged him to 'have a go'. This was easier said than done. Unlike most other major pension funds, BR's money was managed by outsiders, mostly by merchant banks, so it seemed natural to look for an expert intermediary. The obvious choice was Sotheby's, 'which we thought of as the premier auction house, but also as a source of expertise', says Lewin. The opportunity was made to measure for PCW. His reaction was instinctual, even though, by accepting the role of adviser, he publicly abandoned the neutrality that had been the auctioneer's role since time immemorial.

Typically he compounded his eventual problems by recommending as manager for the collection, not an impartial outsider, but someone close to him whom he thought he could control, Annamaria Edelstein. Educated as an international lawyer, this handsome, black-haired Italian lady had originally come to Britain as the wife of a Scottish farmer, had divorced, gravitated to London, remarried a well-known dress designer, Victor Edelstein, and for some years had been working with PCW's younger son Philip on Sotheby's books, most notably the annual *Art of Auction*. She had acquired an excellent all-round education in 'traded art', but it was

209

simply asking for further trouble to choose someone so closely identified with Sotheby's.

In the event the investment policy was institutionalized rather more than PCW might have hoped. Lewin had worked out that the annual turnover of the international art market was about a billion pounds. He was hoping to invest around 3 per cent of the Fund's annual cash flow, or between £4 and £8 million, in works of art, a modest addition to demand, which would not upset prices provided the purchases were sufficiently diversified. BR and Sotheby's formed a series of joint companies (they kept switching them to keep the investment details away from the press, and in particular from Geraldine Norman, who was an early opponent of the scheme). BR kept control: every proposed purchase had to be formally submitted, complete with photograph and price comparisons, through Annamaria Edelstein to a sub-committee which would decide whether to buy, and the maximum price to offer.

The Works of Art sub-committee, which Lewin chaired, imposed a rather loose disciplinary framework. It could provide guidelines, decide on the categories on which to concentrate. It even turned down a few proposals flat, but Lewin knew that 'we had to trust our manager to put together a series of collections, it couldn't be done by a committee, only by an individual, we knew she would make mistakes, it was up to her to judge the artistic merit of the propositions ... she turned out to have a good eye for a bargain.' She was inevitably going to be influenced by PCW's suggestions, but the combination of BR's inevitably cumbersome decision-making process and Annamaria's own independent turn of mind prevented him from exerting the influence he might have hoped. 'He was so transparent', she says.

Insiders did not fret at the Sotheby's links: their worries concerned the slowness of the decision-making process; the sometimes inadequate prices the committee was prepared to allow Annamaria to offer at auction – often well below Sotheby's estimates; and their unwillingness to take risks. This was especially irksome in the field of Victorian painting, where a number of splendid works were on offer because of the financial problems of the City whiz-kids who had 'punted' on them (although the fund did acquire a marvellous Lord Leighton, *Dante in Exile*, from Nadia Gordon, the ballerina wife of one such City financier).

To outsiders the whole thing was a complete ramp. The investment was just getting under way when Christie's and Sotheby's imposed the buyers' premium – which BR had to pay. So the dealers thought of it as yet another attempt to deprive them of a livelihood: 'PCW wanted a monopoly of buyers and sellers', says Julian Agnew.

210

They naturally ignored the new buying power the Fund represented and the large number of important works bought through such firms as Arthur Tooth and Knoedler's. To the art world in general it looked like an attempt by Sotheby's to find a dustbin into which to offload some of their less desirable lots, especially those it owned or on which it had provided an advance or a guarantee. PCW was always going to lose any argument on the subject, partly because the Fund had to keep its operations as secret as possible – Annamaria Edelstein, who was naturally upset by the attacks, gave only one interview during the six years she ran the Collection. So everyone was free to assume the worst. And given PCW's reputation and Annamaria's close connection with Sotheby's, of course they did.

The Dick collection provided a classic 'no-win situation'. There were bargains to be had at the later sales, although the Fund snapped up only a couple – a Stubbs and a Ben Marshall included in the exhibition of some of the Fund's paintings shown at Agnew's in late 1984. In theory it was highly convenient for Sotheby's to have a 'tame' buyer on hand in difficult times especially for works in which it had a direct financial interest. The Fund could also act as the honest under-bidder, forcing up the only truly 'outside' buyer. The trouble with these theories was that, officially, not even PCW knew when, or how much, the fund was going to bid. Indeed Annamaria took great pleasure in devising increasingly elaborate stratagems to keep him in the dark. Sometimes, obviously, he could guess. On one memorable occasion she had placed her commission with a friend in New York, and as the bid came over the phone PCW announced '£X thousand from New York' nodding to her as if to say 'Gotcher'.

The very first purchase was a seventeenth-century Italian illustrated book on architecture, the first of a large number of books and manuscripts, some of them bought for little more than £100, not only because Lewin felt comfortable with them, but also because they seemed especially good value at the time, Numerically the Fund was well enough spread over fifteen hundred items. They covered every possible 'serious' field of collectibles, superb Egyptian bronze heads, eighteenth-century French furniture, including a Louis XV commode bought for £65,000 at the Mentmore sale, Chinese porcelain and bronzes, German Renaissance gold jewellery and classical antiquities. These included a statue of Poseidon allegedly smuggled out of Italy and sold for £500,000, initially to Marcus Linell, through an art dealer, Robin Symes. This created no end of fuss: but Annamaria was saved from embarrassment by the strict rules Lewin had laid down where such works were concerned. She had to produce not only a provenance, but a certificate from Interpol that no hint of suspicion attached to the piece. In cash terms it was rather

211

unbalanced: a third of the money was spent on Old Masters; another 10 per cent on Impressionists – an investment limited because Lewin though prices were rather high; the same proportion was of Chinese porcelain, partly because Julian Thompson was one of the most helpful of the experts she could call on (one of the most useful was not an expert at all, but a porter, Jock Campbell). Outside these three fields its impact on the market was marginal.

Nevertheless the collection was – and remains, for very little has been sold – unique. Other collections were private, corporate or public. This was institutional, for pure profit, not for show, or use, or decoration. It was not truly personal, for Annamaria could not allow her own feelings free rein, although it reflects them to some extent, especially in drawings, the field in which she now specializes. It was not educational-didactic, like that of a good museum. Nor was it flavour-of-the monthish, reflecting merely the fashion of the moment. Lewin applied the same investment criteria to the art collection as he did to shares, he tried to weight the items by sectors of the market. He did not succeed entirely, but they did build a number of specialized collections within a safe, solid, selection of the best works of art available at the time.

Geraldine Norman and the dealers were the first to criticize the idea. They were soon followed by a maverick Labour Member of Parliament, Andrew Faulds, and a number of trades union leaders. These included Dave Bowman, leader of the National Union of Railwaymen, which represented the majority of BR's workers – though the workers' representatives on the investment committee were generally happy with the idea, they grew particularly fond of 'our Annamaria'. But the first sign of real trouble came early in 1977, when the Comptroller and Auditor-General, the government's top financial watch-dog, expressed his concern about pension funds' 'almost unfettered powers of investment' and wondered whether the government ought not to have some say, either in the appointment of trustees, or in framing investment policies.

Criticism mounted throughout the year, leading to an official hearing by a committee of the House of Commons early in 1978. By then the policy had few defenders, partly because its natural allies in the art world had been alienated by the Sotheby's connection. But at least one of the criticisms, that the whole collection was sterilized in a London vault, turned out to be largely unfounded. Because the loans were anonymous, no one realized that a third of the fund's collection – worth two-thirds of the total – is now on view. It was both generous and imaginative in loaning items to many museums, mostly smaller ones in the provinces. Proportionately the biggest beneficiary has been Doncaster, a railway town with very little in its Museum – and

Leeds Castle was always available if no one else wanted an item. Some major British museums were too sniffy about the commercial connections to accept loans, so some pieces are in a few favoured foreign institutions, like the Detroit Museum. This was no easy matter. BR could not insure the works and only a newly-introduced government indemnity scheme enabled the smaller provincial museums to accept the loans.

By the end of 1977 every major purchase the Fund made seemed to attract publicity. An early Picasso, *The Blue Boy*, for which BR had paid £585,000, was allegedly worth less than £400,000 at the time. Some Parmigianino drawings were bought (at Sotheby's, which didn't help) for several times their real worth – though this has multiplied after the sale of the Chatsworth drawings in the summer of 1984. But even at the time the Fund was thought to have a bargain with its single biggest investment, the £1 million paid for Old Master drawings from the Duc de Talleyrand. Nevertheless, the climate of opinion had changed. Lord Leightons might have soared in value, but so had the stock-market, which had more than doubled from the dark days of 1974 when the scheme was hatched. The bargains in the stock-market in 1974–75 proved to be greater than those available in the art market. This is not to say that Annamaria Edelstein will be proved wrong in the long-term: indeed in terms of pure capital appreciation her overall judgment will probably be vindicated. But it is still unclear whether the capital appreciation will be adequate to compensate for lost income. George Ross-Goobey, a much respected figure in the pension fund movement, put the matter with character-istic bluntness: 'Personally I view these investments very poorly. They are probably unique and I hope they remain so ... One great advantage of pension funds is freedom from tax on their income. Works of art produce a negative income in that they cost money to be insured, preserved and stored. Capital appreciation may do enough to eventually make up for this loss, but it is a very big handicap to start with.'

But the game was given away by one of the Fund's defenders, a Mr J. F. Flower, in a letter to *The Economist*. It needed, he wrote, '*only* [my italics] an average annual rate of inflation of 14.7 per cent between now and 1999 for the work of art to be a better investment than a government stock for a tax-exempt pension fund.' So once investors were expecting less than this hyper-inflationary rate in the future, the case for investment in works of art looked decidedly thin.

It was a point of view with which Marsh's successor, Sir Peter Parker, undoubtedly agreed. Parker is a businessman with a keen eye to the prevailing wind of political opinion. He wanted the Pension Fund to be directly managed, cutting out intermediaries of all descriptions. He also knew that the Fund's investment in art, by then nearly £30 million, was a 'campaign that could not be won', an unnecessary additional burden. 'If that's what they're doing with their pension fund, what are they doing about the railways?' was the reaction which worried BR.

So Parker brought in an experienced fund manager from Rothschild's, John Morgan. Himself an art lover – the walls of his sombre City office are brightened by two Miro lithographs bought a quarter of a century ago – Morgan's clear, if unspoken, brief was to stop the experiment. This did not mean selling, nor abandoning any further investment – Morgan was prepared to commit funds up to the original total of £40 million – less than 1 per cent of the total value of the fund – but it did mean that the adventurous phase was over (not surprisingly, Annamaria Edelstein left BR a couple of years later). Morgan, like Parker, had been shaken by the depth and bias of the press comment, but he was also appalled by the problem of how on earth to sell any substantial part of the collection. It was difficult enough even to value – it is still in the books at cost price. Insurance values provide only a rough guide and the very disadvantages – notably the inability to find out comparable prices on a regular basis – that militated against buying works of art in the first place also prevented any proper valuation. But the money will not be needed until early in the next century when the fund will be running down (because the number of railwaymen has been falling for many years). So Morgan can follow a purely neutral policy, selling a very little, and leaving the collection virtually intact.

Morgan is clearly glad that he does not have to sell the collection now and fears that his successors will have an appalling task disposing of several hundred million pounds' worth of art. The argument goes that once the Fund were seen to be selling, prices would tumble in anticipation. Both Edelstein and Julian Thompson believe the precise opposite: that the collection would be relatively easy to sell and would even attract a premium rating, that the times, so carefully chosen, would have a cachet all of their own.

In that case the worst problem would be the 'national interest', however it may be defined in the twenty-first century: the indubitably English paintings by Stubbs and Ben Marshall, the Gainsborough that the Fund bought back from the United States, the manuscript material relating to British authors, and the sometimes delightful English landscapes done by foreign painters – the views of Henley by the seventeenth-century artist Jan Siberechts and of the Thames at Twickenham by Peter Tillemans are all more fundamentally part of the British heritage than anything at Mentmore.

214

# 3  WAS ART PROFITABLE?

It is now easy to see why and how British Rail came to start – and to stop – investing in art. But why was it the only institution with such a programme? For art has been extremely profitable in the post-war period, and especially in the 1970s. The tables on pages 216 and 217 spell it out: compared with any other measure, prices, or stocks and shares, whatever currency you choose, an investment in works of art in the 1970s proved a winner. Only gold did better. For British investors, in particular, it has proved, as so many of them hoped after the first devaluation of sterling in 1967, to be a hedge against currency fluctuations. For twelve years, until foreign exchange controls were removed in 1979, it also provided the only internationally traded commodity available to law-abiding British citizens.

Nevertheless, the tables provide a first clue as to BR's solitary splendour. Sotheby's used a dollar base because the demand for statistical information has come almost exclusively from the United States. Once you adjust the figures to allow for currency fluctuations you can see how investors in art from Britain or other countries with relatively weak currencies, like France and Italy, did far better than their American equivalents. To make comparisons more realistic I have weighted the figures for the 10 per cent commission paid when selling a work of art, against the 2 per cent or so paid on ordinary quoted investments. This additional charge emphasizes that the art market is not a smooth, orthodox one. It is a series of small, difficult, usually imperfect, markets. English eighteenth-century silver was chosen as a speculative medium because it was one of the few artistic areas where there was a continuing, reliable market price. There weren't many alternatives.

John Marion provides a shrewd assessment of why. He was obviously the first port of call for any American looking for advice on investment in art over the years. To him: 'wealth and education had brought an interest in the whole gamut of artistic works, ballets, museums and so on. Then there were the tax advantages. So in the late 1960s there were lots of funds proposed, lots of media attention as to what a good hedge against inflation they were. But the buyers weren't very sophisticated, they bought brand names.' Then senti-

## WAS ART PROFITABLE?

### – For the British

September 1970 = 100

| | Sotheby Index | Adjusted for currency fluctuations | Adjusted for selling costs | UK prices | UK shares* | Gold in £ |
|---|---|---|---|---|---|---|
| 1971 | 124 | 121 | 111 | 110 | 140 | 113 |
| 1972 | 145 | 141 | 130 | 117 | 148 | 185 |
| 1973 | 190 | 184 | 170 | 128 | 101 | 289 |
| 1974 | 185 | 191 | 176 | 148 | 47 | 447 |
| 1975 | 161 | 182 | 168 | 184 | 110 | 520 |
| 1976 | 179 | 241 | 222 | 215 | 104 | 403 |
| 1977 | 206 | 283 | 260 | 249 | 143 | 566 |
| 1978 | 265 | 324 | 298 | 297 | 138 | 726 |
| 1979 | 350 | 372 | 342 | 306 | 122 | 973 |
| 1980 | 408 | 405 | 372 | 361 | 139 | 1769 |
| 1981 | 394 | 513 | 472 | 404 | 156 | 1570 |
| 1982 | 405 | 557 | 513 | 438 | 175 | 1570 |
| 1983 | 444 | 707 | 650 | 458 | 228 | 1883 |
| 1984 | 487 | 892 | 821 | 481 | 280 | 1656 |

*Financial Times 30 share Index

The new Sotheby's Index was devised in the late 1970s using 1975 as 100. However figures for most of the dozen or so constituent sections go back to 1970 (the exceptions were chiefly American paintings and artefacts). So I have taken the liberty of extrapolating back to 1970, weighting the index to allow for the missing sections. At a guess, if these were included, the rise would have been rather faster than appears here

216

# WAS ART PROFITABLE?

## – For the Americans

September 1970 = 100

| | Sotheby Index | Adjusted for selling costs | US prices | US shares* | Gold in $ |
|---|---|---|---|---|---|
| 1971 | 124 | 114 | 104 | 111 | 116 |
| 1972 | 145 | 133 | 108 | 133 | 190 |
| 1973 | 190 | 175 | 114 | 108 | 298 |
| 1974 | 185 | 170 | 127 | 76 | 433 |
| 1975 | 161 | 148 | 139 | 96 | 459 |
| 1976 | 179 | 165 | 147 | 118 | 300 |
| 1977 | 206 | 190 | 156 | 106 | 413 |
| 1978 | 265 | 244 | 168 | 108 | 593 |
| 1979 | 350 | 322 | 187 | 123 | 916 |
| 1980 | 408 | 375 | 211 | 156 | 2634 |
| 1981 | 394 | 362 | 234 | 139 | 1206 |
| 1982 | 405 | 373 | 249 | 160 | 1142 |
| 1983 | 444 | 408 | 257 | 189 | 1182 |
| 1984 | 487 | 448 | 268 | 189 | 977 |

* Standard & Poor's Industrial

217

ment crept in: 'In good times people held back from selling and then in bad times they preferred to sell "unemotional" investments, like REITs' – the usually unprofitable Real Estate Investment Trusts fashionable in the early 1970s. The punters were often people like 'stockbrokers on a roll, adding a dimension to the quality of life', and they did not want to lose that dimension. In virtually every case they could not strip investment in art of its historic overtones – love, show, decoration – motives which lured even one of Jim Slater's acolytes when Salter Walker moved so heavily into Chinese ceremaics. (He fell in love with Annamese ware.)

In the past few years Marion has been advising Citibank, which is including works of art in investment portfolios designed for those – like athletes or pop stars – whose earning peak is inevitably going to be short and sharp. But, again, the human element intervenes. They can't be cold-bloodedly objective: their personal artistic preferences keep intruding. Virtually all these institutional attempts have been short-lived; the major exception has been Artemis, which is often treated as though it were an art investment concern. It isn't: it is a well-run, large scale, highly sophisticated art dealer, backed by a couple of banks – most notably the Banque Bruxelles Lambert. Artemis originally called itself an art investment trust to appease the prejudices of the founders, who preferred the idea of art as investment to art as tradeable beauty. In the hands of a group of experts including Eugene Thaw and the late David Carritt, whom he lured from Christie's in 1970, it has behaved as a highly sophisticated dealer. Many other banks bankroll dealers (how else can they get their money?) and take some of the profits: it's just that Artemis conducts its affairs more publicly – and on a larger scale – than the others.

So British Rail remains a unique case, an exercise which I think unlikely to be repeated for a generation. But the underlying reason is not sentiment. It is simply timing. It was set up in the dark days of 1974–75, when virtually nobody in Britain believed that rational investment in orthodox instruments was profitable any more. The moment that belief became the accepted doctrine, it ceased to be true – the *Financial Times* index is six or seven times the low point it reached that dreadful winter. Once people believed that there was no alternative to investment in art, the belief ceased to be true. For I believe that once any trend is officially declared unstoppable, it promptly stops and reverses itself, quite sharply, and over quite a long period. I first applied this theory in 1970–71 to the balance of direct investment between the United States and the rest of the world. At the time it was assumed that the imbalance was permanent, that the Americans would gradually take over the rest of world business. This doctrine was being promulgated (most publicly by Jean-Jacques Servan-Schreiber in *Le Défi Américain*) just as the tide was turning, and European investment in the United States was beginning to rise faster than the flow in the opposite direction. So it was with the allegedly unstoppable rise of the dollar in 1982–85. So it has proved to be with the rise in the price of art, and above all in the profits to be made from holding it.

The best comparison, perhaps, is with the price of gold, that other refuge in time of trouble. Because the price had been held down for thirty-five inflationary years, it has given an even better return than works of art over the period 1970–84, although not for the shorter period 1975–84. For in the first five years of the decade gold was simply catching up on a generation of neglect. The connection is not unreasonable. In the 1970s, as Robert Hughes has pointed out, a succession of exhibitions – 'The Treasures of the Vikings, the Gold of the Gorgonzolas – helped to reinforce the illusion that art was basically a kind of bullion'.

But even this exceptional period exhibited many of the permanent features of the art market: a tangled web of long-term neglect and short-term fashion. Chinese ceramics are the best example: outstanding performers since 1975, but, allowing for inflation, you would still be out of pocket if you had invested in 1973, or, in some cases, in 1913. For the tables underline a fundamental lesson obvious to percipient investors since the 1930s: that investors in art unload less in time of trouble – partly for emotional reasons, but also because the market dries up – than in other investments. So art is a superb defensive investment if you are generally pessimistic about economic prospects. But it is much less satisfactory if the economic wind is favourable and inflation under control: art has notably under-performed in both London and Wall Street in the early 1980s.

For the art market's performance in the 1970s was unprecedented; even in the decade before 1914 prices had not risen so fast, nor over such a wide range of categories – though it is important not to compare too closely two periods, in one of which no one dreamt that inflation could ever be a factor in everyday life, the other a decade dominated by the fear of hyper-inflation, the annihilation of all values except the most basic. In retrospect too the 1970s may turn out to have been an aberration in the history of the art market. The 1950s and 1960s can now be seen as a time of catching-up, like a series of beacons catching light from each other: 'look there goes Gauguin, there go netsuke'. The rise in the 1970s was a mirror of the unparalleled fear that gripped all the inhabitants of industrialized countries who had any wealth to protect. With the 1980s we can see a return to normal. It too brings its own profits. The rise in the price of contemporary American paintings has far outstripped the average – in notable contrast to silver, that refuge of the timid and fearful.

But every boom brings the seeds of its own destruction. The problems of over-supply and shifts of fashion are inherent in any boom involving contemporary artists. The fashionable painters of New York could well suffer the fate of Rosa Bonheur, whose prices have still not regained those she could command in her own lifetime. For Robert Hughes believes, reasonably enough, that:

> We are repeating one of the peculiarities of the Victorian art market, though on an industrial scale. By and large historical art is better value than contemporary art; and contemporary art is overpriced ... Nobody of intelligence in the art world believes this boom can go on forever. There is a jittery feeling that we are heading for something like the slump that hit the once-dominant French art market in the Fifties. Except that instead of one Bernard Buffet, we have twenty. And except, too, that when the shakeout comes, it will be much more traumatic.

Other contemporary fashions could be as transient as the Duveen boom, with *nouveaux riches* buying their own social security. The exaggerated prices paid for any object which is both Old and American, be it furniture or paintings, originates from the same well-springs of social insecurity. The love of the Luminists could be as transitory a phenomenon as the portraits of the Duveen era, bought with the same idea in mind. Nor should the idea of the supply drying up be taken too seriously. Whatever the theorists may say, auctioneers and dealers alike are adamant – often to their own amazement – that the rising prices of the 1970s produced a growing flow of increasingly important items in almost every category.

For the art market, in the long run, love conquers all. Reitlinger made the point in 1971, though he exaggerates the number of speculators who were sensible enough to sell at the right time:

> It cannot be denied that enormous profits have been made in the past two decades by those who followed fashionable trends, regardless of cost, in order to sell out a few years later, but these are not investors but speculators. The only investors are those who never meant to invest at all. Those who bought some twenty years ago, preferring such things as English eighteenth-century draw- ings, the 'primitives' of English pottery and porcelain, Mughal miniatures, early Japanese porcelain and Chinese blue and white of the early Ming dynasty, may have seen their treasures multiply in value in some cases two or three hundred times over.

220

Reitlinger, the eternal pessimist, went on to predict the end of true collecting. But his underlying distinction between speculation and investment remains valid: in the long run the only sure way to profit from art is to love it, to find a category not greatly in demand. Even PCW knew this: 'If you're going to buy works of art from an investment point of view', he said in 1970, 'to my mind you've got to buy with your eyes and your heart, you've got to buy what you love. If you buy with your ears and your intellect you're just buying what everyone says is fashionable and you may come unstuck' – friends said, unkindly, that he could only buy what was out of fashion, and then not the best, because he was so mean that he would not pay high prices.

René Gimpel tells the marvellous story of Bernard Franck, a French army contractor who spent thirty years collecting eighteenth-century dance cards. News of the collection came to the ears of Pierpont Morgan, who paid $200,000 for them. Franck promptly started another collection of dance cards. Then: 'hoping for other such Americans, he built up still other collections of needle cases, music boxes, etc, pouring no end of money into objects which today aren't worth a quarter of what he paid for them; the miraculous Morgan sale was the worst transaction of his life.'

The history of the art market is composed of just such contrasts. For sudden booms and equally sudden collapses are routine – even when consumer prices were absolutely stable for a generation or more. In the dozen years after Turner's death in 1851 the price of his paintings multiplied some fifteen times – double that rate for watercolours. Turner was not alone: the landscapist David Cox enjoyed a fantastic vogue, which multiplied the prices of his landscapes fifty-fold in as many years; and the vogue for Italian paintings increased their value forty times or more between the 1880s and the 1920s. Nor was the opportunity for profit confined to pictures. A Book of Hours from the Yates Thompson collection jumped from £300 to £11,800 in one man's collecting lifetime. And a first edition of Bacon's *Essays*, which cost just £13 5s in 1870, fetched £1,950 forty years later ('£1,000 an ounce' said the headlines).

The reverse cases are even more illuminating. In the first decade of the nineteenth century Claude was by far the most expensive painter on the market. A merchant from Bristol, the great centre of the slave trade, had paid £12,600 for the famous 'Altieri Claudes' (*The Sacrifice to Apollo* and *The Landing of Aeneas*). They did not regain their price level for another 160 years. Even worse is the case of Van Dyck, worshipped by Duveen's American clients as the master behind their favourite portraitists. His fall was correspondingly greater than the painters he inspired. In 1906 he became the most expensive painter in the world. Six years earlier Morgan had paid $500,000 (£100,000) for a Raphael. Widener promptly paid $15,000 more for Van Dyck's portrait of the Marchesa Grimaldi-Cattaneo. It is important not to sneer at such prices and the men who paid them. How they are remembered is partly a matter of accident. Their posthumous reputation is less secure than that of Doctor Albert Barnes, whose invention, Argyrol, saved thousands of French soldiers from the horrors of syphilis. He repaid the French by buying many of their finest pictures for relatively small sums. He could boast, legitimately, to Joseph Alsop, one of the few visitors he permitted, that 'you are seeing the Old Masters of the future'. But he also bought an immense number of paintings by the now totally forgotten Pascin.

The list of fashionable artists, sculptors and craftsmen who proved appalling investments is endless, but then they were originally bought to impress, not to be profitable and, in any case, fashionable investments are rarely profitable. Maurice Rheims compared the rise in prices since the 1880s of shares in Royal Dutch Shell and Impressionist pictures. But neither were fashionable at the time. In the 1880s fashion was to buy Rosa Bonheur – and the bonds being issued in such tempting quantities by the Tsarist government of Russia and the railway companies of Imperial China.

Now, a hundred years into the modern art market, we are seeing a similar flow from China: an enormous number of ancient Chinese funeral wares. The supply, which was negligible, is not only growing, but could continue to grow for decades. Geraldine Norman explained how:

> The Chinese have been burying their dead for several thousand years and up to about 1600 a supply of pottery accoutrements for the afterlife was buried with them. The great tombs of the Tang dynasty with their pottery horses, camels, musicians and women are among the major tourist attractions of China today.
>
> In the push to modernise China new construction projects are constantly unearthing forgotten tombs. These are supposed to be reported to the authorities and their contents removed to a local warehouse.

The way was clear for local robbers to get to work. They are linked to the international art market by gangsters operating from Hong Kong and Macao, getting guidance as to values from well-illustrated auction catalogues. For in the 1980s collecting will continue to be fashionable fun, but it will not be automatically considered profitable fun. That idea died at about the time PCW deserted Sotheby's.

# 4 HIRSCH: THE LAST HURRAH

For all his talk of investment and profit, PCW remained to the end an auctioneer. So he naturally believed that the high point of his career was the sale in June 1978 of the works accumulated over the preceding sixty years by Robert von Hirsch, a German industrialist long resident in Switzerland. The sale fetched £18,468,300 ($33,981,672) in only eight sessions, nearly treble the Mentmore total, breaking thirty-nine world records on the way. But to a professional auctioneer the money was less important than the knowledge that it was an historic event – PCW compared it with the Hamilton Palace sale, the first and most glamorous of the auctions of the possessions of the British aristocracy nearly a century earlier. Von Hirsch had more 'associative value' than any other sale PCW ever conducted. Most of the pieces with the Mentmore name attached were of no great artistic importance. Those in the von Hirsch sale emphatically were, and PCW made the most of the chance, using the occasion to orchestrate an unparalleled series of auctions: that week in June the whole world of art danced to his tune.

Von Hirsch was yet another of the German-Jewish refugees whose possessions had formed the foundation of PCW's career. An unusually canny watcher of the political weather, von Hirsch had set up a branch of the family leather business in Basle in the late 1920s. The day after the elections that brought Hitler to power he sought permission to leave Germany from Goering, then Gauleiter of Prussia. Goering agreed on condition that he gave the German people (i.e. Goering himself) a Cranach, *Judgment of Paris*, from a collection that was already famous. Von Hirsch was fifty when he left, but lived on in Basle for nearly forty more years, surrounded by his treasures.

Many collectors are happy for their name to be immortalized in a museum – or failing that, a separate wing of an existing institution – named after them. Duveen, later boosted by the American tax authorities, had made this procedure the norm amongst American collectors. But there is another sub-class, those collectors who do not mind if their possessions are scattered after their death, provided that they are for ever associated with their name. Erasmus, the great

Renaissance scholar, established the class in a letter to Grolier, a leading French public servant of his day, an ambassador and director of the Royal finances, who is now remembered for the books he collected: 'You owe nothing to books', wrote Erasmus, 'but books will ensure your immortality.' Three centuries later the French writer Edmond de Goncourt made the point even more elegantly. He did not want 'the works of art which have been the joy of my life' to be consigned to the 'cold tomb of a museum and the uncultivated glance of the indifferent passer-by. I want them to be sold under the auctioneer's hammer, so that the joy the acquisition of each one of them has given me shall be given again, in each case, to some inheritor of my taste.'

Von Hirsch's idea of immortality was association with a famous sale. According to Dr Jorge Wille, Sotheby's man in Zurich: 'One of von Hirsch's last wishes, was to make good prices.' 'Even a sober Swiss banker had caught Wilson's disease', wrote Eugene Thaw in *The Times* after the sale, 'clearly he suspected what would happen since he specified long ago when making his will that Sotheby's should sell his collection. His name was known for years to some cognoscenti, but now he is really famous, an apotheosis as a collector far more spectacular than any he could have achieved by donating the whole lot to a good museum.'

PCW was well placed to play on his vanity. He had been at school with von Hirsch's step-son and had first met von Hirsch himself in 1938. Sotheby's had regularly valued the collection for insurance purposes and Dr Jorge Wille was a friend, spending much of his time with the old man. They had two rivals: the city fathers of Basle with whom Hirsch quarreled; and Georg Swarzenski, the curator of the Frankfurt Museum who had advised him over the medieval German artefacts he acquired between the wars, far the finest group in private hands. Obviously Swarzenski had hoped they would go to his beloved museum. But the hopes died with him.

For most of his life von Hirsch was a typcial German-Jewish bourgeois of the old school, mondain, liking jokes, the theatre, concerts – numbering Bruno Walter and Rudolf Serkin among his friends. But in old age, like many other rich men, von Hirsch tended to be surrounded only by cronies. Several of his friends told Thaw that visiting him had become an ordeal of 'paying court', of uncritically admiring, 'instead of the easy civilized exchange it should have been' – a description which makes him sound like the Basle equivalent of Graham Greene's Dr Fischer of Geneva.

Although the medieval objects were the unique centre-piece of his collection, he had also accumulated a large number of pictures, a Toulouse-Lautrec (his first acquisition) bought in 1907, an early

224

Picasso, a scattering of Impressionists, a marvellous collection of drawings, including four by Rembrandt. But everything he owned, even the furniture he used in daily life was fine.

A lesser impresario than PCW would simply have organized a small number of special sales for the medieval objects and the pictures, since there were simply not enough books or porcelain, for instance, to justify separate sales. Instead, PCW and Stanley Clark turned the last seven days of June in 1978 into the 'von Hirsch week', the supreme example of hype – complete with an 'Olympic-sized press centre'. In doing so they benefited, not only von Hirsch's heirs (his step-children) and Sotheby's itself, but also other collectors whose possessions were included in the sales, and the other sale-rooms – not only in London, for that miraculous week records were freely set in Paris and Switzerland as well.

By the time the collection had done its triumphal tour of the cities where likely buyers were to be found, some people inevitably felt the publicity was already too strident. Thaw, the respected dealer swamped by the resources his rival could muster, was in the van. He complained that it was a 'media event', in which expertise was drowned

> by the tidal wave of Hirsch publicity ... as a media event the Hirsch sale caused some farcical activities on its periphery that had nothing to do with the art being sold. One became aware of art market 'groupies', as determined a band of camp followers as those that surround rock stars. They would wheedle and cajole sale-room tickets, determined to see and be seen even though they had no interest in buying. There were Hirsch parties and everywhere there were cameramen. Wherever one looked, a lens was looking back. I don't blame Sotheby's. They did a superb job of merchandising, which is their responsibility to the consignor. I blame the current philistine approach to art collecting as investment, which has taken away our society's ability to look at art without $ signs in our eyes.

As so often, the lament that a trend was irreversible immediately preceded the turning of the tide, as the belief in art as an investment gradually ebbed. So it is highly unlikely that we shall ever see such a concentration of sales again, ever see fine art news dominate the front pages for a whole week.

The Hirsch sales occupied eight sessions between the 20th and 27th. But the aura they created was spread right through the sale-room world. A list of sales that week gives an idea of how far the Pied Piper, PCW, had led his flock over the twenty years he had been chairman of Sotheby's. 'On the fringe' Sotheby's Belgravia had sales of fine French and Continental furniture, clocks, works of art and bronzes, English and foreign silver, fine and inexpensive wine and vintage port, and fine Victorian paintings, drawings and water-colours. At their sale-room in Torquay, they were offering collectors items, dolls and toys, firearms, microscopes, cameras, clocks and watches, in Zurich fine and rare wines: while von Hirsch's books were included in a sale at Hodgson's Rooms, which combined them with books from the 'Kelmscott, Doves, Ashendene, Golden Cockerel, Nonesuch and other presses' – it is difficult to know which was the 'magic' name in this galère, probably not that of von Hirsch himself.

Christie's were not idle. In Florence they had arranged a sale of the contents of the Castello di Brignano-Frascata, involving furni-ture, objects of art, paintings, prints, carriages, saddles and harness, the property of Count Bruzzo. There were seventeen sales at South Kensington, including traditional items like English and Continen-tal pictures, Japanese prints and Chinese scrolls, European ceramics and silver. 'Collectibles' included 'cigarette cards, postcards, Baxter prints, Stevengraphs, dolls and doll's houses, photographs, motor-ing, aeronautical and railway art and literature.'

But these were peripheral. The first von Hirsch sale was scheduled for the evening of Tuesday 20th. Even before PCW mounted the rostrum the fever had taken hold. Earlier that day, thirty-four manuscripts from the collection of Major J. R. Abbey had been sold for £239,430 ($440,550), with no lots unsold. A late fifteenth-century illustrated manuscript of the Old Testament in Greek, written and decorated with twenty-one large miniatures had fetched £22,000 ($40,480) – against estimates of £4,000 to £6,000. At Sotheby's, too, Chinese export porcelain had fetched £143,975 ($264,914) with only 6 per cent unsold. At Christie's, coins had gone for £125,973 ($231,790), only 2 per cent unsold – a Milanese ducat showing Galeazzo Maria Sforza had fetched £9,500 ($17,480), nearly three times the estimate. A sale of English watercolours at Christie's 'saw generally very competitive bidding' and totalled £166,010 ($305,458) with only 1 per cent unsold. A new record of £19,000 ($34,960) was paid for a Paul Sandby, against an estimate of between £8,000 and £12,000, and other pictures, including a Richard Dadd and a tiny Rossetti had fetched three times their estimates. The magic had spread to Paris where Ader and Picard 'saw prices consistently above expectations for routine pieces of eighteenth-century and French furniture'.

By the evening session at Sotheby's: 'the atomosphere had more in common with a casino than a fine art auction house.' Even the grumpy Thaw was in attendance, and paid £95,000 ($174,800) for one of the few Raphael drawings still in private hands. But the top price was paid by PCW's old friend and mentor, Marianna Feilchenfeldt – £640,000 ($1,177,600) for the last Dürer watercolour in private hands, a rough, quick sketch of an isolated rock on the banks of the River Adige. She also paid £300,000 ($552,000) on behalf of the Karlsruhe Museum for another Dürer, *Christ on the Mount of Olives*. The Cleveland Museum paid £160,000 ($294,400) for a Rembrandt sketch. The evening's total, £2,777,000 ($5,109,680), with nothing unsold, was above any estimate (the Dürer drawing had been expected to fetch £200,000) and well above even the reserves – which themselves had been set far higher than the estimates.

Dr David Wilson, the director of the British Museum, chose the Wednesday to make a passionate and rather pathetic appeal to the auction houses at least to waive their commissions when national institutions spent more than, say, £50,000 on a single item. He blamed their 'razzmatazz' for driving up prices, believing that Mentmore had started the process. But his appeal was drowned by more records from the sale of von Hirsch's Old Masters for nearly £1.75 million. Baron von Thyssen was prominent among the buyers, acquiring a fourteenth-century Adoration of the Magi for £75,000 ($138,000), a fine small Rubens oil sketch for £95,000 ($174,800), and an important early German work for £120,000. ($220,800). Christie's had a couple of sales, of books and manuscripts and fine clocks and watches, and at Belgravia French and Continental furniture went for £235,120 ($432,620). Not all the buyers had come to London: at Parke-Bernet a large Tiffany bronze lamp with a shade in the shape of a flowering lotus fetched a record $60,000 (then £32,250), double the estimate; and in Paris the Greek government paid a record £404,761 ($744,760), over double the estimate, for *Un Grec à Cheval*, the finest Delacroix seen in the auction rooms since 1945.

The next day it was the turn of the German government to buy back their heritage. The medieval objects were sold at a morning sale – PCW knew that evening sales were for the Beautiful People, interested in the Impressionists and later pictures, the professionals preferred the mornings. That morning two small enamels dating from the twelfth century fetched £1.1 million ($2.02 million) and £1.2 million ($2.2 million) respectively, the highest prices ever paid for objects, and, even more remarkably, prices at which no one (not even Eugene Thaw) cavilled. PCW took the enamel up with his usual rhythm: 'One million, one million one hundred thousand, 1150, 1200, 1200 at one million two hundred thousand, your bid, sir', in a tone designed to reassure Sir Geoffrey Agnew that he really had

227

secured the piece. The underbidder – another well-known London dealer, Eskanase – was acting for 'a private European collector'. Sir Geoffrey was acting for the buyers of a number of other crucial lots – a ring of German museums orchestrated by the formidable Dr Hermann Abs, the retired chairman of the Deutsche Bank. He needed all his authority to ensure that they did not bid against each other and that each piece found a home – a century earlier the Germans had shamefacedly to return many of the books they had acquired at the Hamilton Palace Library sale because none of their museums or libraries had the funds to buy them. The occasion was also noteworthy as the last time the British Rail Pension Fund made a major purchase at an auction – a twelfth century gilt bronze candlestick for £550,000 ($1.01 million), the only object in the collection which the British Museum was prepared to put on show. The total over the two sessions was an amazing £7,248,990 ($13,338,141). Only three lots were bought in, for a mere £11,280 ($20,755).

But there were buyers left over, for a sale of musical instruments at Sotheby's totalled £204,166, ($375,665), with £56,000 ($103,000) paid for the Graf van der Golz Stradivarius. At Christie's South Kensington: 'a series of scrap albums referring to the motoring and aeronautical activities of C. S. Rolls from 1899–1910' was sold. At Neale's of Nottingham the Derby City Museum paid £1,900 ($3,496) for a 'rare Derby canary yellow cylindrical chocolate cup and cover'. A sale at Lawrence's in the little West Country town of Crewkerne totalled £77,691 ($142,951), while a bottle of the fabled 1858 Château Yquem went for £700 ($1,288) at a wine sale at Christie's: 'no bottle of white wine had ever matched that price in an English sale'.

On the Friday, the sale of von Hirsch's furniture showed just how far 'Hirsch fever' had taken hold. A 'coiffeuse' made by Roentgen for the Elector of Saxony was bought on behalf of Dr Abs for £200,000 ($368,000). But the remaining 152 lots (which brought £691,356 ($1,272,095) ) were not extraordinary, for they included such relatively mundane items as the chairs von Hirsch actually used: 'the furniture and decorations had a pleasantly used air', noted Geraldine Norman, 'though they were generally good eighteenth-century or Empire pieces the standard was not as high as other sales ... a few minor items in the sale fetched high prices for what they were.'

Over at Christie's there was an object lesson in the fickleness of fashion when a collection of English pictures fetched £1.9 million ($3,496,000). There were four auction records for individual artists, but these included the £120,000 ($220,800) paid for a Lawrence and £40,000 ($73,600) (well below the estimate) for a Zoffany – allowing for inflation still far below the prices of similar pictures in the 1920s.

After the weekend the buyers returned refreshed for a totally new sensation; the sale at Sotheby's of 'the most important extant source of French classical music', the musical scores assembled by the Comte de Toulouse, a son of Louis XIV and Madame de Monte-span, 'transcribed for performance by André Philidor and his family ... in some cases from the works of contemporary composers of whose work no other manuscripts exist.' They were bought for £120,000 ($220,800) by a French dealer, Pierre Berse, who was hoping to get the French national libraries to buy back their heritage.

But the other sales that day – of miniatures, pottery and maiolica and oriental ceramics – were overshadowed by the second evening sale of some of von Hirsch's modern pictures. 'The largest and best-dressed crowd so far attracted by the sales' was in no mood to quibble about prices. Some of the pictures were undeniably fine: Pissarro's 'penetrating and affectionate portrait of the young Cézanne' went for £300,000 ($552,000), against an estimated range of £90,000 to £120,000; and a Matisse, *Nature Morte à la Dormeuse* for £310,000 ($570,400), one and a half times the estimate. But hype ruled and panic had set in so far as the many lesser paintings were concerned. One dealer heard an American lady say to her escort: 'Hurry up, buy something.' Not surprisingly, in Geraldine Norman's words: 'the packed rooms of bidders ran prices on minor pictures regularly far beyond estimates, a reflection of the romance of the occasion. The market in Impressionist and modern pictures has been in a depressed state for several years.'

By the 27th Sotheby's could get away with attaching von Hirsch's name to a morning sale of porcelain that included only a few of his possessions. These were to be sold at 11.00 am, followed by 'Impor-tant Continental porcelain' belonging to lesser mortals at – 11.10 am. Although a Meissen white porcelain figure of a large macaw two foot high went for £105,000 ($193,200), the highest auction price for any piece of European porcelain, and a Giovanni di Paolo 'substantially restored in the 1920s' for £50,000 ($92,000) yet collectors' purses were not bottomless: prices at another sale of Old Master paintings and drawings that day were below expectations.

But that evening, at the final, gala von Hirsch sale: 'the clientele, perhaps sensing that it was the last chance to bid in an historic sale, regularly marked prices to double if not quintuple Sotheby's pre-sale estimates. A Cézanne watercolour *Nature Morte au Melon Vert*, went for £300,000 ($552,000). It provided the means of measuring the normally unmeasurable 'hype factor'. Thaw noted that another Cézanne still life was sold that week: 'also of melons, of the same size and date, fresher in colour and preservation and according to many

229

authorities, a finer example altogether'. It came from the famous Hahnloser collection and brought the high, but rational, price of about $350,000 (£190,217) – just over half the price reached for von Hirsch's *Melon*.

PCW retained his cool: 'Had we said that the collection would have fetched £16 million', he asserted, 'we would have been ridiculed and then the result would have been to depress prices.' Thaw was naturally depressed: 'An event of this kind', he wrote, 'inevitably has a ripple effect over the whole world of art collecting, creating a South Sea Bubble fright, a boom and bust mentality.' Fortunately for art lovers, he was wrong.

# 5  DELUGE

PCW did not see the von Hirsch sale as his farewell performance. Although there had been repeated rumours of his impending retirement – especially when he sold his house in Kent in 1976 – these had been pooh-poohed. He had to weigh his passionate attachment to Sotheby's with his desire not to pay any tax. His attitude to money was paradoxical: he never carried money with him, seemingly indifferent to it. Nevertheless, he felt he had been poor, had suffered from the humiliation inevitable for someone who has lived his life among the very rich. He was notoriously mean, taking the winding country lanes near Clavary rather than pay the tolls on the motorway.

He had hoped to continue living mostly in Britain, but partly at Clavary, without landing his sons with horrendous death duties. He had even discussed the idea of taking the whole company off-shore. But in early November 1979 a leading tax lawyer finally advised him that he risked involving his children in a double set of estate duties, French and British. The solution was to live for most of the year at Clavary, and on the 9th November he resigned, remaining only as a director and as chairman of a rather vague international advisory committee.

His announcement was a dramatic occasion, heralded by a severe thunderstorm as he summoned the staff. The shock was compounded by the announcement that his successor was not to be Peregrine Pollen, still the favourite of many of the department heads, but David Westmorland. Insiders had become reconciled to the idea that PCW's antipathy for Peregrine Pollen had grown so far that 'he simply couldn't bear the idea of Peregrine succeeding him'. And Pollen had steadily lost support over the previous years. 'He was not one of us', says one departmental head: he had been too much of a staff officer, sitting back at the base while the field commanders had to fight the war.

The shock was enormous: some of the porters were in tears; the only positive reaction was Peter Spira's 'little dance of satisfaction'. Most of his associates were incredulous: 'His desertion – four days after the revelations about Blunt' was one director's way of combining bitterness with the old rumours about PCW's supposed treason. PCW knew the chaos his departure would cause. 'He had to be irreplaceable – and he was', says his brother Martin. Someone who had known him for over twenty years explains his departure simply: 'He had had no real life except Sotheby's since he was young: he had never been very close to his sons, he'd never spent much time with them, so he felt he should leave as much as he could to them – he was always hungry for money himself – in addition he was tired, the diabetes had debilitated him.' He assumed that he would still be very much in control.

Clavary was the one true home PCW ever had. Even the unimpressionable Eugene Thaw thought of it as 'an ensemble of Edwardian luxury', which owed a great deal to PCW's 'flair for interior decoration'. And many guests enjoyed rapturously happy summer holidays there, swimming, pottering about in a motor-boat, though PCW, famished for company, would start his restless wanderings at 7.00 am. And some visitors, especially those with children, felt that it was rather oppressive, not really a family home (other guests remember the mosquitoes, attracted by the trees in the park, and the erratic nature of the plumbing, exacerbated by his refusal to pay for a plumber).

He could not be happy once the permanence of his decision had sunk in. No longer at the centre of the world he was alone except for a secretary (who did not stay long) and a chauffeur. Originally he tried to instal a 'tie-line', a permanent telephone link between Clavary and Westmorland's office. When this was laughed out of court he 'spent hours on the phone manipulating everything David Westmorland did'. He naturally assumed he 'would be consulted regularly, and when he wasn't, when he was plainly told "you can't second-guess the people at Bond Street" he became very bitter', says a director. 'I'm going bananas,' he would complain.

Life was not much better back at Sotheby's. David Westmorland had expected to take over on a temporary basis. He had assumed that the senior outside director, Sir Mark Turner, a distinguished industrialist, would soon take over. But Turner was overburdened with bigger business commitments and died in December 1980, finally extinguishing any hopes that Pollen – his cousin and close friend – might have had of running the firm. Westmorland was left increasingly isolated at the centre of a web of intrigue. 'The spymaster general had created his successors and had kept them infighting', says one ex-director, 'and we had what you read about in the papers, an internal power struggle' – for none of those involved, except Spira, were primarily businessmen, they were simply unused to corporate knife-fights and therefore not very skilled at organiza-

232

tional warfare. 'Marcus Linell didn't get on with Graham Llewellyn or Peregrine Pollen', another director told *Fortune* magazine: 'Llewellyn didn't get on with Pollen; Pollen didn't get on with Peter Spira; Spira didn't get on with Llewellyn; I've never experienced anything like it.' Even outsiders noticed. When PCW threw his farewell party at Leeds Castle early in 1980 John Pearson wondered how long Westmorland would last, for he had seen 'some very ambitious gentlemen indeed sipping their champagne'. The managerial merry-go-round during his short chairmanship took its toll: 'the poor chap, amiable, uncommitted, aged ten years in a few months', says one director, like everyone else united in sympathy with the new chairman, so plainly 'decent to the core', but trained as a courtier, not a corporate hatchet-man.

Only insiders knew how vulnerable the company really was. 'I used to think of Sotheby's as a blasted oak tree, kept alive by the external magic of PCW and the experts' was the poetic way one ex-director put it. The shareholders' register told the story more bluntly. In the year he 'deserted', PCW sold off 250,000 shares, leaving him with 400,000, and ignoring an agreement not to sell he had made with the other shareholders at the time of the flotation: Peregrine Pollen sold 175,000, but he still had by far the largest personal holding, 609,000 shares, 5 per cent of the total. Graham Llewellyn, who himself disposed of 38,000 shares, explained rather lamely that the sales amounted merely to an unwinding of the board's holdings as a result of going public.

Even outsiders could see that costs had got completely out of control. PCW was 'an expansionist par excellence'. He once admitted he 'confused sales volume with profitability', and, even before his departure, staff numbers had escalated appallingly. Between the mid-1970s and 1981 the numbers Sotheby's employed world-wide jumped by over 50 per cent to over 1,900. So, although sales kept rising, profit margins declined dramatically. Until 1979 the firm was regularly earning between 4 and 5 per cent of the sales total. By 1981 these margins had been halved. In 1978–79 Sotheby's had earned £8.2 million from sales of £186.4 million; two years later sales had risen by 70 per cent to a record £321 million, and so had gross revenue – the firm was still taking one pound in five realized at its sales. But net profits had actually dropped by 15 per cent to a mere £7 million, the same as the firm had been earning in 1978 when the auctions had brought in a mere half that amount.

Over-hiring was one cause: physical over-expansion was another, for it resulted in an increasing burden of interest and other overheads. In London Sotheby's took the natural opportunity to expand within Bond Street: it bought the old Aeolian Hall the other side of the street from the BBC, as well as the Steinway building.

But the biggest drain was the major expansion in New York. The idea of expansion had been hatched by John Marion during a game of golf with a developer friend Charlie Berenson. Marion had long been irked by the limited physical space available at Madison Avenue. PB '84 had never been a great success, he was looking for a much bigger building to take the majority of sales, including all those in the decorative arts. Madison Avenue would keep the big sales of paintings, sculpture and jewellery. Berenson found an ideal building five blocks east of Madison Avenue on York Avenue. It had originally been built as a cigar factory, then used by Kodak, so was available relatively cheap. But the interior of the building was supported every twenty-two feet by a solid cement pillar; Berenson suggested a way of removing three of them and thus creating enough space for a central auction gallery surrounded by smaller, but still spacious sale-rooms. The idea assumed that sales would expand sufficiently fast to absorb the additional costs: $8.4 million to buy the building, remove the pillars, add a granite façade and all the trimmings to transform a factory into offices, auction rooms and display galleries.

The expansion came at precisely the wrong time. For Christie's had soon bounced back from their bad start. New Yorkers typically loved the competition they introduced, although they still had their critics: 'Look, see, I hate Sotheby's for their goddam arrogance', one dealer told Martin Stansfeld, 'but I hate Christie's for their incompetence'. This was rather unfair to the newcomers. Their first success was the sale of the Ingersoll mansion in Newport, Rhode Island. 'We fought like stink for the sale, it was our first house sale, and we had to make it a success', says David Bathurst – a 'stamp of legitimacy' confirmed by the sale in 1980 of some of Henry Ford's Impressionists. Bathurst and his chairman Jo Floyd proved that they could copy the successes of Peregrine Pollen and PCW on the same circuit twenty years earlier. Christie's were still cautious. They employed only a few people – 'we felt that Parke-Bernet were overstaffed and complacent', says one Christie's director, 'the gulf between management and staff was so great it was almost a joke.'

'By 1979', says one former director, 'that curious process by which a newly public company begins inflicting corporate constipation on its previously entrepreneurial character had begun to take hold'. The 'administrators', Spira's American equivalents, were in the ascendant, displacing more market-oriented executives like Stansfeld and Tom Norton with organization-minded executives who believed, for instance, that 'if you have the right art you can sell it as easily on a street corner in Timbuctoo'. They told still-sceptical colleagues that the move to York Avenue would solve the firm's undoubted administrative problems and at the same time put Christie's in its place.

Christie's success was due, not only to the English contingent, Bathurst, Floyd – and Ray Pearman, the quiet fixer who provided the crucial organizational flair – but also to three American executives. Stephen Latch, a former Warburg man, was sent round to talk to the executors: 'They liked to be talked to by a lawyer or banker', says Bathurst. Somewhat to their own surprise, Christie's also managed to capture a large proportion of the market in Americana thanks to Ralph Carpenter, the guru of Newport furniture. The third challenge was in American paintings thanks to another scholarly figure, Jay Kanter. Bathurst's triumph led to his promotion to running the British end of Christie's, but in mid-1985 a case was brought in New York by a Swiss dealer, Christalline, alleging fraud over the sale of eight Impressionists in 1981. The market had been shaky: only one was sold, but at the time David Bathurst said that three had been. The court threw out the accusations but what Bathurst called this 'exercise in containment against the more sensational elements of the press' led to screaming headlines in the New York press, worries over Christie's licence to conduct auctions, and, inevitably, Bathurst's resignation.

In 1981, however, Bathurst was a hero and Christie's in the ascendant. They were clearly better placed than Sotheby's to benefit from the final compromise agreement with the dealers over the buyer's premium. The long-running argument, ended after a long night's session at Claridge's, had its serious side. 'If Christie's and Sotheby's had been found guilty of collusion', says Christopher Weston of Phillips, 'the art market here would have collapsed because they would have moved to the U.S.'

As part of the agreement both houses agreed to study the idea of reducing the buyers' premium by 2 per cent. Just before Christmas, Christie's decided it could afford the cut, although vendors selling lots for less than £1,000 would have to pay 12.5 rather than 10 per cent commission. Jo Floyd was grinning when he made the announcement, pointing out that his firm would need only an extra 10 per cent business to compensate for the lost revenue. Sotheby's, losing money, couldn't match its rival, and it further inflamed relationships with the dealers by increasing the vendor's premium by 5 per cent to 15 per cent on lots below £500, which still accounted for over three-quarters of the lots sold by both houses. Although the breakeven point was lower at Christie's in South Ken and at the 'fast sales' Sotheby's instituted, lots fetching less than £200 were unprofitable.

Sotheby's was paying the price for over-expansion, and had been hit by a slump which hurt only the more amateur dealers. 'We kept selling the better things', says Julian Agnew, 'whereas in 1974–75 the trade was completely frozen for a few months.' Then – as in 1969–1970 – the slump had merely heralded a new and even less discriminating upsurge in prices and categories. The recession of 1980–82 spelt a return to normality, a period when the fear of losing jobs replaced that of losing the value of your possessions. The premium on prices disappeared with the need for protection against inflation. Within Sotheby's, Peter Spira recognized the point: 'We like inflation', he told *Business Week*, 'we do well when people flee assets for tangible goods.'

'The dealers', in the words of one observer, 'gloated at the failure of Sotheby's "Napoleonic complex"', but they had little reason to gloat over the final solution to the long-running quarrel. Early in 1982 the British Antique Dealers' Association of London Art Dealers agreed to release to the Office of Fair Trading evidence that there had been collusion. It took the Office a mere six weeks to decide that the auction rooms had no case to answer. Counsel hired by a number of leading dealers had already come to the same conclusion, in direct conflict with their learned brethren whose advice had been sought by their official representatives.

The contrast between the two rival auction houses was emphasized by the figures for the opening months of the 1981–82 season. Christie's sales world-wide were up, albeit by only £500,000, to £70.84 million. But Sotheby's refused to release figures. Christie's increased the pressure, launching an aggressive advertising campaign. Sotheby's claimed, with some justice, that comparisons would have been unfair, that the finer lots were still selling and they had no sales in the autumn of 1981 to compare with the disposal a year earlier of the collection of André Meyer, banker (and former shareholder of Parke-Bernet), and a number of spectacular ceramic and jewellery collections. The only well-publicized auction that dreadful autumn was light relief: the sale in November of twenty-four transponders on the satellite Sitcom IV, for which fifty-three television stations were bidding.

By early 1982 Westmorland was desperate for help. The natural man to turn to was Gordon Brunton, a bluff former salesman who had spent twenty years building up the Thomson Organization. He had joined the Sotheby's board a couple of years earlier through Mike Renshaw, a senior advertising executive with Thomson's and an old friend of PCW. Brunton was asked to do a full report on the company's problems. As the situation worsened he had to work fast and, in the event, his study took only six weeks, in which time he managed to interview sixty senior executives, all of whom told him much the same story.

So there were no real shocks when he presented his findings to the directors and then to the staff at the end of March. Nevertheless, the report removed the arrogant gloss that had covered so much. It forced many of the senior people to face reality for the first time. Like them he thought the place 'Byzantine', its management structure worse than non-existent, but its problems had never been openly spelled out, let alone in the blunt language he used. Brunton was used to prima donnas from years of dealing with Thomson's publishing interests and the journalists and printers on *The Times* and the *Sunday Times*. So he could appreciate the high intellectual stature of the Sotheby's staff. He was also able to deliver a favourable verdict on the company's prospects: contrary to reports, it was not financially over-stretched and had a promising future in what was still a growth business.

But those were his only positive conclusions. He was shocked by the individual power bases stemming from personal ambitions, by the lack of regular lines of reporting to superiors, by the bitter divisions between management and experts, often due to the experts' recognition that they were not managers. London and New York were barely on speaking terms, and the European offices, which contributed half London's sales, felt like second-class citizens. There was no management structure: the Group Board was a joke, meeting irregularly, basically for a clubby gossip. The London Board was worse: 'like a Gilbert and Sullivan farce', he kept insisting, with real authority devolved on the Chief Executive's London Operating Committee. And even that was a far from satisfactory body: its membership widely criticized, its function and authority unclear. No wonder those affected by decisions often knew about them only through the grapevine.

PCW, he said, had run Sotheby's in a 'distinctive and autocratic fashion', which was a polite way of putting it. Despite its toughness the report was well received – the applause led by Peregrine Pollen, even though he knew his days were numbered. As a result of the report, Sotheby's was to have a proper managerial structure for the first time in its 228 year history, with a group board supervizing three operating subsidiaries. Brunton had proposed a non-executive chairman: and he was the only director to fill the criteria he laid down for the job. So in April he took over. It was useless looking for an outsider to run the group. A suitable candidate simply could not be available in time. In his appointments Brunton made it clear he was looking, not for professional managerial capacity, because there wasn't any, but for character, for executives who were so trusted that

237

they could thus perform the painful surgery needed to restore the group to health.

Brunton was appointed chairman on 7 April 1982. Peregrine Pollen, Marcus Linell, and David Nash and Robert Woolley in New York left the board. Jay Woolf became vice-chairman – he was by now senior partner of his firm, and had shed all his other clients except Sotheby's – and General Motors. Graham Llewellyn, a solid veteran, who had originally been a jewellery porter at Harrod's, was to be chief executive. Julian Thompson, a virtual outsider since he had spent so much of the previous years in Hong Kong, became chairman of two of the three operating companies into which the business was divided: those covering sales in Britain and sales outside the UK and the Americas. The United States remained separate with Jay Wolff as chairman. John Marion was to remain chief executive but the real authority would be devolved onto Jim Lalley, a graduate from Columbia Business School who had run the Los Angeles sale-room and had then turned himself into an expert as well. Old hands were rather shell-shocked, although they approved the departure of Peter Spira in August and the promotion of his deputy, Andrew Alers-Hankey, perceived by the experts as the only financial figure with any sensitivity towards the business. The new London board had a ghastly job. Every department was encumbered with dead wood, sometimes at the top, and none of the new appointees was a natural hatchet-man. But within a few months the slimming operation had been carried through.

The American operation was in a worse state. Morale had been shot to pieces by lack of cohesion and Christie's success. Marion had already started to sack people in late 1981, but had gone about it in the most cack-handed possible fashion. He had called the staff together and told them that over two hundred people would have to go and that thirty of them would be told every Friday, thus leaving the whole staff in a state of suspense over an unnecessarily prolonged period. Worse was to come. In June he announced the closure of the historic sale-room on Madison Avenue and of the sale-room in Los Angeles. This had always been something of an anomaly. It had opened with a great fanfare in early 1971 with the highly-publicized sale of surplus props and memorabilia accumulated by 20th Century Fox over the years. This set a rather too showbizzy tone and the sale-room never really became an integral part of the Sotheby empire, partly because the market simply wasn't sufficiently developed, partly because secret reserves were illegal in California so Sotheby's could not use them. At any other time its closure would have been seen as a sensible recognition of the limits of Sotheby's American operations. But, like all the other steps taken by the firm that summer, it was perceived as a panic measure, a sign of impending doom.

Abandoning Madison Avenue naturally created problems in turning York avenue into a New York equivalent of Paris's Hôtel Drouot, with junk sales downstairs and classy ones upstairs. For private buyers were looking for a 'bit of class'. The dealers were left stranded without a natural centre for their activities – for Jay Wolff ensured that no other auction house would be allowed to take on the lease ('I may be stupid, but I'm not dumb', he says). It now looks like a deserted shrine, standing four-square and empty surrounded by the dozens of galleries – from Provence Antiques to the Art of Tibet, from Vito Gallo Antiques to Time Will Tell (selling, as you guessed, antique wrist-watches) – reminding passers-by of the all-embracing cult of the objects once worshipped within. Opposite stands the Carlyle Hotel, prominent in its display cases an advertisement for – Christie's. Apart from newsreel clips, the only permanent pictorial record of the glories of 980 Madison Avenue comes in a film starring Meryl Streep, *The Still of the Night,* shot there on location, in which Tom Norton plays an auctioneer. Although plenty of renovation was promised to provide galleries round the York Avenue building, its location, just north of a major hospital, and too far to the East Side to be on the regular beat of mid-towners tells against it. Meanwhile Christie's quietly gloated, pointing to the way that a couple from Kentucky just happened to stroll past their sale-rooms one evening, inspected the Elizabeth Firestone collection of gold boxes on display within and bid $200,000 for some of them next day. Trade like that simply does not pass down York Avenue. For although the art trade had moved uptown with Parke-Bernet years earlier it was (and is) by no means clear that it would shift East to York Avenue. The staff didn't want to move either. David Nash, shaken as much by the unexpected competition from Christie's as by the move, flew to London to beg for the best possible lots for the first sale at the new location. It is, as he says, 'a marvellous machine for conducting auctions in', the first purpose-created auction rooms since 980 Madison Avenue, elegant and spacious, but still looks lonely.

In London the closure of Belgravia was more logical, just as sudden, just as badly handled. For years a number of far-sighted departmental heads (especially Peter Nahum) had recognized that the experiment had worked, that Victoriana was now in the mainstream of collectibility, and that it was logical to re-integrate the Belgravia material into the newly-enlarged premises available in Bond Street. But in the absence of Stanley Clark the planned withdrawal from Belgravia looked like a panic: the employees were

239

given only a weekend's notice and even the press release got it rather wrong. As in New York, the senior people didn't want to move (especially David Batty, naturally forlorn at losing his independent empire). The same slimming operation was carried through, with rather less pain, in the provinces. Six people left the small operation at Chester, ten went at Torquay – saved from closure by its former management, which bought back the sale-room in August 1982 for a fraction of the price Sotheby's had paid a few years before.

Obviously Sotheby's troubles were widely-publicized: 'We lived by publicity and then we died from it', says Lord Westmorland. The most damaging article from Sotheby's point of view (and, by a natural corollary, one of the best) was a major piece in *Fortune* by Gwen Kinkead, published at the end of May, only a few weeks after Brunton had taken the chair. Its incisive analysis under the headline 'Sotheby's Lost Art: management' discouraged always-nervous executors from consigning goods to a firm that appeared to be in worse trouble than it really was. 'All executors are scared stiff that they're going to be sued for negligence', says David Bathurst, 'and what could be more negligent than entrusting your goods to an auction house that appeared to be in trouble?' Even departments like books, which had not been too badly affected in previous slumps, lost business in 1980–82. 'It was a loss of confidence, like a run on a bank', says Peter Spira, '*Fortune* never got round to mentioning the £11 million we had in cash and other liquid assets, but insisted on our £13 million debts.'

Sotheby's had already declared a loss for the first half year. Even so the results for the year to the end of August 1982, released early in February 1983, were dreadful. Sales had gone down by a quarter to £267 million. Revenue was down by slightly less, 20 per cent to £52.8 million: not surprisingly the pre-tax profit of £7 million had been replaced by a loss of £3.1 million. A quarter of the staff had gone although Sotheby's still employed 1,430 people, far more than its great rivals. Nor were their problems over. Buyers had not followed Parke-Bernet to York Avenue and sales there during the autumn had declined from £59 million to £37.2 million. For the unthinkable had happened: within five years of their arrival, Christie's were, just, outselling Parke-Bernet and, for the first time since the early 1950s, were ahead world-wide. But by that time Brunton and the board had worse things to worry about than the competition.

# 6  A FATE WORSE THAN DEATH

By mid-1982 Sotheby's was marked down as a likely candidate for take-over. All the ingredients were there: a glamorous name, the departure of the Great Man leaving a managerial vacuum behind him, together with a business which was clearly capable of rescue from short-term losses. It was especially vulnerable because so many rats had deserted the sinking share register: when the company was floated on the stock-market in 1977 the directors had controlled 53 per cent of the company: by the end of 1982 the figure was down to 14 per cent. The Rothschild Investment Trust, which still had 10 per cent after the flotation, had cut its stake to a mere 1 per cent; and clients of Robert Fleming, a merchant bank specializing in fund management, had disposed of 1.5 million shares. The buyers were a varied collection. They included a Kuwaiti businessman, Shaikh Nassar al-Sabah (who also owned 6 per cent of Christie's), Warner Communications, Henry Macneil, a wealthy American businessman, as well as a horde of professional speculators, smelling a 'special situation' and ready to sell to the highest bidder.

The first vulture to descend on the Sotheby board room, naturally in his corporate jet, was Steve Ross, chairman of Warner Communications. John Marion had been mightily impressed by his hard sell of the possibilities of conducting an auction business from the home, naturally using computers made by Atari, then a Warner subsidiary. Brunton was less enthusiastic, and Ross was politely turned down. The only English firm to show real interest was a major conglomerate, Sears Holdings. But its chairman, Leonard Sainer, was really interested only in a bargain and was soon deterred. The most serious talks were with American Express. John Marion had been in desultory contact with the group for some years in an attempt to mount joint marketing efforts. Superficially a bid made sense: Sotheby's 'fitted in with the lifestyles of the Amex membership', says a director, and Amex was openly looking out for new services to add to its portfolio.

Speculation about a possible bid increased in late November. A rough tough American wheeler-dealer, David Murdock, had started building up his holding in the second half of the year, after the loss for the first half year had been announced, and this helped the shares to double to over £5 in the autumn. Ten days before Christmas the blow fell. Just as the Sotheby team was setting off for New York to negotiate with Amex, two New York financiers, Stephen Swid and Marshall Cogan, announced that they had bought 14.2 per cent of Sotheby's shares (at an average price of 519p). Although they did not announce a full-scale bid, they were obviously only awaiting the most appropriate moment – presumably once the horrid truth of the full year's losses had been spelt out.

The bid immediately transformed two previously unknown businessmen into major players on the international business scene. Swid had been a researcher with a couple of respected investment institutions before teaming up in 1973 with the much better-known Marshall Cogan. He had helped found the aggressive New York stockbroking firm of Cogan, Berlind, Weill and Levitt, which eventually merged with Shearson Hammill and then with American Express. But by that time Cogan had been eased out by his old partner, Sanford Weill, his only consolation a pile of cash. Cogan and Swid's first takeover was GFI Industries, a maker of carpet felt, based in New Jersey, GFI became their holding company and thus the – apparently wholly inappropriate – bidder for Sotheby's. This was rather misleading, for in 1976 they had seized the opportunity to acquire Knoll, the furniture manufacturers, a business which, like Sotheby's, depended on a group of temperamental specialists. Its former owner, Walter Heller, had given the management three months to find the funds to buy him out: they couldn't, but when Cogan and Swid made an offer thirty out of the company's thirty-one all-important designers threatened to quit. But they managed to get two hundred of the employees together to explain their intentions. It was a dramatic occasion: Swid remembers people hanging out of the windows overlooking the courtyard where they were talking. The experts stayed, the company prospered as never before.

Naturally they tried the same tactics with Sotheby's. They had approached Jay Wolff through a mutual friend. He rebuffed them and they were forced to consider an unfriendly bid. They then began to buy in the market in earnest and soon had 15 per cent of the company. This, they felt, gave them a veto right in any other deal Sotheby's might get up to (especially disposing of the Los Angeles sale-room, which had still not been sold). Their position was perfectly logical: the business had been mismanaged and they knew how to turn it round: 'the experts were the curators and they were not being treated as they should have been', says Swid. Yes, they proposed to supervize the business themselves; they would each spend half their time in London, which would remain the centre of the group's

242

activities. And finally, yes, they were tempted to control a business which would give them a more assured, higher profile in society. They were both collectors of modern art and Cogan was chairman of the American Council on the Arts. But they clearly wanted a higher public profile, they were not content with the signed photographs of politicians in their waiting room. For they were – and are – a couple with flair. Their joint office testifies to that. It is on the very top floor of the new Citibank building on 53rd Street and Lexington, just below the unmistakable steep triangular roof. Simply furnished by Knoll, with a stunning view west to the New Jersey hills, it is the office of men interested in the appearance of things.

There was a pause of several months between the original announcement of their stake and the bid, which eventually arrived at Bond Street on April 15. For most of that time the Sotheby board had been lulled into a sense of false security by the promising progress of the negotiations with David Robinson, the Chairman, and Sandy Weill, Cogan's old partner and then President of American Express. But then the negotiations went sour: Andrew Alers-Hankey casually mentioned that Christie's sales had, temporarily anyway, overtaken Sotheby's, and this obviously gave the American Expressmen pause for thought, implying as it did that Sotheby's needed more managerial rejuvenation than they had initially supposed. Then there was the personal element: it was clear that Weill, by now a pillar of the financial establishment, did not relish a fight with a former colleague and rival from earlier, less inhibited days. The negotiations fizzled out and by the time the bid, of 520p a share, was received, the Sotheby Board was largely defenceless.

Their only hope was to prolong the battle. Cogan and Swid had to borrow the money they needed for the bid and for the increased working capital they pledged they would provide. So time was against them: although they could afford the cost of the loans (appropriately from their landlords, Citibank) their need to borrow gave the opposition a handle, suggesting their lack of capital backing, and their inability to sustain a long war or increase the price they would pay. Nevertheless, the bid seemed irresistible: the price was far more generous than anyone had dreamt of during the troubles of 1981–82. Moreover they had hired Morgan Grenfell, one of London's best banks at take-over manoeuvres, and put forward as chairman the highly established figure of the late Lord Harlech. He had been a Tory minister and British Ambassador to Washington during the Kennedy years – thus provoking a rumour that the Kennedys were behind the bid. But he proved an ineffectual champion. (By a strange coincidence, he was married to Pamela Colin, daughter of Sotheby's old antagonist, Ralph Colin. But Colin warned his son-in-law against becoming involved.)

For it was soon clear that they could not repeat their success with Knoll by persuading the experts to accept them. The board's opposition had, predictably, been immediate and ferocious: without any prompting the heads of departments signed a letter threatening to quit if 'Toboggan and Skid', as the bidders were soon named, succeeded. 'Sotheby's experts do not accept items for sale without looking at them personally and making an assessment', the bidders complained, 'but none of the experts have been allowed to look at us.' They tried and failed to meet the key experts – including Thompson and John Marion but, pointedly, excluding Graham Llewellyn. Behind the experts' opposition was the fear of effective, hands-on management, for the bidders were obviously proposing to run the business themselves. There was also a certain snobbery: 'The real reason why they were against the two', says Tom Norton, 'was that they were not using their own money. Their reliance on Citibank triggered the snobbery of the London staff.' 'We would be working for a bank', said one director. Behind the snobbery was the very genuine fear that the couple did not have the long-term backing required to support Sotheby's in difficult times. In New York, Jay Wolff produced a ruling by the Securities and Exchange Commission in which Cogan, although not admitting guilt, had agreed to allow himself to be disqualified as an investment adviser – a damaging blow to the bidders' reputation. Nevertheless they are still convinced they could have won if Brunton had not blocked their path to the experts: 'I'll talk to them', he had said.

For Toboggan and Skid had underestimated the ferocity of the response by the board, a hostility compounded by insecurity and fear of the unknown. Graham Llewellyn was under the worst strain. He felt genuinely miserable at the thought of the takeover and his feelings exploded into the open with the famous remark: 'If they win I'll blow my brains out.' He claims the phrase was a journalistic invention (or, if spoken, an off-the-record joke), but for outsiders the phrase summed up the hysteria underlying the strength of the reaction. The City of London's takeover panel smelt the fear in the air and was concerned that he was going too far. More rationally he could say that 'what sticks in my gullet about all this is that having done all the soul-destroying restructuring of the last year, these two Americans have come along to try and reap the rewards'. The bidders had approached a number of ex-Sotheby directors, notably Peregrine Pollen and Jeremy Cooper, and they tried to contact some departmental heads (including Michel Strauss) through dealers; but their trump card was PCW himself. Pique at being out in the cold, love of adventure and of power, all affected his judgment. They claimed that he was the only director to treat them courteously on the one occasion they did get to meet the board. The others 'treated us like pariahs', says Swid, 'they did everything possible to try to intimidate and frighten us' – although the directors claim they behaved correctly. Relations were inevitably strained, and feelings exacerbated when Morgan Grenfell released to the press details of an early meeting which the Sotheby Board thought was confidential. By contrast PCW tried to persuade the rest of the board to let him negotiate with the two Americans and a number of his colleagues are convinced that, given half a chance, he would have done a deal with them. But Brunton was firm: it was for the board as a whole to negotiate. PCW, who previously had felt that he could charm Brunton into following him, never forgave him.

Brunton's role was crucial. 'He was very different from everyone else in the story', says one adviser, 'he was not impressed by wealth.' Most of the advice came from Spira's old employers, S. G. Warburg. Their team was headed by a senior director, Hugh Stevenson, but the chairman, David Scholey, was personally deeply involved in the defence. This was mounted on two fronts: first the preparation of a document rubbishing the bid, and secondly securing the evidence required to prove to the Office of Fair Trading that the bid should be referred to the Monopolies Commission.

The defence could not claim that Sotheby's assets were undervalued – the bidders were offering a premium of nearly £36 million over asset value for the goodwill attaching to the name; nor could they forecast an immediate and dramatic return to profitability. They could say that staff had been reduced from 2,002, to 1,370, 'almost entirely by reductions in administrative and other non-expert staff'; that a number of major sales, among them the Havemeyer collection of Impressionists and the contents of Hever Castle, were in the pipeline; and, above all, that 'annual operating cost savings of around £8 million have been achieved and consequently the company's break-even point has been sharply reduced. When sales pass this point approximately 80 per cent of revenues flow through to profits attributable to shareholders'. But this point was some way off. Sales in the six months to the end of February 1983 had slumped to £109 million from £143.3 million for the same period the previous year. Inevitably, the main thrust of the defence was concentrated on undermining the bidders' credibility. Appendices emphasized 'their lack of knowledge of the business', Cogan's problems with the SEC and the deficiencies in their claims to be able to help Sotheby's business. Warburg's even drew up a balance sheet for the combined firm showing a net asset deficiency, with borrowings £15 million more than assets.

But they knew their efforts were unlikely to be successful. 'The audience didn't want to hear,' says Hugh Stevenson, 'most serious investors had sold out long ago', leaving only what Wall Street insiders call the 'arbs' (arbitrageurs) totally indifferent to anything other than a quick profit. They were equally unlucky with the OFT. Its officials knew the art market, only eighteen months earlier they had dealt briskly with the dealers in their complaint against the Big Two. They had to recommend whether a proposed bid would constitute a monopoly. They decided it didn't, and sent their recommendation to their political master, the Secretary of State for Trade, Lord Cockfield. These recommendations were rarely overturned, but this particular minister had acquired a reputation as something of a maverick. This was, on the face of it, improbable: Cockfield started as a tax inspector of great brilliance – he still talks with the measured, slightly artificial precision of a tax judge – and had subsequently run Boots the Chemists. Edward Heath had brought him into public life to run the Prices Commission but his precision and objectivity had also commended him to Margaret Thatcher: 'he thought in paragraphs', she once said admiringly. As Secretary for Trade he had shown an alarming tendency to take his own erratic line in deciding on whether mergers should be referred to the Monopolies Commission and then whether its recommendations should be accepted. This was not entirely his fault: he had proposed a framework providing more rational criteria for judging mergers, but this had become lost in the government machinery.

There was no obvious reason for him to overturn his officials' decision, but nevertheless a reference to the Monopolies Commission offered the best hope for delaying Cogan and Swid while they searched for a friendly counter-bidder, a 'White Knight'. By the end of the first week after the bid it was clear that the defence needed to open a new, political front. Paid political lobbyists are a new breed in Britain, and one of the best is GJW, initials standing for three young professionals, Andrew Gifford, Jenny Jeger and Wilf Weeks, all close to different political parties. On Friday 22nd Stevenson phoned Gifford and that Sunday he and Weeks were presented to the board, which was putting the final touches to the defence document. The board dithered as to whether to hire them – typically PCW lightened the mood with mock-astonishment at the idea of hiring someone with so plebeian a name as 'Weeeeeelf'. But in the end they agreed.

Gifford and Weeks saw the problem very clearly. The art market was highly unlikely to rally to Sotheby's defence: 'they have been thrashing around rudderless and have behaved with an extraordinary degree of arrogance – pretending that nothing was wrong,' said Charles Lee, President of the British Antique Dealers' Association. Sotheby's could scarcely claim to be part of the national heritage when, as a Conservative MP put it, 'they've made so much money selling off bits of it'. The only hope was a referral to the Monopolies Commission. Since a third of bidders dropped their bids while the Commission was considering their case and another third found their bids blocked, a referral, in theory, would give Sotheby's a two-to-one chance. In practice, because Cogan and Swid needed a quick victory, the odds were even better.

GJW's basic concept was simple: to sow the seeds of doubt throughout Whitehall and Westminster. In a world obsessed with safety they hoped that officials and politicians alike would feel that reference to the Monopolies Commission was the safest way to allay the misgivings they intended to sow. The directors' reactions varied. Poor Lord Westmorland worried lest their machinations be found out. Others were rather dazed. Julian Thompson, his foot in plaster, was 'very cool and impressive ... we carted him all over the place', says one insider. But the key figure was PCW. He had given up hope of doing a deal with the bidders and had put his name to the defence document. Suddenly he was needed again, it was all good fun, he immediately understood that the battle was political: 'he treated us like experts', says Weeks. PCW was in his element, making instant decisions, fire-fighting on behalf of his Old Boys, who took their cue from him, and were thoroughly accustomed to the crisis atmosphere.

In the House of Commons the defence was orchestrated through a Tory MP Patrick Cormack, a stalwart supporter of the arts, (in *Who's Who* he lists his recreations as 'fighting Philistines'). He put down an 'early day motion' designed to stir up debate on the subject and lobbied MPs. But the crucial front was in Whitehall: they needed to involve other government departments to muddy a superficially simple picture. This is where Edward Heath came in. He was a former protégé of Sir Alec Martin: he had stayed at Clavary and was close both to Earl Jellicoe and to the chairman of the trustees of Leeds Castle, Lord Geoffrey-Lloyd, ('he was a sort of extension of GJW that week, phoning up several times a day, rallying support in the Lords', according to Weeks).

PCW, Weeks (once Heath's personal assistant) and Lord Geoffrey-Lloyd persuaded Heath to go with them to see Paul Channon, the Minister for the Arts. Weeks and Gifford had soon enlisted the support of Andrew Faulds, the temperamental Labour Arts spokesman as well as the MPs assembled by Cormack. By that time Cockfield was battered by a storm of lobbying – most crucially from Heath, the man who had brought him into high office in the first place. Suddenly it seemed safer to refer, and on May 4 he duly did so. Cockfield extracted from the Director of Fair Trading's Report the key phrases: 'the importance of London as the centre of the international art market and the position of Sotheby's in relation to that market' and used them as a reason for referral. The move was greeted with derision as a typical example of establishment manoeuvring, as indeed it was. Typically *The Times* felt that there was 'no evidence' that 'the public interest would be served if the bid were subject to closer official examination'.

The key to the reference was unlocked a week later when Mrs Thatcher announced that there was to be a General Election. Clearly she had not wanted to be saddled with even the smallest irrelevant row, and Weeks and Gifford had ensured that if the bid were not referred it would prove to be an – albeit tiny – stick with which to beat the government. But, inevitably, Cockfield was blamed. The reference may have saved Sotheby's, but not him. He was eased out of the Cabinet after the election. But referral was only buying time: PCW needed a White Knight.

# 7 HOW WHITE A KNIGHT?

The referral came in the nick of time, for it was announced the very morning that the bid was to close. Without the referral Cogan and Swid could certainly have announced that more than half the shareholders had accepted, and that they controlled Sotheby's. Even after the referral Peter Spira is not alone in thinking that had they immediately bought control in the market, they would have been unstoppable – for no one in the Sotheby camp seriously expected to win the case before the Monopolies Commission. But they were clearly anxious not to commit too much of their expensively-borrowed money too early, and they were thus in a position to be out-gunned by a rival with a deeper pocket.

The first glimmer of hope had appeared the previous week through David Metcalfe, an insurance broker. He had worked for decades with Max Fisher, a Detroit millionaire and former chairman of United Brands. He had thus got to know Fisher's old friend Alfred Taubman. Metcalfe interested Taubman in the possibility of a counter-bid but he needed full details of Sotheby's financial prospects. The only man in a position to supply them was Marcus Agius, a director of Lazard's Bank who had acted for Amex and had prepared a complete financial statement for the negotiations. Taubman needed the information that weekend, Peter Spira found Agius at home and, by Monday, Taubman was in possession of the facts. Even before he had them he had bought a few shares in the market.

Alfred Taubman had been one of a long list of possible saviours, but initially had been rejected simply because he was an individual rather than a firm. But as a person, he seemed well fitted to be a White Knight. Trained as an architect, he relied on his father, a builder, to supervize the actual construction work when he turned to a new and specialized type of property development: the suburban shopping malls which effectively sucked the life from the down-town shopping streets of the United States in the thirty years after the war. His centres were always big enough to accommodate expansion (sometimes too big at first so retailers felt they were rather rattling around), but they were well-designed – even the haughty New York firm of Brooks Bros has stores in four of them.

Until the late 1970s he was known only in a rather restricted circle, but he leapt into the public eye when he formed a syndicate of fellow Detroiters to buy up the Irvine Ranch. This was an extraordinary anachronism: nearly 78,000 acres bordering the Pacific Ocean within easy commuting distance of Los Angeles. Through the paternal ownership of the Irvine family, only 5,000 acres had been developed. Much of the rest was still grazing land or orange groves. After a hard-fought battle (against Mobil Oil amongst others), the estate was bought by Taubman's group, which included the controversial Wall Street banker Herbert Allen, and an old friend, Max Fisher. The story was a glamorous one; five years after the bid the investors sold out at a gigantic profit. On an equity investment of perhaps $25 million the partners walked away with over $500 million. Taubman's share, together with the profits from his twenty-one shopping centres, had put him firmly into the ranks of the richest men in the United States. He could easily afford the $100 million or so required to buy Sotheby's.

By the time he had divorced his first wife and married a former Miss Israel, Judy Mazor, fondly remembered by the staff at Christie's in New York where she had worked on the front counter for a couple of years. Kibitzers, puzzled at the bid, suggested that she had asked her new husband to buy Sotheby's as a present. In fact the bid made perfect sense. Gordon Brunton – now Sir Gordon – who had worked for an even richer man than Taubman, Roy Thomson, understood the rationale perfectly. The same reasoning, the same fascination with a national institution, had led his old boss to buy *The Times*. But there the parallel ended, for Taubman and the small group, including Henry Ford and Max Fisher, who shared control with him, clearly expected to get both fun and profit from their investment. They could also hope for status: indeed all the motives that led rich Americans to buy art, or to seek trusteeships with major museums, applied to Taubman's purchase of Sotheby's.

Taubman 'made up his mind in ten minutes, against the advice of his financial advisers' according to one witness. At first the directors hesitated simply because they knew so little about him. Only David Westmorland had ever met him, and then only casually while on holiday. Once they had explored his background they welcomed him eagerly. The British public were naturally intrigued. They respectfully noted his wealth, his position as trustee of the Whitney Museum and the Smithsonian; they wondered at how he sparred every morning, although in his late fifties, how he had bought the Michigan Panthers, a football team now part of the new United States League – and how his enthusiasm for his footballers was the only time he had been seen to lose his natural cool.

He immediately started buying shares in the market and at that point Swid and Cogan knew they had serious competition. They were already in trouble with the unions at GFI (who said in effect: 'Hey, if you've got the cabbage to buy Sotheby's, why aren't you giving us the pay raise we asked for?'). 'We had bid 520p', says Swid. 'Once the bid was referred we thought the price would fall to the 325–365p range, in fact it dropped only to 420p although both the London and New York markets were falling. Then the shares crept up to 440p against the general trend, even though the market could have had our shares dumped on it. Then the shares started to move up' – there were a number of buyers, British and American, in the market at above the bid price.

By that time they suspected they were outgunned. Taubman officially announced his presence on 10 June and a couple of days later they raised their bid by over £1 a share to 630p. They saw one glimmer of hope when the City's Takeover Panel ordered Taubman to include the shares held by the Sotheby's directors with his own, thus limiting any further purchases. But at the end of June they gave up and persuaded Taubman to buy their stake at 700p a share, far more than he had thought of paying only a few weeks previously, and giving them a profit of £7 million amid suspicions that they had never intended the bid seriously in the first place. This was untrue: they were manifestly interested in 'high-profile' businesses; eighteen months later they spent the profits on buying one of New York's best-known restaurants, '21'. Once they had left the scene, the Monopolies Commission enquiry became a mere formality although the report took until the middle of September. Taubman deeply impressed the Commission, but made it clear that for tax reasons he would turn Sotheby's into a privately-owned company based in the United States.

In the event Taubman proceeded slowly and cautiously. His first step was to install as chief executive officer Michael Ward, a senior partner with Touche Ross, who had audited Taubman's own accounts for several years. To outsiders the step might be puzzling, but it was perfectly sensible. If you have taken over a firm notorious for its lack of managerial control and cohesion, it is natural to install an accountant to look under stones, do the dirty work before a permanent chief executive is appointed., Within a few months Ward had been replaced by Michael Ainslie, head of the National Trust for Historic Preservation – the American equivalent of the British National Trust. Ainslie had acquired a considerable following in the steamy politics of preservation: he was considered a tough Boston Brahmin with a decidedly soft side – the care he showed for his step-children even after he had divorced their mother was legendary.

Like all successful entrepreneurs Taubman was lucky in his timing. The economic recovery cheered the market in that old stand-by, Impressionists, and sellers were emboldened to bring them out again after a particularly successful, if largely unnoticed, sale of the pictures belonging to the Havemeyer family in May 1983. The froth from the bull market on the world's stock exchanges spread to the art market, and records were being achieved with every major sale – not only at Sotheby's, the Duke of Devonshire's drawings from Chatsworth fetched £30 million at Christie's in the summer of 1984.

But the balance between London and New York was changing, and not only because of the continuing strength of the dollar. The newly privatized Sotheby's did not provide a division of sales figures, but Christie's did: in the opening six months of 1984, sales in New York exceeded those for the rest of the world. But even in dollar terms the rise was impressive: by over a third to $113 million – a mere seven years after Christie's had opened in New York. Moreover it had managed to double the sale space available in New York without moving away from its central location.

Accompanying the shift was a subtle change in the direction in which Sotheby's was heading. This was not a matter of people. To an astonishing extent the continuity has been maintained. In their first two years in control Taubman and his associates have lost only a few key people: Derek Johns, Peter Nahum – now both successful dealers – and Andrew Alers-Hankey. But the shift to New York could well be accompanied by an increasing emphasis on the big vendors. Although Ainslie has gone on record confirming his belief in the small client, yet in one department, wine, the trend was the other way. Wine had been the only department where the buyer's premium had not been imposed in 1975: in early 1984, before Ainslie's arrival, the premium was imposed, basically to close the gap with Christie's, the historic leader in the field. Although the premium has enabled Sotheby's to capture some major trade sales, this was at the cost of losing the head of the department, Pat Grubb. And even before the takeover the books department was trying to cope with increasing costs by making up very large lots – not the most efficient way of selling from the vendors' point of view. Indeed Sotheby's could lose a great deal of business to Bloomsbury Book Auctions, a firm with much smaller overheads set up by Frank Herrmann and Lord John Kerr, the former head of the books department. This sort of division between big and small vendors could be on the increase, an abandonment of the Stanley Clark hankering after the '£100 client'.

Another sign of the renewed emphasis on the truly rich came with

252

the strengthening of Sotheby's real estate interests, a natural interest for a property developer like Taubman. These had grown, largely unnoticed, since 1976, with eight regional offices, and sales had reached $136 million. But profits had been minimal, because John Marion's original deal had allowed most of them to go to Sotheby's partner. Taubman appointed Bruce Wennerstrom, an expert in luxury real estate development, to run the firm instead.

Taubman lost no time in surrounding himself with an appropriate galaxy of star directors. Henry Ford became vice-chairman, and Max Fisher, richest of the Detroit group and the only colleague capable of arguing with Taubman as an equal, became a member of the executive committee. It took over a year to assemble the full supporting cast for the Al Taubman show. The majority were, of course, Americans; from the West Coast came Ann Getty, wife of one of the richer Gettys, from Palm Beach a stockbroker, Earl Smith, together with a publisher and a real estate developer from New York. Internationally the cast was starrier: from Germany via Switzerland came Baron Thyssen-Bornemisza, some of whose collection was naturally exhibited at York Avenue; from Japan one of its richest department-store magnates, Seiji Tsutsumi, chairman of the Seibu Group, and from Spain, in early 1985, the King's elder sister.

The star-studded board enabled Taubman to break down the historic barriers between the auction room and the classier museums. He was even able to induce the Director of the Metropolitan Museum to organize a joint Gala, an unthinkable partnership only a few years earlier. Cynics claimed that the style had gone, that Taubman behaved like a *nouveau* – presenting a cheque for $50,000 to the Director in person and saying he'd match it, 'just as he would at a Jewish charity do', said an unfriendly Kibitzer. The sneer, although unjustified, was a fair reflection of Sotheby's continuing position relative to Christie's. In the United States, as in Britain, Christie's have become auctioneers by appointment to the older aristocracy, leaving Sotheby's with the jet-set.

The historic contrast was embodied in the two most newsworthy sales of the spring of 1985. Christie's sold a Mantegna belonging to the Marquis of Northampton for £8.1 million ($10,000,000); a week later John Marion sold the collection of one of PCW's Riviera neighbours, Mrs Florence J. Gould. She was an amazing link with nineteenth-century New York, the widow of Frank J. Gould, younger son of that archetypal Robber Baron, Jay Gould. In the 1920s she and her husband had virtually invented the idea of going to the Riviera in the summer, unthinkable only a few years before Scott Fitzgerald made it the natural summer haunt of Dick and Nicole Diver. She had continued to live in her Riviera villa in regal splendour and after her husband's death in 1955, had started collecting Impressionists, bought mostly from Daniel Wildenstein. So her collection was not an historic one: it had been built up during the Wilson era and included a few works bought at Sotheby's. PCW had naturally been a close friend, and although the trustees gave Christie's – who had already sold her magnificent jewels – a chance to compete, no one really doubted that Sotheby's would sell the Impressionists and her other pictures. Indeed PCW's introduction to the catalogue could serve as a memorial, full of slightly malicious fun (he fully appreciated how the stools on which her guests were seated relegated them to the level of courtiers).

Taubman's resources enabled him to mount an amazing world tour and ensure that the sale itself was surrounded by a social whirlwind that not even PCW in his heyday had been able to mount. But in a sense the pictures let him down. The total, $32.6 million (£26.5 million) was a world record, and Van Gogh's *Landscape with Rising Sun* sold for a record $9.9 million (£8.05 million). But none of the pictures went to a museum, for they were pretty rather than important. Even so the hype had served its purpose, to indoctrinate another generation of the rich with the idea that Impressionists, above all those bought at Sotheby's, were an important adjunct to social aspirations.

PCW was not there to see his lessons being taught by another teacher. He had died from leukemia on 3 June 1984. Friends claim that the fate he feared most for Sotheby's was for it to become a rich man's plaything, but once Taubman had been exposed to the PCW magic during a short stay at Clavary they became firm friends. PCW had become increasingly lonely: 'Looking through his address book was like walking through a cemetery', said an old friend. He had been flagging for some time: 'The worst thing about old age', says his brother, 'is the loss of energy and he missed it in his later years.' He finally collapsed – with the words – 'Je n'en peux plus', 'I can't go on any more' – in the Paris apartment of an old friend, an art dealer from Aix-en-Provence, a town he greatly loved. He was taken to hospital, and Earl Jellicoe recounted how: 'his last act, as he slipped into unconsciousness in his final illness was, when the telephone rang beside his hospital bed, instinctively to stretch out his hand to grasp it.'

Jellicoe was speaking at the memorial service held a few weeks after PCW's death at the church round the corner from Sotheby's, the glorious eighteenth-century St George's Hanover Square.

> All the photographed living were there,
> and the dead were listening

in the words of W. H. Auden. The normally cynical art trade joined *en masse* to roar the old favourites 'O God our help in ages past' and 'For all the saints', to appreciate Jellicoe's crisp, unsentimental, and therefore intensely moving, address, and to shed real tears at the passing of the Godfather of their trade. 'After singing the Nunc Dimittis', wrote Geraldine Norman, 'the assembled company poured out into George Street to gossip, trade, invite each other to lunch and keep Mr Wilson's creation, the art market, alive and well.'

Taubman had done his bit to fertilize his predecessor's crop into somewhat artificial growth by his offer of a formal, public package of financial support for vendors and purchasers alike. The idea was not as new as people thought, but the package was more open, bigger, and, unlike previous schemes, available to anyone doing business with the firm. The money was eagerly welcomed. In 1984 alone, Sotheby's lent about $30 million to 130 vendors, a 30 per cent rise on the previous year. Taubman is taking a sceptical view of future prices, for the loans are never more than 40 per cent of a low estimate of the value of the objects on offer. This is a sensible precaution, for an art market which depends on fashionable whims, new – or borrowed – money and tax deductions will always be vulnerable. By 1985 the American Internal Revenue Service was querying the value of up to three-quarters of all the deductions claimed on charitable contributions of art; and the shake-out in the oil industry was bringing recent collections onto the market – the toys accumulated by fashion-conscious Americans can never be reliable vehicles for long-term investment.

Even in Britain the pessimism expressed by investment in art had faded, a change emphasized when over two million investors applied for shares in British Telecom, the previously nationalized telephone system, in late 1984. Greed and hope were now attracted to the stock-market, not the art market. Records were still being set, but often in areas – like old glass – which had never been considered investment opportunities, and therefore to the benefit of those who collect for the love of it. For despite PCW's appetite for novelty, there are still hundreds of categories where the market is still narrow, providing plenty of scope for his successors.

For whatever happens to Sotheby's, to the relative positions of auctioneers and dealers of London and New York markets, PCW's creation looks to be permanent. Taubman's purchase bore witness to that. To PCW art was profit as well as fun. And although he was incapable of the simplest managerial tasks, he left behind a major business in a world that he himself had transformed into big business. It remains a world acutely dependent on the flair of a few individuals, but the art world now knows that it has to take note of the laws and institutions that govern the world of business –

including trades unions. In the spring of 1985 the workers by hand and brain at Bond Street were even contemplating joining a trades union to represent their interests.

This was a world away from the cosy family firm that PCW had joined less than fifty years earlier, for like all revolutionaries, he had destroyed as well as created. 'Each man kills the thing he loves', and PCW duly killed the great love of his life. Whatever the undoubted qualities of Taubman and his staff, Sotheby's will never again be capable of the unique combination of scholarship and business which was PCW's inheritance. It will not have the capacity to be unique: but, thanks to PCW, it served to change not only the art maket but also our visual perceptions, now covered with a film of monetary appreciation. And, thanks to human nature as much as PCW himself, the mist shows no sign of clearing.

256

# ACKNOWLEDGMENTS AND SOURCES

Any book centred on Sotheby's inevitably depends heavily on the official history: *Sotheby's: Portrait of an Auction House* by Frank Herrmann, published by Chatto and Windus in 1980. It is an invaluable work and, although it was sponsored by the firm itself, it is, as the author says: 'my personal reconstruction after years of research'. Although I have been content to follow the author's reasonings, especially in the three historical chapters ('The Making of an Auction House', 'The Making of an Auctioneer', and 'The Making of a Triumph') which depend heavily on his book, obviously, Frank Herrmann himself cannot be held responsible for my – even more personal – interpretation of his work.

He was kindness itself in elucidating problems and providing further invaluable information. Like him, many of the people I talked to obviously know far more about the subject than I do, but were (mostly) tactful enough not to point this out. These interviews provide the flesh and blood for the work.

The skeleton was created largely from newspapers and magazines. The art world does not appreciate how lucky it is in the quality of the specialist writers on the subject and I have relied greatly on the work of the key members of the 'art press corps' especially Edwin Mullins, Geraldine Norman of *The Times*, Donald Wintersgill of the *Guardian*, Souren Melikian of *The International Herald Tribune* and Anthony Thorncroft of the *Financial Times*. Among other useful publications were *Fortune* and *Business Week*. Another invaluable source was the transcripts of the many radio and television programmes featuring Sotheby's or PCW himself. These were pursued with terrier-like persistence through the BBC's tangle of archives by Ms Carol Evans. The final book owes a great deal to the patient work of Caroline Tonson-Rye, who retained her equanimity when lesser editors would have hit me.

I am grateful to the publishers and copyright holders for permission to quote from the following works: *The Rare Art Traditions* by Joseph Alsop (Thames & Hudson/Harper & Row); Enid Bagnold's *Autobiography* (William Heinemann/Little Brown & Company); *Diary of an Art Dealer* by René Gimpel (Hodder &

Stoughton); *The New Antiques* by Bevis Hillier (Times Books Ltd); *The Economics of Taste* by Gerald Reitlinger (Barrie & Rockliff); *Lock, Stock and Barrel* by Douglas and Elizabeth Rigby (Harper & Row); *The Elegant Auctioneers* by Wesley Towner. Copyright © 1970 by the Estate of Wesley Towner. Reprinted by permission of Farrar, Straus and Giroux, and Victor Gollancz Ltd; *Dear Youth* by Barbara Wilson by permission of Sir Martin Wilson; two articles by Eric Hodgins and Parker Lesley in December 1955 and January 1959 issues of *Fortune*. The quotations from 'On Art and Money' by Robert Hughes and 'The Art Biz' by John Bernard Myers are reprinted with permission from The New York Review of Books © 1983, 1984 Nyrev Inc.; I am grateful to Philip Norman for permission to quote from 'After the Sale was Over' *Sunday Times* 29 May 1977, and to Mollie Panter-Downes for permission to quote from 'A British Morning at Sotheby's, *The New Yorker* 10 August 1957. The quotations from the articles by Geraldine Norman and Eugene Thaw are reprinted by permission of Times Newspapers Limited. Every effort has been made to contact the copyright holders of *The Proud Possessors* by Aline Saarinen (Weidenfeld & Nicolson) and *The Art Game* by Robert Wraight (Frewin) without success. Should any omission have been made, we apologise and will be pleased to make the necessary acknowledgment in any future edition.

The extracts from BBC interviews come from the following programmes: BBC2, 'An Empire in Art', 4 March 1972; Third Programme, 'Art and the Intermediary', 12 September 1964; Radio 4, 'The Money Programme, 17 May 1966; Radio 4, 'Woman's Hour', 30 September 1970; External Services, 'London Art Market', 27 January 1976 (LP 36984); and Radio 4, 'Desert Island Discs', 4 August 1966.

There are surprisingly few books on the history of collecting. I have used a simple star system to indicate their relative usefulness;

** Alsop, Joseph: *The Rare Art Traditions*, Thames & Hudson, 1982
** Behrman, S. N: *Duveen*, Hamish Hamilton, 1952
* Burnham, Bonnie: *The Art Crisis*, Collins, 1975
** Burnham, Sophie: *The Art Crowd*, David McKay, 1973
* Carter, A. C. R: *Let Me Tell You*, Hutchinson, 1940
** Cooper, Jeremy: *Under the Hammer, The Auctions and Auctioneers of London*, Constable, 1977
* Cooper, Jeremy: *Dealing with Dealers, The Ins and Outs of the London Antiques Trade*, Thames & Hudson, 1985
de Coppet, Laura, and Jones Alan: *The Art Dealers*, Potter, 1984
*** Gimpel, René: *Diary of an Art Dealer* translated by John Rosenberg, Hodder & Stoughton, 1966

** Hillier, Bevis: *The New Antiques*, Times Books, 1977

* Hobson, Geoffrey: *Some thoughts on the organisation of the art market after the war*, Batsford, 1946

* Keen, Geraldine: *The Sale of Works of Art*, Nelson, 1971

* Lynes, Russell: *The Tastemakers – the shaping of American popular taste*,Constable/Dover, 1980

* Maas, Jeremy: *Victorian Painters*, Barrie & Jenkins, 1978

* Maas, Jeremy: *Gambart, Prince of the Victorian Art World*, Barrie & Jenkins, 1975

* Marillier, H. C: *Christie's*, Constable/Houghton Mifflin, 1926

* Myers, John Bernard: *Tracking the Marvellous*, Random House, 1983

* Norton, Tom: *100 years of Collecting in America. The Story of Sotheby Parke Bernet*, Abrams, 1983

**** Reitlinger Gerald: *The Economics of Taste*, Barrie & Rockliff, 1961–70

   Vol i: *The Rise and Fall of Picture Prices 1760–1960*, 1961

   Vol ii: *The Rise and Fall of Objet d'art Prices since 1750*, 1963

   Vol iii: *The Art Market in the 1960s*, 1970

*** Rigby, Douglas and Elizabeth: *Lock, Stock and Barrel: The Story of Collecting*, Harper & Row, 1944

* Rush, Richard: *Art as Investment*, Prentice Hall, 1961

** Saarinen, Aline: *The Proud Possessors*, Weidenfeld & Nicolson, 1959

** Taylor, F. H: *The Taste of Angels*, Little Brown, 1948

Taylor, John Russell and Brian Brooke: *The Art Dealers*, Hodder & Stoughton, 1969

*** Towner, Wesley: *The Elegant Auctioneers*, Gollancz, 1971

** Wraight, Robert: *The Art Game*, Frewin, 1965


*** Sotheby's *Annual Review*: 215th–218th seasons 1958–1962
   *The Ivory Hammer, The Year at Sotheby's*, Longman, 1962–66
   *Arts at Auction*, Macdonald, 1966–70, Thames & Hudson, 1970–72, Sotheby Parke-Bernet 1970–84.

Especially:

** 1970–71: *Sotheby's of London, New York: The Early Days, Some Egotistical Reminiscences* by John Carter

* 1972–73: *Return of the Duveen Market* by Gerald Reitlinger

** 1973–74: *The Sale of The Allen Funt Collection of Paintings by Sir Lawrence Alma-Tadema* by Russell Ash

** 1974–75: *The Art Market: Now and Then* by Frank Herrmann

** 1975–76: *Amsterdam: Three Centuries of Collecting* by Willem A. van Geffen

* 1970–71: *Sotheby Parke-Bernet Los Angeles* by Edward J Landrigan III

Articles:
* 'On Art and Money' by Robert Hughes in *The New York Review of Books*, 6 December 1984
* 'The Art Biz' by John Bernard Myers, *The New York Review of Books*, 13 October 1983

# INDEX